Jews and Human Rights

Jews and Human Rights

Dancing at Three Weddings

Michael Galchinsky

ROWMAN & LITTLEFIELD PUBLISHERS, INC.
Lanham • Boulder • New York • Toronto • Plymouth, UK

ROWMAN & LITTLEFIELD PUBLISHERS, INC.

Published in the United States of America
by Rowman & Littlefield Publishers, Inc.
A wholly owned subsidiary of The Rowman & Littlefield Publishing Group, Inc.
4501 Forbes Boulevard, Suite 200, Lanham, Maryland 20706
www.rowmanlittlefield.com

Estover Road
Plymouth PL6 7PY
United Kingdom

British Library Cataloguing in Publication Information Available

Library of Congress Cataloging-in-Publication Data

Galchinsky, Michael.
Jews and human rights : dancing at three weddings / Michael Galchinsky.
p. cm.
Includes bibliographical references.
ISBN-13: 978-0-7425-5266-1 (cloth : alk. paper)
ISBN-10: 0-7425-5266-7 (cloth : alk. paper)
ISBN-13: 978-0-7425-5267-8 (pbk. : alk. paper)
ISBN-10: 0-7425-5267-5 (pbk. : alk. paper)
1. Human rights. 2. Jews—Politics and government. I. Title.
JC571.G234 2008
341.4'8—dc22 2007019504

Printed in the United States of America

∞™ The paper used in this publication meets the minimum requirements of American National Standard for Information Sciences—Permanence of Paper for Printed Library Materials, ANSI/NISO Z39.48-1992.

To

Judge Herbert H. Galchinsky, whose briefcase I carry,
Arlene Galchinsky, chief fire-stoker, and
Elke Wolf Davidson, who keeps courage and makes maps.

Contents

Acknowledgments

Every book is a journey; this one has been an odyssey. I could not have brought it to an end without the substantial help of numerous individuals and institutions.

The Jacob Rader Marcus Center of the American Jewish Archives at Hebrew Union College in Cincinnati awarded me the Rabbi Joachim Prinz Memorial Fellowship for 2006–2007 for work on chapter 3. Thanks to Dr. Gary Zola, Kevin Proffitt, Fred Krome, and all the archivists for their quiet, excellent assistance. In summer, 2006, at just the right time in the life of the project, the Brandeis University Summer Institute for Israel Studies admitted me as a participant. Thanks to Ilan Troen, Sylvia Fuks-Fried, and all the participants for this stimulating boot camp in the field's latest developments. The Hilda and Jacob Blaustein Research Library at the American Jewish Committee in New York permitted me to use their archives. Thanks especially to the head librarian, Cyma Horowitz, for her kind and thorough assistance. Thanks to Judith Baskin, president of the Association for Jewish Studies, who led a delegation of Jewish studies professionals to Russia, enabling me to learn about Jewish life in the Former Soviet Union. The University of California at Los Angeles Department of English admitted me as a visiting scholar enabling me to use the university's substantial collections on Soviet Jewry. Emory University Law School, in particular professor Johan van der Vyver, permitted me to sit in on classes in international human rights and humanitarian law, from which I acquired necessary concepts and tools.

This book would have lacked much of whatever depth it has were it not for the perspective of the activists, lawyers, funders, technical assistance providers, curators, and scholars who gave me hours of their time in interviews and discussions: Rabbi Arik Ascherman, Lily Baxter, Michael Broyde, Felice

Gaer, Daphna Golan-Agnon, Tamar Hermann, Dorit Karlin, Sybil Kessler, Leonid Lvov, Ruchama Marton, Ruth Messinger, Jessica Montell, Rolly Rosen, Dr. Harris Schoenberg, Dan Yakir, Neta Ziv, and Gila Svirsky.

I am grateful to the academic institutions that invited me to deliver presentations on this material: Ludwig-Maximilians-Universität Munich, University of Haifa, Emory University, Hebrew Union College–Jewish Institute of Religion, Brandeis University, the University of Florida, and the Association for Jewish Studies. Fellow participants at these events provided me with advice and support: Shaul Kelner, Michael Brenner, Sander Gilman, and Judith Page.

I am also grateful to the nonacademic groups with whom I was able to try out my ideas: the University of Judaism Elder Hostel Program and Senior Summer Institute in Los Angeles, as well as Mount Scopus Hadassah and Congregation Shearith Israel in Atlanta. In addition, my own private advisory board saved me from many errors of fact and tact: Randy Malamud, Rabbi Noah Shapiro, and Jeff Allen. Kevin Kelly and Jessica Kirkwood sustained me with their love and support.

This project would never have been sustained without the aid I received from Georgia State University, in the form of professional leave, a research initiation grant, a summer research award, IRB certification, and travel and research assistance. Thanks particularly to deans Lauren Adamson and David Blumenfeld, and my chair, Matthew Roudané. My competent and self-directed research assistants, Angela Hall-Godsey and Natalie Trice, collected and annotated endless submissions to UN human rights bodies.

Chapter 4 previously appeared in article form as "The American Jewish Committee and the Birth of the Israeli Human Rights Movement," *Journal of Human Rights* 5, no. 3 (2006): 303–321. Thanks to the journal's editor, Thomas Cushman, for permitting me to reprint a revised version of the essay.

My family reorganized itself throughout the six-year process to make my research trips possible. My kids' grandparents, Arlene and Herb Galchinsky, Mayer Davidson, and Roseann Herman, and their aunt, Cindy Sales, flew across the country as needed. While I was away, my sons, Gideon and Rafael, mostly continued playing the mysterious "hakakoocheh" and dancing in the living room after dinner. Elke stayed up many late nights arguing with me and holding me to a higher standard. My deepest thanks to all.

Introduction

> You can't dance at two weddings with one pair of feet; nor can you sit on two horses with one rear end.
>
> —Yiddish proverb

TRIPLE LOYALTIES

In the first two decades after the Holocaust, Jews made some of the earliest and most important contributions to the formation of the international human rights system. In 1945, the American Jewish Committee (AJC) led a coalition of nongovernmental organizations (NGOs) that succeeded in convincing states' representatives at the San Francisco Conference that human rights should become one of the central components of the United Nations Charter.[1] Raphael Lemkin, an international lawyer who was also a Polish Jew, coined the term "genocide" and with his lobbying efforts almost single-handedly achieved the General Assembly's adoption of the UN Genocide Convention in 1948.[2] René Cassin, president of the Alliance Israélite Universelle, played a key role in the drafting of the UN Universal Declaration of Human Rights (UDHR), a document that since 1948 has come to be seen as the founding text of the international human rights movement.[3] Hersch Lauterpacht, an international lawyer, drew up the first proposal for an international bill of human rights, which had a large impact on the European Convention on Human Rights. For two generations after the Holocaust, Jewish activists contributed to drafting and ratifying human rights treaties, monitoring states' compliance, lobbying states on human rights questions, and creating coalitions with other human rights activists, all in order to build a global safety net that would prevent a future Nazi-like state from focusing its sights on Jews and other minorities.

Often, these activists were associated with Jewish NGOs like the AJC, World Jewish Congress (WJC), International Council of Jewish Women (ICJW), and B'nai B'rith. Some of their members saw their commitment to international human rights not only as one of the cornerstones of their Never Again program, but in many cases as the natural outgrowth of core Jewish values like *tikkun olam* (repair of the world), *b'tselem elohim* (the belief that all human beings were created in God's image), *ger lo tilhaz* (the command not to oppress the stranger), *kevod haberiyyoth* (the honor due to all creatures), *mippene darkhe shalom* (what must be done for the sake of the ways of peace), and *ben adam l'havero* (the ethical responsibilities of one person toward another).[4] These Jews believed that the Jewish experience of victimization, and/or the values inscribed in Jewish sacred texts, called them to work on behalf of universal norms for promoting and protecting human dignity.

At first, and then sporadically thereafter, many of these activists saw no conflict between their support for international human rights and their commitments to Jewish nationalism and domestic pluralism.[5] Here, the term "international" refers to the political community whose members are comprised of multiple nation-states and the individuals and groups within those states, and whose interactions are mediated by global and regional intergovernmental institutions like the United Nations, the African Union, the European Union, the Organization for Security and Cooperation in Europe, and the Organization of American States.

Nationalism refers to the ideology by which individuals and groups within a sizable common territory imagine themselves to be members of a single political body whose interactions are mediated by the common institutions of a state—administrative, legal, economic, military—as well as by its communicative institutions—factual and fictional media and common symbols.[6]

Sociologists distinguish pluralism from other sociopolitical arrangements (such as assimilationism and multiculturalism) by which a given national culture tries to produce peaceful and harmonious interactions among its diverse ethnic, religious, linguistic, and racial groups. Whereas assimilationist cultures try to integrate diverse citizens to a common pattern, pluralism recognizes the right of individuals to form distinct cultures within the nation on their private time, so long as the group adheres to basic civic duties in the public sphere. By contrast, multiculturalism promotes a celebration of diversity in the public sphere itself, whether through distinct languages, dress, foods (multiculturalism light), or through direct state support of diverse educational, religious, and cultural projects of particular groups (multiculturalism heavy).[7] For the purposes of this book, all of these arrangements will be referred to as "pluralist" in the sense that they all seek to establish harmony among the diverse cultures within a given nation. While international institutions establish and seek to enforce universal *human rights*, national institutions establish and seek to enforce *citizenship rights,* including civil, political, economic, social, and cultural rights, which in the Unites States and Israel are referred to together, somewhat confusingly, as "civil rights."

The book's argument can be stated succinctly: Diaspora Jewish activists enthusiastically embraced international human rights in the 1950s and 1960s, but since the mid-1960s, and especially after Israel's Six-Day War in 1967, their enthusiasm has declined due to the conflicts among their commitments to international human rights, Jewish nationalism, and domestic pluralism. At the same time, Israeli Jewish activists' enthusiasm for both human rights and citizenship rights has increased from almost nothing in the early years of prestate Palestine and the first forty years of statehood to a visible, sustainable presence on the Israeli political scene. Both trends can be accounted for through analyses of the external and internal pressures Jews have experienced. Jews in the international arena and in Israel have been responsive to external historical pressures—such as the rise of an anti-Zionist alliance at the UN and the threat posed to Israel by Palestinian nationalists and Arab states—and they have also been responsive to internal pressures, such as American Jews' suburbanization and move toward political centrism or neoconservatism, or the fragmentation within the Zionist national consensus during the past quarter century.

In the initial years after World War II, international Jewish human rights activists often saw the UDHR and the state of Israel as the twin births of 1948—both dedicated to making Jews safe from persecution. At the same time, they thought that protecting the rights of disfavored groups around the globe went hand in hand with advocating for the rights of minorities, immigrants, refugees, asylum-seekers, and diaspora members in their home countries. Many of these activists in the 1950s and 1960s were based in the United States and espoused internationalism combined with a domestic policy of citizenship rights advocacy on behalf of African Americans.[8]

Yet, while the hope of these Jews in international human rights bloomed early, it began to wither during the early 1960s, as the new UN majority—including the Communist bloc, the Arab states, and newly independent African and Asian states—started to manipulate the emerging human rights mechanisms to turn Israel into an international pariah. The General Assembly's infamous "Zionism=Racism" resolution of November 10, 1975 is only the best-known example, and it led to forty years of ceaseless claims of Israeli rights violations by various UN charter bodies, treaty bodies, specialized agencies, and conference programs. Until the UN Commission on Human

Rights was abolished in 2006 and replaced by a new Human Rights Council, it observed a ritual each spring of condemning Israel's alleged human rights violations, holding Israel to a far higher standard than it did states that had demonstrated far less commitment to the Geneva Conventions and the UN Charter.[9] While the Zionism=Racism charge was officially repealed in 1991, it resurfaced in August 2001 in the final program of the UN World Conference against Racism in Durban, South Africa.[10] Again and again, legitimate questions about specific alleged Israeli rights violations have been turned into pretexts for a broader campaign to ostracize the state of Israel.[11] For good reasons, many who love Israel have honed their contempt for the international community's misuse of human rights treaties and institutions. How Jews should respond to the UN, an organization that has promised so much on human rights but delivered so little, has been a vexing question.

If the activities of the anti-Israel alliance have challenged Jewish human rights advocates from one side, Israel's sometimes questionable practices with regard to Palestinians in the occupied territories and minorities inside Israel itself have challenged activists from the other. For, apart from the UN's many false or trumped-up charges and overgeneralizations, there have been numerous well-documented occasions when a member of the Israeli government, or the Israel Defense Forces, has actually committed some specific violation of a treaty to which Israel has obligated itself. A commission led by former Israeli Supreme Court Justice Moshe Landau found that the General Security Services had engaged in the systematic torture of Palestinian detainees between 1967 and 1984. International tribunals, human rights NGOs, and treaty-monitoring bodies have found Israel in violation of Palestinians' rights to self-determination, use of natural resources, equality, property, adequate standard of living, work, health, education, freedom of movement, and, not least, in violation of the prohibition against resettling civilian populations in occupied territory. Israeli soldiers and guards have engaged, in some cases while following orders issued from the highest levels of the chain of command, in violations of humanitarian law (the law of war) such as extrajudicial executions, collective punishments, ill-treatment of prisoners, and excessive use of force.[12]

Even a cursory glance at the case law in the European Court of Human Rights demonstrates that no democracy is free of rights violations. But when the violating state in question is Israel, Jewish human rights activists often experience excruciating tension because their commitment as Israeli citizens or members of the Diaspora to the security of the homeland may appear to conflict with their commitment as rights advocates to pluralism at home and universalism abroad. For example, while American Jews have remained far more liberal on most issues than other Americans who share their socioeconomic status, a majority have, since 1967, taken a line on Israeli politics that is concerned less with Israeli democracy than with the state's security.[13] What kind of response can human rights–oriented Jews frame for themselves when their commitments become opposed? If they stand too staunchly in the solidarity camp, ignoring reliably attested evidence, will they betray their own ideals and lose friends in the social justice communities abroad and at home? If they stand too naively in the international human rights and domestic citizenship rights camps, will they sell their birthright for a mess of lentils?

In response to such conflicts, Jewish human rights activists, both in the Diaspora and in Israel, have tried to dance simultaneously at three different weddings: internationalism, Jewish nationalism, and domestic pluralism. This book focuses on the actions and self-justifications of international Jewish NGOs at the UN and regional human rights bodies; state-based NGOs in Israel, the United States, and Russia; and well-placed Jewish individuals in national government, the judiciary, the military, and the international human rights system.

The first half of the book analyzes the contributions to international human rights made by NGOs with explicitly Jewish platforms. Topics include, among others, Jewish contributions to drafting, ratifying, and monitoring human rights treaties; the role of Jews in the development of enforcement machinery; how a network of Jewish organizations emerged to advocate on behalf of Soviet Jews' human rights; what happened to that network after the dissolution of the USSR; and finally, in a meditation on the force and content behind Jewish universalism, how Jews have responded to genocides in which no Jewish victims were involved. In each case I consider how Jewish human rights activism has been conditioned and limited by the rise of an anti-Israel alliance at the UN, as well as internal/domestic pressures within the Jewish community itself.

The second half of the book analyzes the question of how human rights have been addressed in Israel—Israel's approach to the protection of human rights in the occupied territories, the historical development of the Israeli human rights movement, the role of the Israeli courts in interpreting international human rights law, the conflicting interpretations of the same law made by international bodies, the constraints required by the national security context, and the transnational relationship between Israel and the Diaspora regarding allegations of rights violations.

As a whole, the book aims to raise the profile of Jewish international and transnational studies in a manner accessible to a broader public. It analyzes the role of Jews in global and regional intergovernmental bodies, nongovernmental bodies, and courts, and the relations among Jews across national borders. The study of Jews' participation in these arenas has been surprisingly underdeveloped. To be sure, international law experts like Hersch Lauterpacht, Natan Lerner, Louis Henkin, and Yoram Dinstein have provided analyses that undergirded Jewish NGO activism with respect to particular rights, treaties, committees, or situations.[14] These legal analyses help to discern the changes in formal law and practice, but often preclude the historical context that could flesh out the law. Activists like Anatoly Sharansky, William Korey, Harris Schoenberg, Nehemiah Robinson, Felice Gaer, and Daphna Golan-Agnon have published memoirs and chronicles of their activities that constitute rich, indispensable resources for those interested in the field.[15] Yet works written by participants are necessarily partial, in both senses of the term.

What has not yet appeared, by and large, are the social, scientific, and historical studies—by sociologists, political scientists, and historians—that would (1) set the human rights activism of the Jewish community in a comparative context with the activism sponsored by other minority communities; (2) trace the ideas and tactics Jews have learned from their encounters with human rights; (3) highlight the unique ideas and tactics they have brought to the table; and (4) determine how significant their contributions have been, both to their community's self-perception and to the human rights movement overall.[16]

There are two readily comprehensible reasons for the absence of such analyses. First of all, the interdisciplinary field of Jewish studies has largely been dominated by religious studies scholars, philosophers, literary critics, and cultural historians, for whom human rights, when it appears on the radar at all, is likely to do so in intellectual expressions in cultural texts rather than in a particular history of organized activity. Second, the field has been set up primarily along national and linguistic lines, making unlikely the conceptualization of global and transnational relations among Jews from different nations or language groups. However, recent studies, like David Schneer and Caryn Aviv's *New Jews* and the magisterial set of commentaries on *The Jewish Political Tradition* edited by Michael Walzer et al., are moving beyond the national model. Marrying the study of Jewish and international politics can result in mutual benefit. On the one hand, international studies can illuminate a significant aspect of postwar Jewish identity as well as a whole range of intra-Jewish relations (e.g., homeland/diaspora, religious/secular, elite/grassroots, and Ashkenazi/Sephardi); on the other hand, Jewish studies approaches can help lawyers, activists, and policymakers understand the complex role that the Holocaust, Jewish voluntarism, and Israel's human rights record have played in the making of the UN and the development of the human rights system. The study of Jewish NGOs can also contribute to a larger endeavor, one which has barely even been attempted to date: rather than merely trying to find out what human rights workers do, we can get glimpses of how their activities are conditioned by their national, ethnic, religious, and/or racial identities.

HUMAN RIGHTS IN THE JEWISH TRADITION

Here, Jewish tradition refers both to a complex, centuries-old religious tradition as well as to the no less complex historical tradition of Jewish political thought. Is human rights activism consonant with Jewish religious tradition? Legal theorists, philosophers, policymakers, and theologians have produced a large literature arguing that it is. Basing their claims on the Hebrew Bible, the Mishnah, the Talmud, and subsequent commentaries, these "Judaism and human rights" projects have sprung from two different inclinations: (1) the desire to find justifications for one's own human rights activism within traditional sources, and (2) the prophetic or prescriptive desire to use the rights implied or stated in the tradition as a way to criticize current international, Jewish, or Israeli practices.

Many of these projects argue that secular human rights concepts are grounded in Judaic theological concepts. For instance, while acknowledging that the positive legal framework for human rights is a modern product of Enlightenment natural law, the philosopher Eckart Otto still traces the human rights found in the two United Nations "Covenants" of 1966 (i.e., the Covenant on Civil and Political Rights and the Covenant on Economic, Social, and Cultural Rights) to the influence of the Hebrew Bible. He stresses that ancient Greek proponents of democracy did not produce the only concepts that became the "cradle of human rights," but that "Judean intellectuals" responding to the imperialistic royal theology of the Assyrians around the time of the Babylonian exile in 586 BCE also produced central concepts. The "confluence of biblical and Greek motifs" in the Netherlands and England during the sixteenth and seventeenth centuries was "decisive" for the conceptualization of human rights.[17] Drawing less on biblical motifs and more on kabbalah and folk understandings, Irwin Cotler, formerly a professor of international law at McGill University and head of the Canadian Ministry of Justice, has written that "if human rights has emerged as the new 'secular religion' of our time, then the Jewish religion is at the core of this new secular religion of human rights—the whole symbolized by the normative exhortation in the Jewish religion of *Tikkun Olam*—the responsibility to 'repair the world.'"[18] Cotler also cites the biblical concept of *b'tselem elohim*, that all humans are made in the image of God, which he says is "the essence of a religion organized around the inherent dignity of the human person and the equal dignity of all persons."[19]

Similarly, Milton Konvitz, who was a law professor and founder of the periodical *Midstream*, wrote in the introduction to an edited collection of essays, *Judaism and Human Rights*, that although the term "human rights" appears nowhere in the Hebrew Bible, the ideal of human rights is very much present there, such as when Abraham intercedes with God to protect the lives of the righteous individuals in Sodom.[20] One can get a good idea of Konvitz's perspective from the titles of some of the chapters in his book, like "Foundations of Democracy in the Scriptures and Talmud," or "Conscience and Civil Disobedience in the Jewish Tradition."

Religious studies scholars and philosophers have also sought to find the basis for human rights in Jewish tradition. Peter J. Haas, chair of religious studies at Case Western Reserve University, has contributed a volume on the Jewish tradition to a series entitled *Human Rights in the World's Major Religions*, discussing texts from the tradition that can be seen as precursors of various rights in the UDHR.[21] Haas recognizes that the concept of human rights is nowhere explicitly articulated in the Bible, Mishnah, or Talmud. The Bible does not promulgate a human rights concept because the covenant between the Israelites and God assumes that the authority both to give and take away all rights and privileges, including the right to life, rests with God rather than with human beings. As products of rabbinic Judaism, the Mishnah and Talmud do not theorize human rights because they are concerned with how to act in particular cases, not with abstract formulations of human dignity. Nonetheless, Haas argues that one can "tease out" from these sources certain dispositions—unevenly expressed—toward pluralist tolerance, protection of certain disfavored classes (e.g., widows, orphans, and strangers), and respect for the dignity of the human person. These dispositions can serve as "human rights resources in the Jewish tradition."[22]

A similar approach, with different outcomes, is *Judaism, Human Rights, and Human Values*, by Lenn E. Goodman, a philosopher from Vanderbilt who traces "the metaphysical foundations of the idea of human rights in the classic Jewish sources" to determine ethical norms on a variety of hot-button issues, such as abortion, nationalism, and hate speech.[23] For these scholars, the texts of ancient and medieval Judaism provide potent material that can be adapted for modern human rights discourse.

At least one prominent human rights activist argues that Judaism cannot accurately be portrayed as a rights-based tradition, much less a foundation for modern rights talk. No less an authority than René Cassin denied that the Tanakh and the Talmud had formed the basis for the modern conception of human rights. For Cassin, the Bible and Talmud are exemplified by the Ten Commandments and the halakhah. The Tanakh and Talmud demand duties; they do not confer rights. They outline what one must do, not what one is entitled to expect.[24]

Yet the former Israeli Supreme Court Justice Haim Cohn replied to Cassin that every duty implies a right. If I have the duty not to kill you, then you are entitled to demand that I not kill you. You have the right to life. For Justice Cohn, a tradition based on ethical commandments is still by implication a human rights tradition, and in two books he goes on to find in Judaism the implied rights to equality, religious freedom, asylum, freedom of speech, and a host of others.[25] Having quoted the first paragraph of the UDHR, he writes, "The equality between people, and the declaration that all people were born free and equal, are not the inventions of the authors of this declaration; their basis, as with that of the vast majority of basic human rights, lies in Jewish sources."[26]

At times, Justice Cohn adopts a prophetic/prescriptive posture as well. Writing in 1989 in response to the first intifada, Cohn sought to lay an intellectual foundation for the bourgeoning human rights network in Israel. Although he makes no mention of the Israeli/Palestinian conflict, certain passages implicitly criticize his country's treatment of Israeli Arabs. For example, he writes of the attitudes toward the "stranger" prescribed for the ancient Israelites, but then shifts to describe the attitudes that should be normative for modern Israelis:

> As we had gone through this bitter experience, this trauma of being "strangers" in a strange land, who were exploited terribly throughout, we were commanded in the Torah, not once but twenty-four times, to love the strangers living in our midst, not to exploit them and not to force them to engage in heavy manual labor, and to permit them to enjoy those benefits granted us. . . .
>
> And if at the time this referred primarily to the stranger who came from the outside, the stranger who found or who sought refuge among us from persecution, hunger, or any other type of distress, how much more must this be true with the people who were already living here when we came here.[27]

It seems clear that in tracing human rights to Jewish sources, Justice Cohn is looking both outwardly and inwardly, both to defend Israel as a state steeped in a rights-based tradition and to criticize the state's practices toward Israeli Arabs. He is simultaneously describing an ancient system of justice and prescribing norms for the present. It is no surprise that Justice Cohn helped found two Jewish human rights organizations, the Association for Civil Rights in Israel and the International Association of Jewish Lawyers and Jurists.

"Judaism and human rights" books like these serve useful purposes. A thorough knowledge of selected human rights resources within the tradition can help Jewish activists, members of the judiciary, rabbis, and policymakers articulate what makes their mission distinct within the human rights field, and can attract other Jews to their cause. Yet such projects can have their limitations. First, in order to link Judaism and human rights, such projects often present the tradition as a stable repository of beliefs from which an essential, unchanging, and positive human rights orientation might be derived. This idea can result in the loss of historical perspective and reduce the tradition's inner complexity. While Milton Konvitz, in *Judaism and Human Rights*, is aware of this danger, he argues that "it is a calculated risk which the philosophic or historical mind can hardly avoid," and goes on to develop an ahistorical and essentialist account of "Judaism's" take on human rights.[28]

Second, philosophical and theological projects often assert that ancient texts envision human rights, which is historically inaccurate.[29] Humanity did not begin to be conceptualized in its modern political sense—as a category applied by states and intergovernmental organizations that transcends social factors like one's race, religion, gender, or nationality—until the late seventeenth century. As a matter of fact, human rights were embodied in an international legal and institutional framework only after World War II. Philosophies and theologies of Judaism and human rights tend to confuse the rights of monarchal subjects, in biblical times, or of members of a *kehillah* in the medieval period, with international human rights in the contemporary era. While the rights found in ancient and medieval texts were certainly human rights precursors in their concern for justice and the individual's dignity, they did not conceive of themselves as global in scope and reach. The term "state" ought not to be used interchangeably for an ancient monarchy and a modern nation-state.

Finally, such undertakings can sometimes seem to defend Jewish tradition with the sort of partisanship that excludes contrary evidence from consideration. It is true that one can find in the Tanakh many universally applicable ethical norms, such as the Noachide laws, the duties relating to the widow, the stranger, and the orphan, the collection of personal ethical duties referred to as *gemilut hasadim* (acts of lovingkindness), and the prophetic injunction to "let justice well up like water, righteousness like an unfailing stream."[30] One can find the Jubilee provisions releasing slaves and canceling all debts, and the passion for *tsedek* and *tsedakah* (justice and charity) of institutions like the Sanhedrin, the *kahal*, and the *bet din*.[31] One can celebrate the prophets' practice of shaming Israelite kings who engage in injustice, such as when Nathan castigates King David for sending Uriah the Hittite to an early grave.[32]

However, in "Judaism and human rights" books one rarely encounters extended discussion of passages like the following from Deuteronomy about the Israelites' treatment of Canaanite peoples:

> You must destroy all the sites at which the nations you are to dispossess worshiped their gods, whether on lofty mountains and on hills or under any luxuriant tree. Tear down their altars, smash their pillars, put their sacred posts to the fire, and cut down the images of their gods, obliterating their name from that site.[33]

This kind of passage demands a particularist stance based on the concept of Jews' chosenness rather than a universalist stance based on all humans' equality before God. It could not be the source for the international right to religious freedom.

In Jewish human rights theologies one finds references to the Bible's battlefield ethics, such as its prohibition against Israelites destroying the fruit trees of cities they conquer.[34] Yet one hears less about Moses's destruction of King Og of Bashan and King Sihon of the Amorites, together with all their people and possessions; or the thirty-one Canaanite kings, with all their people and possessions, whom God commands Joshua to put to the sword.[35] There is little mention of Moses's rage at the soldiers who refuse his order to destroy the Midianites completely, and leave the civilian women, children, and property unharmed.[36] The norms displayed in such passages can hardly serve as sources for the UN Genocide Convention. Peter Haas, whose book is an exception to the apologetic trend, remarks that "the Israelites are commanded to exterminate certain peoples. There is no question in the Bible that the Israelites are committing . . . wrong by fulfilling these explicit words of God. . . . [T]he lesson is clear. There were no human rights per se, only certain protections, obligations, and expectations imposed by the community as agent of the divine and as spelled out in the covenant."[37]

Moreover, as Emory University law professor Michael Broyde has pointed out, the focus on finding human rights resources in the Bible misses a profoundly important point—that normative Judaism developed not directly out of the Bible but out of later rabbinic materials—the Mishnah, the Talmud, the Midrash, and later commentaries.[38] Jewish philosophers, including even the radical modern thinker, Baruch Spinoza, did not always value the prophets who criticized the reigning powers. As Spinoza put it: "even devout kings often found prophets intolerable because of their assumption of authority to decide what action was pious or impious."[39]

As is the case with every ancient philosophical and theological corpus, Judaism is comprised of a multitude of sources, often separated by hundreds or thousands of years. Not all of this material can be assimilated comfortably to a contemporary human rights perspective. One can find support in the tradition for any of the three modern positions: universalism, nationalism, and pluralism. Every group of Jews has had both the freedom and responsibility, within the constraints of its social position, to choose which way it would go.

Thus Jewish human rights activism always begins with the endeavor of selecting a usable past.

Rather than trace the genealogical development of human rights concepts from ancient Judaism, this book traces the interaction of modern human rights institutions with Jews. The subjects of the study are individuals and groups acting at specific moments in time from their contingent understandings of Jewishness, in all its ethnic, religious, linguistic, national, and diasporic complexity. These understandings can and do change from individual to individual, from group to group, from era to era, depending on which aspects of Jewish identity are emphasized or excluded. Jewish identity is an unstable compound, flexible and indeterminate, the relative emphasis given to any particular aspect changing with the circumstances. Rather than elaborating a set of Jewish human rights norms that persist through time, this book analyzes the interdependence of norms with circumstances. It records the religious and philosophical self-justifications of the individuals and groups in question, not as testimonies to a dimension of Jewish belief that transcends time, but as provisional gestures in a dynamic historical narrative.

This approach is closer to the analytical framework set out by the editors of *The Jewish Political Tradition*, but there are some differences. Michael Walzer, Menachem Lorberbaum, and Noam J. Zohar are concerned primarily with recovering and commenting on a repository of political theories from all periods of Jewish history. Their approach (as Walzer explains in the introduction to Volume 1) is normative, demonstrating that these texts comprise a "tradition" of political thought because they self-consciously refer or allude to previous texts—biblical, rabbinic, and modern. While the texts' responses to political questions vary, the editors demonstrate that the questions themselves remain largely stable through time. As the editors write, this focus on stability through time means that their "primary aim" is not to tell a story with "historical verisimilitude," but to meditate on Jewish political theory. By contrast, this book's main aim is largely historical rather than theoretical; it seeks, in Walzer's words, to be "faithful to local customs and practices, . . . local political struggles and intellectual debates"—except that here "local" is expanded to mean specific national, regional, and global struggles.[40]

Like other works of normative political theory—such as Jack Donnelly's *Universal Human Rights in Theory and Practice*—the texts recovered in *The Jewish Political Tradition*, and the commentaries on them, do frequently illuminate post-Holocaust Jews' choices about rights, dignity, individualism, nationalism, and pluralism, and will be referred to from time to time throughout the book.[41] However, in general the subjects of this book are not deliberately acting with reference to political theory. In the majority of cases they are not aware of it, and are not especially concerned with placing themselves within it. (This is a given, considering that many of the texts the editors of *The Jewish Political Tradition* recover have been translated into English for the first time from Hebrew or Aramaic.) Rather, the activists associated with NGOs that espouse an explicit Jewish platform identify themselves as part of a history of organized activity, which has its roots in the nineteenth century—in emancipation activism, Yiddish socialism, and Hebrew nationalism—and is based largely in a secular, ethnic identity devoted to the "civic religion of human rights." Hence, if the activists are not always self-consciously engaged with Jewish political theory, they typically *are* aware of their place in the history of Jewish activism.

Alongside well-known identity categories (ethnicity, nationality, language, religion, diaspora), it will be necessary, from time to time, to introduce a newer category that informs contemporary Jewish self-understanding: transnationalism. This category arises because the term, Diaspora, in its traditional formulation, is no longer suited to world Jewry in every situation. In its traditional sense, the Diaspora is understood as a scattered community with a common history and myth of return, related to Israel as the periphery is to the center. Yet, as Caryn Aviv and David Schneer have demonstrated in *New Jews: The End of the Jewish Diaspora*, most Jews outside of Israel—in the United States, Europe, and the former Soviet Union—have resisted seeing themselves as members of a Diaspora in this traditional sense.[42]

The theoretical term "transnationalism" captures certain aspects of the contemporary self-understanding of Jews outside of Israel. A transnational person has a foot, literally or imaginatively, in both the homeland and the land to which he or she has migrated. Transnationals might own homes in both Israel and another place, might have dual citizenship, might travel back and forth and send faxes and emails and pictures. The number of actual transnationals among Jews is probably quite small, but the number of Jews who traverse the space between, say, the United States and Israel *imaginatively*—through purchases of Israeli literature and music, attending Israeli Independence Day events, participating in Israel-supportive fund-raising, engaging in homeland tourism—is large and well established.[43] A transnational person tends to think of his or her relation to the homeland, not as a relation of periphery to center, but as the relation of interdependent co-equals.

When, from a political perspective, the relation actually takes on a co-equal character, when key decisions affecting Israelis and world Jewry are made jointly by Israelis with Jews outside of the state, then it is probably best to recognize that they are not members of a diaspora or even transnationals, but members of a globally dispersed set of Jewish political communities. As we will see below in the chapters on Soviet Jewry activism and Israeli human rights activism, the concept of a set of global Jewish political communities can help isolate some of the features of human rights activism that are probably unique to the Jewish case, and at the same time can point out ways in which other large, well-organized sets of global political communities might benefit by comparison with Jews.

A BRIEF HISTORY OF JEWS AND HUMAN RIGHTS, 1645–1945

Jews have played every role in the human rights drama: they have been victims, advocates, violators, and judges. For much of diaspora history, Jews suffered as serial victims of abuse, often directed by the rulers of the city-states, kingdoms, nation-states and empires in which they resided. One might therefore imagine that the struggle to protect themselves from abuse of their rights as an ethnic, religious, and linguistic minority has been a permanent feature of Diaspora Jewish history. Yet while it is useful to look for precursors to human rights concepts in ancient and medieval Jewish sources, one should not assume that Jews or any other group in Europe had begun thinking about human rights much prior to the French Republic's Declaration of the Rights of Man and Citizen in 1789. For most of human history, Jews—like everyone else—did not articulate an explicit concept of human rights, because they did not conceive of their humanity as having a political dimension. As Lynn Hunt, the former president of the American Historical Association, has demonstrated, the human rights concept had to be invented and then institutionalized, and these processes did not really begin until the later Enlightenment.[44]

Until the end of the seventeenth century, the very fact that one was human was not considered reason enough for one to deserve political entitlements. Prior to that, individuals were bequeathed entitlements based on much narrower considerations: because they lived within a given territory, because they spoke a given language, because they worshipped a particular God and observed *these* and not *those* ritual practices, because they were classified as members of a race, because they were positioned in a given caste, or class, or gender that shared a common history. In the public square, they did not think of themselves primarily as human beings, but as Christians or Muslims or Jews, Englishmen or Frenchmen, males or females, aristocrats or serfs. They did not possess basic inherent entitlements by virtue of the fact that they had been born; rather, the local ruling powers granted them limited, temporary privileges based on changeable criteria and subject to repeal.

From a legal standpoint, European Jews in the seventeenth and eighteenth centuries were not considered full participants in the Christian political community, and the restricted condition of their rights to vote, to own property, to conclude contracts, to operate businesses, to testify in court, and to run for office reflected that status. Yet at the same time, Jews were beginning to serve as objects of humanitarian concern in early Enlightenment documents such as the Treaty of Westphalia (1648) and John Locke's Letter concerning Toleration (1689).[45] During the later Enlightenment, the idea of a transcendent and politically charged humanity began to take hold. Political philosophers like Voltaire, Rousseau, and Jefferson were beginning to conceive of a political category—called humanity—that transcended race, class, religion, gender, and even (in theory at least) nationality. Writers and statesmen such as Pierre Bayle, Wilhelm Christian Dohm, and Stanislas de Clermont-Tonnere saw Jews as the test of a state's commitment to freedom, equality, and brotherhood, particularly in the wake of the French Revolution.[46] When Napoleon swept through Europe he put in place new enlightened law codes in which Jews were guaranteed the same rights as other citizens. At every historical juncture in the West since the Enlightenment, Jews have continued to serve as the litmus test of the strength of a state's guarantee of basic citizenship rights.

Yet, while the idea of a universal set of entitlements that each individual deserved regardless of where he or she lived had been launched by Enlightenment philosophers, in practice an individual still had only those rights that had been conferred by a given state. If a state decided to torture a person or take his life or property, there was not much he or his family could do about it. If a state decided to refuse to grant religious Jews the right to slaughter their cattle according to the laws of *kashrut* or bury their dead in a Jewish cemetery, the Jews would simply have to make do. If a state, like Russia under the czars, issued a series of decrees limiting Jews' freedom of movement to a certain Pale of Settlement, they had no choice. They had to move. There was no authority outside of the state that could enforce the human rights of Jews or any other group, either collectively or as individuals.

Limited as their citizenship rights often were, many Jews, starting in Germany in the 1750s and spreading to France, England, and Russia through the subsequent century, rushed to embrace such rights. These modernizing Jews, known in Hebrew as *maskilim*, or enlighteners, became advocates for the community's civil emancipation efforts, calling for emancipation, for example, at Napoleon's Sanhedrin (1806), the Congress of Vienna (1815), the Treaty of Paris (1856), and the Congress of Berlin (1878).[47] In fits and starts, European Jews won or were granted rights by the states in which they lived, sometimes only partially. Jews were not always able to exercise the rights they were granted in every situation, and there were many legal and political setbacks. For example, many of the German states that adopted the Napoleonic code did not enforce the rights it guaranteed their Jews. After Napoleon had been defeated, Jews formally demanded citizenship rights at the Congress of Vienna. A conservative backlash took place throughout Europe, leading in Germany to one of the first instances of modern anti-Semitism when the Hep! Hep! riots broke out in 1819. By the late nineteenth century, modern anti-Semitism had become a staple of political discourse, spread via the scientific racism of the 1870s, the czarist pogroms of the 1880s, the institutionalization of racist anti-Semitism in Germany, and the Dreyfus affair in France of the 1890s. There were limits to the empathy that would transcend ethnic, religious, and national differences.[48] Many Jews became convinced that there was nothing to hope for from European states' commitment to their legal rights.

In the wake of their perceived failure to gain the full rights of citizenship, especially after the Dreyfus affair, some European Jews at the turn of the twentieth century turned to Socialism and Communism, some to political Zionism, and some to the liberal League of Nations, in the hopes that one or the other would finally prevent discrimination and protect their rights. For their part, the new Communist systems, after a brief experiment in tolerating Jews, either banned Jewish religious and cultural practices outright, or imposed severe restrictions on such practices (see chapter 2).

A growing number of Jews in the early twentieth century were attracted to political Zionism as an expression of a nationalist movement that would give Jews state power to protect their own rights. Although the first inklings of the Zionist movement began to appear as early as the 1840s, the movement became professionalized after Theodore Herzl, a Viennese journalist who reported on the Dreyfus trial, organized the first Zionist Congress in Basel, Switzerland, in 1897. Herzl's call for Jews to find a state that might succeed in protecting their rights where the European states failed appealed at first to Jews in Eastern Europe. Successive waves of *aliyah*—or migration to Palestine—occurred, at first from Eastern Europe, where Jews had been subject to restrictive czarist and then Communist laws and attacks. Gradually, Central and Western European Jews were attracted to Zionism, as they witnessed the increase in racial anti-Semitism, the erosion of liberalism, and the rise of Nazism in Weimar, Germany. Once the state was established, Jews throughout the Arab world—Iraq, Yemen, Syria, Morocco, Iran—fled persecution in their home countries to the new state in the 1950s. Eventually they were joined by Ethiopian Jews and the massive Russian immigration of the 1980s and 1990s.

In pre-state Palestine migrants set up agricultural settlements, built cities and roads, and gradually increased their population until the local Arab population began to take note. Even before World War I, Palestinian Arabs had rejected the Zionist movement's aim to create a Jewish state in Palestine, and in the 1920s and 1930s they organized mass revolts against the British Mandate and the Zionists. Although there were some Zionists, like Ahad Ha-am, Yitzhak Epstein, and David Ben-Gurion, who wished to work with the Palestinian Arabs to protect their rights in a Jewish state, others, like Vladmir Jabotinsky, the founder of Revisionist Zionism, called for armed struggle, if necessary. After 1945, Holocaust refugees and Jews fleeing their homes in Arab countries that had been aligned with Hitler amounted to some 700,000 persons, roughly equal to the number of Jews already in Palestine. Due to restrictive immigration policies in the Allied countries, including the United States, and, of course during the British Mandate, Jewish refugees had nowhere else to turn. The impending end of the Mandate brought tensions with the Palestinian Arabs to a head, and when Israel declared its independence in 1948, a war broke out that resulted in 700,000 Arabs fleeing the territory that had been the British Mandate. Most of these people fled voluntarily (according to typical Zionist history), or both chose and were forced to flee (according to New Historian Benny Morris), ending up in Lebanon, Syria, Jordan, and in refugee camps in the West Bank and Gaza, where they and their descendants largely still live. The state designed to protect the rights of Jews ran into the problem of how to protect the rights of its own minority Arab population.[49]

Zionism was an expression of the Jewish people's right to self-determination, guaranteed by the General Assembly Resolution 181 (the UN Partition Plan) of November 29, 1947. It was also an attempt to give Jews a state in which as the majority their citizenship rights would be protected. Yet not all Jews migrated to the new state for protection or intended to do so. Sizable Jewish communities still existed as minorities in Eastern and Western Europe, the United States, the Arab world, and in Africa. These groups needed protection, yet until the end of World War I no individuals or groups had the standing to appeal to an international arbiter, which in any case did not exist.

It was not until 1921 that the League of Nations tried to protect some Jews and other minorities in a small part of the world, although only with limited and short-term success. The Comité des Delegations Juives had argued for the League's imposition of minorities treaties on the Eastern European states that had lost World War I, as well as new states like Poland, stipulating that the League's Committee of Three would develop a system for reviewing petitions claiming violations had been committed. These were the world's first multilateral human rights treaties. Yet such treaties only applied to a small number of countries—they were regional rather than universal in scope—and when the League of Nations evaporated, the treaties were no longer enforced.[50]

Practically, the only hope of relief that victims had in most cases was that another state would embark on a humanitarian intervention on their behalf. As a mechanism for addressing human rights violations, humanitarian intervention was and is highly unreliable, depending as it does on the noblesse oblige of states rather than on permanently codified law and enforcement procedures. Still, Western European Jews in the nineteenth century had in fact laid the ground for support of humanitarian concern across borders, through their efforts to persuade their countries to help Jews in Algeria, Persia, Syria, Romania, Russia, Switzerland, and Hungary.[51] Yet, while sometimes tolerated, state-led humanitarian interventions were generally discouraged by international lawyers, since they could easily be used as a pretext for hostilities with other, less noble, ends, such as territorial expansion.[52] In any case states were unlikely to compromise trade and military alliances by bringing human rights complaints against other states, even when the ill-treatment was of such magnitude that it offended the conscience of the world.

Prior to World War II, voluntary humanitarian efforts were the best international law could do to protect citizens from their states. Then the Nazis made it absolutely clear that such paltry measures were useless in the face of a state committed to genocide. Jews' victimization during the Holocaust demonstrated to the world the need for something more universal and international than citizenship rights, a rights system operated from beyond any individual state's jurisdiction and equally accessible to all. In the International Military Tribunal at Nuremberg, the fourth Geneva Convention, and the Genocide Convention, the world community tried to give the laws of war international stature, permanence, and structure. In the United Nations Charter, the nonbinding UDHR, and the series of binding treaties that followed, the United Nations sought to do the same for laws protecting each individual's dignity and fundamental freedoms.

JEWISH HUMAN RIGHTS ACTIVISM SINCE 1945

Those who, since 1945, have advocated international human rights can be described as promoters of a type of cosmopolitanism, which in its modern political manifestation is a belief in the potential of universal standard-setting and enforcement machinery to help states avoid conflict and alleviate the mistreatment of disfavored individuals and groups anywhere in the world. In its political dimensions, cosmopolitanism today is far different from what it was prior to World War II. The Holocaust changed the perceptions of the international community about the potential and practical structure of cosmopolitanism. While Jews made important contributions to post-Holocaust cosmopolitanism, certain constraints prevented them from working to their full potential in this new arena.

The context in which a cosmopolitan worldview can be expressed has changed dramatically since Immanuel Kant first articulated an enlightened cosmopolitan ideal in the late eighteenth century. In 1784, Kant envisioned a peaceful union of democratic nation-states interacting by means of a "league of nations" in which "each can be assured of its right."[53] Kant could not have foreseen the development, after World War II, of structures of world governance that would depend, not only on the bilateral interaction of states, but also on the interaction of multilateral *regions* like the European Union or the Organization of American States or the African Union. He could not have foreseen the establishment of intergovernmental institutions like the United Nations, or permanent regional military alliances like NATO, or NGOs like Human Rights Watch and the International Committee of the Red Cross, or global financial institutions like the International Monetary Fund and the World Bank, or the intricate system of international treaties, laws, and courts in place today.[54] He could not have foreseen the gradual movement from an inter-*national* system of governance based on state sovereignty and independence, to a *global* system of governance based on shared sovereignty and interdependence. In short, he could not have foreseen the slow and messy process known as "globalization."

Kant's cosmopolitanism spoke to a world that has come and gone. Today's complex world order is the ground from which a new, post-Kantian cosmopolitanism is growing. Articulated by political leaders, activists, and theorists, this new cosmopolitanism promotes not only a peaceful union of states and regions, but also a peaceful and secure position for individuals and disfavored groups. This new cosmopolitanism envisions ways to prevent and rectify some of the injustices experienced by these individuals and groups. David Held, the Graham Wallace Professor of Political Science at the London School of Economics, has called this new orientation "cosmopolitan democracy."[55]

In practice, cosmopolitan democracy seeks ways to democratize global governance and justice. International institutions are still largely designed to serve the political and juridical interests of states rather than those of individuals or private groups. For example, the UN General Assembly hears only the concerns of states, not those of individuals or groups. In a similar way, the International Court of Justice in The Hague hears only complaints between states, not those of individuals or groups. To reform the UN, supporters of cosmopolitan democracy have advocated for the right of individual and group petitions to various UN bodies, especially those dealing with human rights violations. With regard to global justice, supporters of cosmopolitan democracy successfully worked to create the International Criminal Court (ICC), established in 1998, a mechanism for securing justice for victims of genocide, war crimes, or crimes against humanity. In the ICC, individuals can be held culpable for their crimes, and individuals and groups have standing to bring information about potential crimes to the prosecutor, who then decides whether to pursue the complaint.

No goals are more important to advocates of cosmopolitan democracy than to prevent the violation of the rights of individuals and (to a more limited extent) groups, and to provide victims with appropriate redress. The international human rights system is legally grounded in the 1945 UN Charter, in the 1948 UDHR, and in subsequent international treaties. It has been overseen and implemented by complex UN machinery, including bodies designated in the charter, such as the Economic and Social Council, its Commission (now Council) on Human Rights, and the commission's Subcommission on the Promotion and Protection of Human Rights. These bodies have in turn created various thematic mechanisms, working groups, and special rapporteurs. Each human rights treaty has established a committee to monitor states' compliance, including the treaty bodies associated with the international covenants on Civil and Political Rights, and Economic, Social and Cultural Rights (CP Covenant and ESC Covenant, respectively) as well as more specialized treaties like the Convention on the Elimination of Racial Discrimination (CERD), the Convention on the Elimination of Discrimination against Women (CEDAW), the Convention against Torture (CAT), and the Convention on the Rights of the Child (CRC). Since 1994, the UN system has been administered by the Office of the High Commissioner for Human Rights. Having developed alongside the ad hoc international criminal tribunals for Yugoslavia and Rwanda, the ICC has become a permanent structure dedicated to international criminal justice.

The movement for cosmopolitan democracy has had evident relevance for Jews. Each Jewish Diaspora community is inextricably linked with other ethnic and religious minorities and immigrants. International and regional conventions on the freedoms of religion, movement, establishment, and association; on torture, genocide, war crimes, and crimes against humanity; on slavery, forced labor, and racial discrimination; on the individual expulsion of nationals and the collective expulsion of aliens—all of these conventions serve as significant safeguards for Jews as much as for other groups. Jews' historical suffering, especially during the Holocaust, has given them both the moral justification and the platform from which to act in this arena. And by acting to build a rights system in the postwar period—when they themselves have been relatively secure and influential—Jewish human rights activists have hoped to put safeguards in place to help themselves and others when times of insecurity arise.

Of the twenty-seven Jewish NGOs that have been affiliated with the UN, twenty-three are located in the Diaspora, most of these in the United States. The following eight organizations espousing human rights platforms have had consultative status with the UN Economic and Social Council, which oversees the human rights program. This status enables them to make oral and written submissions to human rights bodies. The year in which they first received consultative status is listed parenthetically:

Consultative Council of Jewish Organizations (CCJO), including the American Jewish Committee (AJC), Anglo-Jewish Association, and Alliance Israélite Universelle (1947)
Coordinating Board of Jewish Organizations (CBJO), including B'nai B'rith International, the British Board of Jewish Deputies, and the South African Board of Jewish Deputies (1947)
World Jewish Congress (WJC) (1947)
International Council of Jewish Women (ICJW) (1969)
International Association of Jewish Lawyers and Jurists (IAJLJ) (1995)
American Jewish Committee (AJC) (1997)

Most of these NGOs worked historically at the international level at least as far back as the League of Nations. Although the AJC only recently received separate consultative status, it has worked at the UN since the organization's founding as a constituent member of CCJO. Similarly, from 1947 until its dissolution in 2000, B'nai B'rith International worked as a member of CBJO. The IAJLJ is a relative newcomer, having been established in 1969 by Haim Cohn from Israel, Arthur Goldberg from the United States, and René Cassin from France. Although not technically a human rights NGO, World Union for Progressive Judaism (WUPJ) has also been heavily involved in specific human rights areas, such as the effort to reestablish Jewish life in the former Soviet Union. Because of their international scope and explicit human rights missions, these organizations are ideal subjects for this book's analysis of post-Holocaust Jewish cosmopolitanism.

The goals of these NGOs have varied widely, but some persistent items on the agenda will be identified in chapter 1. In general, they have sought to establish and sustain those aspects of the international human rights system that promote and protect the rights of Diaspora Jewish communities and individuals worldwide. They have also participated in the more general work of human rights activists, including:

- contributing to UN and regional standard-setting and treaty drafting
- advocating for their states' ratification of international human rights treaties
- lobbying policymakers

- monitoring states' compliance with treaties through site visits, information-gathering, and oral histories
- providing UN and regional human rights bodies with information on states' compliance
- using television, radio, school curricula, and conferences to educate the public on the value of human rights and mobilize the public to shame noncompliant states
- giving pro bono defense services to human rights victims
- raising funds on behalf of human rights causes
- tying in with other NGOs to form coalitions on particular issues.

In addition to its concern with international Jewish NGOs, this study attends to Jewish groups and individuals working for human rights at the level of the state, whether Israel, the United States, or Russia. In Israel, the book traces the emergence of a domestic human rights network from the late 1970s through the first intifada, including the Association for Civil Rights in Israel, B'Tselem, Physicians for Human Rights—Israel, HaMoked, Rabbis for Human Rights, and the Public Committee against Torture in Israel. In the United States, it is concerned with state-based NGOs like the National Conference for Soviet Jewry, Union of Councils for Soviet Jews and the National Council of Jewish Women, where their agendas overlap with international human rights issues. In Soviet and post–Soviet Russia, it analyzes the role of organizations—the Hebrew Circles, the Helsinki Watch Committee—and individuals in the struggle for Jews' freedom of movement and cultural and religious rights.

From time to time, this book touches on the numerous mainstream human rights NGOs and independent jurists who contributed substantially to efforts on behalf of Jews. Many of the general human rights NGOs were themselves founded, headed, and largely staffed by Jews: Human Rights Watch (Robert Bernstein, founder; Kenneth Roth, executive director), Helsinki Watch (Aryeh Neier, executive director), the International League for Human Rights (Roberta Cohen, its first executive director), and the Lawyers Committee for Human Rights (Michael Posner, founder and executive director). In addition, many US officials working on human rights issues had close affiliations with Jewish NGOs, including Supreme Court Justice (and later US ambassador to the UN) Arthur J. Goldberg; Rita Hauser, a Nixon appointee to the UN Commission on Human Rights; Morris Abram, a one-time president of AJC as well as US ambassador to the UN Commission on Human Rights; and Max Kampelman, ambassador to the Conference on Security and Cooperation in Europe during the Helsinki process. Many Jewish legal scholars have contributed to the development of human rights. Their contributions will be noted throughout the book, particularly when they act explicitly in reference to their Jewish identity.

Throughout this book, I attempt to clarify the areas in which NGOs specialized, coordinated activities with one another, competed with one another, or opposed one another. I scrutinize the relations among Jewish NGOs in Diaspora, state-based Israeli NGOs, the Israeli government, and individual "lone rangers" in order to understand how human rights questions in Israel have affected Israel/Diaspora relations. How are the political relations among the global Jewish political communities on human rights questions affected by the decision of the members of the Diaspora not to be "gathered in" through immigration to the state? I trace the degree to which Jewish NGOs at the UN formed coalitions—either among themselves or with other nongovernmental or governmental partners—in order to advance their aims. Paying close attention to the NGOs' inner dynamics enables an assessment of how unified Jewish political projects have been since 1945.

In this book, I try to clarify wherever necessary the political orientation of the actors. The initial impulse may be to assume that human rights activism springs from the progressive/liberal wing of Jewish politics, but this linkage cannot be made in every case. While many Jewish human rights activists founded their activism on concepts associated with the Jewish radical left, many others founded it on politically liberal or conservative concepts such as anti-Communism or Zionism. A good example of the anti-Communists were activists who worked to free Soviet Jews: Jewish neoconservatives (often associated with *Commentary* magazine) engaged in rights activism, not because they especially valued the UN human rights system—which they thought had been degraded and made repulsive by its anti-Zionism—but because the plight of Soviet Jews was the example par excellence of how Communism conflicted with the civil liberties outlined in the American Constitution.[56] Neoconservative Zionists also questioned the good of rights.[57]

Nor can we confidently associate human rights activism with the level of an individual's religious observance. To be sure, most of the Jewish human rights NGOs have been of the secular-liberal type, and most of the more religiously conservative Jewish sects, from modern Othodoxy to Chabad, have rejected the human rights discourse as a rationalist outgrowth of modernity and the Enlightenment rather than a discourse well grounded in Torah.[58] Yet one of the earliest Jewish human rights organizations, Agudat Israel (established 1912), was represented during the first years of the UN by Rabbi Isaac Lewin, who sought to persuade the UN to protect Jewish religious rights such as *shechitah* (ritual slaughter), *eruv* (the right to place a boundary around a Jewish community for ritual purposes), and burial rights. The individuals in Rabbis for Human Rights, a state-based NGO in Israel, and the World Union for Progressive Jews, an international alliance among Reform and Reconstructionist Jews, emphasize that their human rights activism is grounded in specific interpretations of Torah. Even activists in secular-liberal organizations, like the AJC, have from time to time defended their activism with reference to Jewish theological concepts or religious experiences. The division between secular and religious is sometimes hard to draw. A number of multidenominational organizations, such as the WJC and the ICJW, have developed human rights programs. In these cases, the type of political activity chosen necessarily results from interdenominational dialogue and struggle.

Finally, this book is concerned with the efforts by Jewish human rights activists to reform the UN human rights system. Since the 1960s, Jewish NGOs have expended at least as much energy and resources combating the anti-Zionism and anti-Semitism they found at the UN as on promoting their human rights agenda. This circumstance has influenced Jewish human rights activists to lead the charge for reform of UN procedures to ensure that anti-Israel rhetoric can no longer derail human rights efforts.[59] Jewish NGOs worked hard to get Israel included in one of the UN's regional groups and to get recognition for anti-Semitism as a prohibited form of discrimination.[60] There is still much to be done in order to rid the international human rights system of its ingrained bias against Israel and Jews. Yet many Jewish activists have concluded that the system has too much potential to abandon without a fight. With upwards of forty thousand human rights complaints flowing into the UN from around the world each year, these activists have held out for a fair and effective human rights system that could respond to at least the most egregious situations.

METHODS AND CHAPTER OVERVIEW

My research program has included trips to archives such as the Jacob and Hilda S. Blaustein Human Relations Research Library in the AJC building in New York, and the Jacob Rader Marcus Center of the American Jewish Archives at Hebrew Union College in Cincinnati, and extensive work with UN documents as well as documents from regional intergovernmental organizations such as the Organization for Security and Cooperation in Europe. The book has benefited greatly from the generosity and insight of the many activists I interviewed in Israel, the United States, and Russia.

To date, much of the work on Jewish human rights activism has proceeded in a number of directions. Studies have:

- described the broad spectrum of activities these NGOs have undertaken, but without an overall understanding of their relative weight or significance;
- analyzed their contributions with respect to one particular right (e.g., the right to leave any country, the prevention and prohibition of genocide, the elimination of racial discrimination);
- investigated Jewish human rights work apart from Jews' other political commitments, without reference to the full context of Jewish political history;
- investigated NGOs' activities in the context of human rights activism in general without reference to Jewish history, and without acknowledging or analyzing the Jewish sources by which the actors have been driven.

My approach is to synthesize aspects of all these approaches in order to examine human rights work as part of a total system of Jewish political commitments, a system characterized by the dynamic interdependence of its parts. I try to understand how this system is shaped by both human rights history and Jewish history. I also try to understand how particular components of the total system shift according to the specific needs of particular actors in given situations, and how those shifts ripple through the system as a whole.

In a book on a large and rather sparsely investigated subject, one's first impulse might simply be to take a chronicler's approach and tell about as many incidents as possible in their chronological order. Alternatively, one might try to avoid getting lost in the mass of details by gathering all of the observed phenomena under several broad headings, each of which could then be reduced to a number of common principles or elements. I have decided not to go either route, instead seeking a dialectical method through which the specifics and the generalizations inform and limit one another. I have selected for discussion relatively few types of activity that, in my judgment, call attention to critical aspects of the subject as a whole. In each instance I work from the ground up, where the "ground" consists of the multitude of positive details that occurred. Having established the ground in a particular setting, I then try to grapple with the overall significance of the specific events to my understanding of the whole sphere of activities I call "Jews and human rights." By concentrating on a limited number of activities, in both their specificity and their comparative significance, I try to imply (rather than provide) a view of the whole. Regardless of the particular subject at hand, I analyze the path Jews have taken to balance their commitments to the three weddings: nationalism, internationalism, and pluralism.

The first three chapters analyze the goals, strategies, and structure of international Jewish human rights activism. In chapter 1, "Building Human Rights,"

I trace the waxing and waning of Jews' enthusiasm for the new international human rights system that was born with the United Nations. Having described the historical emergence of the major international Jewish organizations, I then turn to the NGOs' activism in the first two decades after World War II. I show that Jewish leaders in Israel and the United States, Australia, France, and Britain were committed to the development of international human rights, making significant contributions to UN standard-setting and enforcement machinery. Yet as the UN majority changed, a bourgeoning anti-Israel alliance used many of the very treaties and enforcement mechanisms that Jews had built to condemn Israel, in many cases without evidentiary foundation. This led many Jews to wash their hands of international human rights. Others stayed on to fight to try to reform the system, believing that Jews still had much to gain from participation in the international community and the creation of a world human rights order. The paths of Jewish internationalism and Jewish nationalism begin here to diverge.

In chapter 2, "Freeing Soviet Jews—and After," I analyze the network of human rights actors that formed, both inside and outside of the Soviet Union, to work on behalf of the human rights of Soviet Jews. This network represents the preeminent example of Jewish human rights activism on behalf of a vulnerable part of the Diaspora. I show that each part of the network operated sometimes independently, sometimes in coordination, and sometimes in competition with or opposition to other parts. Each group used Soviet Jews as symbols for its own ends, producing tension between the Zionist impulses of the Israeli officials and the human rights impulses of the Diaspora activists. After the Soviet Jews' mass emigration in the wake of the dissolution of the USSR, Soviet Jews ceased to be human rights symbols, and the advocacy network mostly turned toward other matters, with negative consequences for those Jews remaining in the former Soviet Union.

If chapter 2 showed how Jews were able to employ the language of international human rights for the particular defense of their own group, chapter 3, "Jewish Responses to Non-Jewish Genocides," asks to what degree Jews have been involved in human rights struggles on behalf of non-Jewish populations—in a nonparochial, universal sense. The chapter details the contributions made by Jews, in the wake of World War II, to naming, defining, and prohibiting genocide; monitoring and publicizing outbreaks; advocating for intervention; and establishing accountability for the perpetrators. From the Genocide Convention to the Nuremburg Tribunal to the establishment of the ICC, Jews have mounted a variety of disparate responses, on a mostly unsystematic basis. Historically, these responses were more outspoken in the 1960s and 1970s, more muted in the 1980s and 1990s. Jews' response to the genocide in Darfur, although somewhat slow to kindle, eventually developed into a full-throated example of grassroots activism. Here, too, however, the response raises questions about the gradual decline of Jews' commitment toward international human rights.

Having established the global dimensions, strategies, and structure of Jewish human rights activism, I then analyze Jewish activism focused on human rights questions in Israel. In chapter 4, "American Jews and Violations in Zion: A Case Study," I show that in the wake of the Zionism=Racism resolution of 1975 and other manifestations of the hijacking of the UN by the anti-Israel alliance, the AJC was increasingly caught in a triple bind: its commitments to international human rights, the state of Israel, and American civil rights increasingly seemed in conflict with one another. At the same time, AJC's constituency was responding to internal historical pressures by moving toward the center/right with regard to internationalism and Zionism. I demonstrate how AJC's staff negotiated this fraught territory by standing publicly in solidarity with Israel against its enemies, while privately helping to establish the first Israeli domestic human and civil rights organization, the Association for Civil Rights in Israel. This episode had implications both for the transnational relationship between the Israeli government and American Jews, as well as for how far diaspora/ethnic minority NGOs can go in calling into question the human rights practices of their homelands.

I then turn to chapter 5, "Israeli, Jewish, Human," to explore the inner dynamics of the Israeli human rights network. If American Jews tried to apply the international human rights norms to the case of Israel, how did Israeli Jews react to the international human rights system? Basing my analysis on access to archival documents of Israeli human rights organizations as well as firsthand interviews with many of the principal activists, I tell the story of how a collection of individuals and small groups operating independently formed Israel's domestic human rights network in the late 1980s. I profile the groups involved and examine their developing stratification in the context of Israelis' continuous perception of existential threat and the tensions within Israel's constitution as "a Jewish and democratic state."

The book's brief conclusion, "The Road from Durban," contemplates the continuing failures of the international human rights system with regard to Israel, but also its remaining potential to achieve the hopes that had been placed in it by its earliest Jewish supporters. Recalling the negative aspects of the UN system, as exemplified by the re-emergence of the Zionism=Racism charge at the 2001 World Conference against Racism in Durban, South Africa, the conclusion goes on to consider the episode's ironic, and perhaps hopeful, aftermath.

While this book tells the story of how Diaspora Jews'optimism about human rights turned to ambivalence and pessimism, there is reason to imagine that a reverse process is still possible. The current international human rights system has numerous problems, to be sure, but many Jews remember how precarious the life of a minority community was in a world that lacked external checks on states' behavior, and many would rather work to make the current system better than revert to that world. The history traced here demonstrates that protecting human rights has been a persistent, if not always predominant, feature of Jews' political activity in the world. Whether they observe Jewish religious practices or are worshippers of the secular religion of human rights, activists would undoubtedly subscribe to the Mishnah's demand: "Yours is not to complete the work: but neither are you free to desist from it."

1

Building Human Rights

DANCING AT THREE WEDDINGS IS EASY

In the wake of the Holocaust, the international community was determined to build a new infrastructure that would prevent the horrors of genocide from happening again. The Nazis' drive to deprive Jews systematically of all their rights—including their right to life—was intolerable and cried out for a new kind of international law that would bind states to do several things: recognize and defend the fundamental rights and freedoms due every human being, codify and promote human rights standards in every nation in the world, protect individuals and minorities from their own governments if necessary, and bring violators to justice. This was an international mission that Jews were deeply inclined to support.

The International Military Tribunal at Nuremberg began to assert the need for an international legal order with the power to sanction states that violated the rights of those in their control. For the first time, states sought legal ways to protect victims of war crimes and crimes against humanity. In the words of Benjamin Ferencz, lead prosecutor during the trial of the Einsatzgrüppen, the soldiers who ran the Nazis' mobile killing units, "We seek here a judgment . . . reaffirming under law the basic rights of man."[1] The four principles that emerged from Nuremberg were that aggressive war is a crime, that some "crimes against humanity" are so egregious that they offend the conscience of the world, that "superior orders" is not a good defense, and that even a head of state can be held individually liable for the most atrocious crimes. These principles became the basis for all subsequent humanitarian and human rights law.[2] The United Nations Charter (1945) went further to codify them, as did the (nonbinding) Universal Declaration of Human Rights

(UDHR) (1948), the Convention on the Prevention and Punishment of the Crime of Genocide (1948), and the four Geneva conventions (1949). States that became parties to the newly forming international order perceived their postwar duty as giving greater international standing to individuals, both to protect them and hold them accountable when necessary.[3]

Although in the wake of World War II states agreed that something had to be done, they were wary about committing themselves to international protections for human rights. At the San Francisco Conference, the United States and the United Kingdom, among others, resisted the proposal to include human rights in the United Nations Charter, on the grounds that such a mission would permit the erosion of state sovereignty by encouraging international intervention into states' relations with their own citizens.[4] But even before the war, Jewish nongovernmental organization (NGOs) were working to ensure that the postwar world order would meaningfully address human rights.

Many of the NGOs that would go to work drafting rights standards in the early days of the UN had their roots in much earlier civil rights struggles. The earliest of the Jewish rights organizations were the Board of Deputies of British Jews (established in 1815) and the Alliance Israélite Universelle (established in 1840). The former, while primarily an association to advocate for Jews' emancipation at home, undertook under Moses Montefiore a number of missions to alleviate the sufferings of Jews abroad, in Syria, Palestine, and Romania. Established in France by Adolph Crémieux, the Alliance's initial aims were "to work everywhere for the emancipation and moral progress of the Jews" and "to lend effectual support to those who suffer through being Jews."[5] The Alliance fulfilled its mission by building schools and social services for Jews in North Africa and the Levant and by advocating to the local rulers for amelioration of Jewish disabilities. Its president during World War II, René Cassin, went on to become one of the drafters of the UDHR and win the Nobel Peace Prize.

B'nai B'rith International (BBI) was founded in New York 1843, soon after the Alliance, and in reaction to the same catalyst: the revival of the blood libel in Damascus in 1840, which led to a massacre of Syrian Jews. The BBI's main business during its first half century was the founding of local lodges (parallel to Masonic and other lodges exclusively open to Christians), and it also established hospitals, libraries, cemeteries, homes for the aged, and homes for widows and orphans. It became involved in rights defense in reaction to the Russian pogroms of 1903–1906. When the United Nations was formed in 1945, BBI joined with the British Board of Jewish Deputies and the South African Board of Jewish Deputies to form the Coordinating Board of Jewish Organizations (CBJO), which received consultative status in UN human rights bodies in 1947.

The National Council of Jewish Women was formed in 1893 as a social welfare and philanthropic organization, in line with the expectations of the time that women would engage in nurturing public activity. The Council formed women's auxiliaries, multidenominational religious associations, and social reform associations. Under Rebekah Kohut, the organization became increasingly interested in civic affairs and social legislation. In 1923, Kohut called the first international conference of Jewish women's councils. Thereafter the National Council became increasingly internationalized. After World War II, it joined with other women's organizations abroad to form the International Council of Jewish Women (ICJW), and in 1969 it received consultative status at the United Nations.

The American Jewish Committee (AJC), which, along with the World Jewish Congress (WJC), was to become the most influential international human rights organization, and was formed amid the Russian pogroms of 1903–1906 and the establishment of anti-Semitic nationalist organizations like the Union of Genuine Russians. Its purpose from the outset was to defend the citizenship rights of Jews throughout the world. The AJC commissioned Professor Hersch Lauterpacht of Cambridge University to write a treatise on "An International Bill of the Rights of Man" as early as 1942 and used his resulting book, *The International Bill of the Rights of Man* (1944), in its advocacy efforts.[6] In February 1945, the AJC published a booklet, *To the Counselors of Peace*, asserting that human rights must be a principle purpose of the United Nations. It joined with the Alliance Israélite Universelle and the Anglo-Jewish Association to form the Consultative Council of Jewish Organizations (CCJO), through which it was granted consultative status at the UN in 1947.

The WJC began as a federation of national organizations. For example, the American Jewish Congress (AJCongress) was formed in 1917, and reorganized in 1920 under the direction of its charismatic leader, Rabbi Stephen S. Wise. Its activities mirrored those of the AJC but served a different constituency. While the Committee was considered the elite organization, formed by the German-Jewish elite, the Congress was formed by Russian Jews who were at that time closer to the immigration experience and less well off as a whole. In 1936, the WJC was formed in Geneva to try to address the rise of the Nazi Party. With affiliates in over one hundred countries, the WJC has sought to become the voice of world Jewry to defend Jews' rights. It received consultative status at the UN in 1947.

Finally, two religious organizations, the World Union for Progressive Judaism (WUPJ) and Agudas Israel World Organization (AIWO), were awarded consultative status in UN human rights bodies. The WUPJ was founded by Lily Montagu, one of the leaders of Liberal Judaism in Great

Britain (analogous to Reform in the United States), in 1926. Gradually, it gathered members from throughout the Jewish world. Theologically, the WUPJ's members held a number of liberal beliefs: (1) the theory of progressive revelation—that God continuously reveals himself in every generation in an evolving way, and hence the tradition is always evolving; (2) that God's unity was revealed, or should be revealed, in the unity of human beings, for which it was Jews' task to strive; that every human being was made in the image of God; (3) that human beings were intrinsically good and perfectible; and (4) that Judaism's holiday cycle and its central ritual practices encoded beliefs of a universal character. All of these tenets tended to make the WUPJ enthusiastic about the United Nations. Although much of its work was on the educational and social aspects of the UN's work, it also participated selectively in human rights issues. In a sermon called "Religion and the United Nations" on October 25, 1958, Lily Montagu called human rights advocacy "religious work" and asserted that it was the duty of all Jews to support.[7]

Orthodox Jews, too, initially supported the United Nations through the AIWO. Established in 1912 as the political arm of Ashkenazi orthodoxy in Eastern Europe, the AIWO was responsible for negotiating the Status Quo Agreement with the secular founders of Israel delimiting the line between the religious and secular characters of the state. Its first UN representative, Rabbi Isaac Lewin, made submissions to human rights bodies arguing for the protection of religious freedoms.

Jewish nongovernmental organizations (NGOs) played perhaps the key role in ensuring that human rights would be a major commitment of the new United Nations organization. The AJC, working with the British Board of Deputies and the WJC, sent a "Memorandum on Certain Matters of Specific Jewish Interest," to the state delegates at the San Francisco Conference, asserting that the UN must commit to human rights.[8] The AJC's president, Judge Joseph Proskauer, corresponded with US secretary of state Edward Stettinius, and, together with Jacob Blaustein, the chair of the AJC's Executive Committee, the two led a delegation of forty-two Jewish, church-based, and civic NGOs to persuade the Americans and British to write broad rights protections in the charter. Judge Proskauer made an impassioned plea to the delegates that proved persuasive.[9]

Once the United Nations had committed itself, Jewish NGOs threw themselves into the standard setting that was then the major task of the newly established UN Commission on Human Rights (CHR) and its Subcommission on the Prevention of Discrimination and the Protection of Minorities.[10]

If Jewish activists thought the UN would provide a quick fix for threats to human rights, however, they soon learned otherwise. Although states were fond of declaring their commitment to human rights, the UN's CHR determined as early as 1947 that it had no power to take any action in regard to complaints of human rights violations, and its parent body, the Economic and Social Council (ECOSOC) , affirmed this decision.[11] This was called "the self-denying rule." Although from 1947 to 1957, CHR received some 65,000 human rights complaints, it abided by its determination that it could do no more than receive them.[12] In short order the subcommission made it equally clear that it would focus only on the first half of its title—preventing discrimination—while all but neglecting the latter half—protecting minorities. Establishing norms, rather than enforcing them, would become the heart of the UN human rights program, at least until 1967, after which more effective procedures for addressing complaints began to be developed.

International Jewish activists were not dissuaded by the states' initial reluctance to live up to their rhetoric. Jews were inspired by their religious tradition, by the negative example of the Holocaust, and by self-interest. During the 1950s, many American Jews went to work on behalf of civil rights in order to strengthen America's pluralism. Civil rights at the national level were analogous to human rights at the international level: an attempt to balance the abstract needs of governance with the concrete needs of the individuals and groups being governed. No doubt, then, American Jews' experience of civil rights activism prepared them to understand and support the aims of the new world order.

For all these reasons, members of Jewish human rights NGOs were disposed to see the international community as a potentially effective hedge against their own insecurity, dedicating considerable resources to crafting rights they conceived as universal in application and indivisible in substance. Jewish activists believed that Jews would best be protected against human rights violations if everyone were protected. For example, when Sidney Liskofsky, the director of the Foreign Affairs Department of the AJC, drew up a plan for what was to become the Jacob Blaustein Institute for the Advancement of Human Rights, he wrote:

> The ethical ideals of Judaism and the historical experience of the Jewish people bear witness that human rights and Jewish rights are of one warp and woof. As was said of Jacob and Benjamin, their souls are bound up one in the other. . . . Therefore, while attentive to specific Jewish concerns and vigilant in the defense of Jewish rights, we are devoted to the movement for recognition and protection of human rights and fundamental freedoms for all of mankind.[13]

While working on an international treaty to eliminate statelessness, he wrote that "the needs of Jewish stateless persons will be best served by international agreement on standards held to be helpful to stateless persons generally."[14] Universalist internationalism could serve specifically Jewish ends.

At the same time, the birth of the state of Israel (1948) seemed to give Jews a safe haven where their rights could be protected at the national level. If before the war Jews chose either Jewish nationalism, loyalty to their own state, or internationalism, in the first years of the postwar period choosing did not seem necessary. Jews in international NGOs worked for the expansion of international human rights at the UN, the development of the homeland in Israel, and the extension of civil rights and civil liberties in their country of citizenship. In other words, they exhibited triple loyalties to three weddings. For a time, all three priorities seemed to be aligned.

DRAFTING AND PROMOTING UNIVERSAL STANDARDS

After the UN had been established, Jewish leaders jumped at the chance to make the human rights promises in the charter real. In the first decade of the UN, Jewish NGOs with consultative status at the UN made literally hundreds of written and oral submissions to the ECOSOC, the CHR, its subcommission, and specialized agencies like the International Law Commission, World Health Organization, UNESCO, and UNICEF.[15] Perhaps their most significant work was in the relief of vulnerable Jewish populations, as well as in the struggle to define, prohibit, and punish genocide (to be discussed in chapters 2 and 3, respectively).

In addition to their work at the UN, Jewish NGOs mounted campaigns to educate the public to support human rights. In the 1950s the CCJO worked with UNESCO to create an extensive program of human rights education, bringing the message of human rights to Americans through radio, television, film, school curricula, church and synagogue activities, and local chapter events.[16]

From the beginning of the United Nations, Jewish NGOs forged informal working relationships with one another. As a report of the CBJO put it in its 1950 "Report of Activities,"

> CBJO has from time to time worked with Agudas Israel World Organization, the Consultative Council of Jewish Organizations and the World Jewish Congress in respect of matters of common interest, such as human rights, problems of Jewish war orphans, and such. Although there is no formal agreement or system of coordination, a considerable degree of cooperation exists on an *ad hoc* basis among consultants for Jewish consultative organizations.[17]

This informal arrangement was, paradoxically, the product of careful negotiations. After the Jewish NGOs worked so well together at the San Francisco

Conference, CBJO and the AJC proposed the formation of a Council of Jewish Delegations, with an executive governing the whole organization. This would have provided a much more formal structure than actually emerged. But WJC rejected the proposal, "as this might undermine the existence of the World Jewish Congress itself."[18] In its bid to be recognized as the sole voice of world Jewry, WJC filed alone for consultative status with the UN, arguing that it should be the only Jewish NGO to receive such status; if it had been successful, the practical effect would have been that all Jewish organizations would have had to make proposals through WJC.

As it was, WJC's separate action caused other Jewish NGOs—BBI, AJC, British Board of Deputies, South African Board of Jewish Deputies, and WUPJ—to form their own alliances for consultative status.[19] As a result, although all Jewish NGOs shared information informally, in the first years of the UN they managed to issue only one joint memorandum, on the Declaration of the Rights of the Child. Similar tensions cropped up from time to time. In 1969, Phil Baum, the executive director of WJC's American chapter, did not think WJC should honor Arthur J. Goldberg, then-president of AJC, because "the Committee's excursions into international affairs are unseemly and ill-advised."[20] (The recipient of the letter, Rabbi Joachim Prinz, chair of the AJC's Commission on International Affairs, disagreed.)

While developing these informal working relationships among themselves, Jewish NGOs also made alliances with non-Jewish international NGOs through attending the conferences of international NGOs held by the UN Department of Public Information, as well as the general conferences of consultative NGOs and other similar meetings. AJC had extensive working relations with the International League for the Rights of Man, and later, Human Rights Watch. Each organization's national affiliates formed relationships with other national groups. BBI worked extensively with the Carnegie Endowment for International Peace and the American Association for the United Nations.[21] Forming such alliances was useful, both to avoid the ghettoization of Jewish NGOs at the UN and to amplify their influence at home. As relatively small NGOs, with neither the staff nor the clout of larger human rights organizations, Jewish NGOs could not always sway the international community in and of themselves. By "tying in" with the statements of broad-based NGOs like Human Rights Watch, they could also promote issues of Jewish concern under the cover of a more general universalist agenda.[22]

Jewish NGOs were influential with the general NGO community out of all proportion to their size and numbers, from the UN's early days to the present. Kenneth Roth, executive director of Human Rights Watch, remarked in May 1977 that AJC's Jacob Blaustein Institute "has become no less than the nucleus around which the US-based human rights movement works out its strategy on major UN issues, not to mention a unique source of inside information and activist ideas based on extraordinary access to serious officials."[23] A measure of this influence is that Blaustein's director, Felice Gaer, was the first woman and first American to be named to the UN Committee against Torture.

Jewish NGOs have also succeeded by collaborating on particular issues with international law experts and government officials. For instance, in 1977, Blaustein's Sidney Liskofsky wrote a draft proposal for a book-length collection of articles by noted jurists on the International Covenant on Civil and Political Rights (CP Covenant, entered into force in 1976), to be edited by Louis Henkin, the well-known Columbia University international law professor. Liskofsky then arranged for the AJC to provide $9,000 toward publication.[24] Blaustein worked closely with sympathetic State Department officials (such as Rita Hauser, Roberta Cohen, and Richard Gardner), members of the judiciary (Arthur J. Goldberg, Thomas Buergenthal), the US Delegation to the UN (Marietta Tree, John Carey, Morris Abram) and the UN Human Rights Division (John Humphrey, Egon Schwelb).

While contributing substantially to the UN's effort to create universal norms, Jewish NGOs engaged in a forty-year effort to persuade states, especially the United States, to ratify the human rights treaties adopted by the international community. Having established an NGO coalition called the Ad Hoc Committee on Human Rights and Genocide Treaties, Jewish human rights activists like Sidney Liskofsky, William Korey, and Harris Schoenberg worked tirelessly, convincing figures like Arthur J. Goldberg, US ambassador to the UN and former Supreme Court justice, to join the fight, advocating at the American Bar Association, and lobbying members of Congress and the White House.[25]

A comprehensive report of all the activities in which Jewish NGOs engaged would cover many volumes. For our purpose, it is enough to present an overview of the most significant categories of activity, focused on the first decades after World War II but in many cases continuing to the present. The overview attests to the broad range of issues with which Jewish human rights workers concerned themselves.

Civilians and Refugees

Jews' immediate task was to protect the rights of survivors of World War II, in the process ensuring that future victims of genocide, war crimes, and crimes against humanity would not face the same postwar difficulties Jews did. Jewish NGOs worked diligently on treaties establishing the rights of refugees, the right to a nationality, the right of asylum, the right to restitution of property, protection from statelessness, prohibition of forced labor, and prohibition of slavery. The work of the WJC, CBJO, and WUPJ on behalf of the principle of self-determination was also crucial to the establishment of that right as Article 1 of both the UDHR and the CP Covenant.[26] The codification of this right would be indispensable to the UN's recognition of the state of Israel, although ironically it would be the basis for later condemnations of Israel for denying Palestinians the same right.

Jewish NGOs worked to ensure that all these rights would be codified in the Geneva conventions and the general human rights treaties, not only the CP Covenant but the International Covenant on Economic, Social and Cultural Rights (ESC Covenant), and the International Convention on the Elimination of All Forms of Racial Discrimination (CERD).[27] Their draft articles for these treaties were often summarily incorporated, or served as the basis for delegates' deliberations.

Jews' concern for protecting civilians has continued to the present. In keeping with its historic concern for children and women, the ICJW was a principle architect of the Ottawa treaty prohibiting landmines, weapons often left behind by militants to be tripped later by civilians.

Religious Freedoms

Immediately after the end of the war, Jewish NGOs sought enforceable protection of the rights to freedom of worship, conscience, religious belief, and association. The AIWO, led by Rabbi Isaac Lewin, was an orthodox NGO that argued for protection of Jews' religious practices, including kosher slaughtering, Jewish cemeteries and burial rituals, study of Jewish religious texts, and the right of religious minorities to educate their children.[28]

The WUPJ, especially its first honorary secretary, Lily Montagu, was particularly active in this area in the early decades of the UN. In 1945, immediately after the San Francisco Conference, WUPJ sent a "Statement from the World Union for Progressive Judaism to the Governments of the United Nations," demanding protection for religious freedom.[29] After the right was guaranteed by the UDHR in 1948, WUPJ continued throughout the 1950s to make oral and written submissions to the ECOSOC and the CHR, pressing for this freedom to be included in the CP Covenant. In 1957, the NGO produced an impressive country-by-country analysis of the state of religious freedom in fifty-four countries, which it submitted to special rapporteur Arcot Krishnaswami, who was preparing a report on the state of the right for the subcommission.[30] From the 1950s until today, WUPJ has played a leading role among NGOs working on this right. Betty Golomb and Norma U. Levitt, WUPJ's UN representatives, served in official positions on the broad-based Committee of Religious NGOs throughout the 1970s and 1980s, tracking threats to religious freedom around the world, mapping out common political strategies for addressing them, and holding multidenominational observances.

While the UN was eager to adopt treaties and declarations prohibiting racial discrimination, the Soviet Union and many of the decolonized and Arab states were less eager to adopt prohibitions of religious intolerance, because they were themselves engaged in religious persecution at home. The Commission's original plan was to draft a treaty prohibiting *both* racial and religious intolerance, but when this proved politically impossible, its members decided to split the work into two treaties. In the end, only the CERD was adopted (1964). The UN has never been able to come to consensus on a religious freedom treaty. Both AJC's Blaustein Institute for the Advancement of Human Rights and the ICJW participated in a decades-long struggle for some kind of legislative recognition of the right. While a binding treaty was never possible, Blaustein's first director, Sidney Liskofsky, was a leading force in drafting a Declaration on the Elimination of All Forms of Religious Intolerance, which was adopted by the UN General Assembly in 1981. Although lacking the binding force of a formal treaty, the declaration would enable NGOs to exercise some moral persuasion on states that abused religious freedoms.[31] In 2001, Blaustein's second director, Felice Gaer, continued the NGO's tradition of activism in this area when she was appointed by House Minority Leader Richard Gephardt to the United States Commission on International Religious Freedom. She was reappointed by House Minority Leader Nancy Pelosi in 2004, and served as chair (2002–2003) and vice chair (2003–2006) of the commission.[32]

Protection of Minorities and Prevention of Discrimination

From the 1940s until now, Jews have acted to protect minorities and to prevent all forms of discrimination. They have tried to draft rights protections, monitor specific abuses, and advocate for international solutions, particularly where the vulnerable minority in question was Jewish.

In terms of standard-setting, Jewish NGOs were indispensable participants in the debate over whether to include rights protections for ethnic, religious, and linguistic minorities in the UDHR and the CP Covenant. The arguments against such protection were strong: if the new actor on the international stage was the individual human person, then members of minorities could have rights only as individuals rather than collectively. Conferring rights to a protected class would entail enormous fiscal obligations on states, because such rights require state support of minority educational facilities, language resources, community centers, and so on. Many delegates participating in the debate found that defining a "minority" raised insurmountable problems. As Moses Moskowitz, the first secretary of the CCJO, noted, states often have an interest in assimilating their minorities to prevent internal unrest, to prohibit internal attempts to undermine state sovereignty, and to create a homogeneous national identity: this interest is fundamentally at odds with the maintenance of minority group identity.[33] Jewish NGOs were, however, ultimately successful in arguing for inclusion of some minority group protection in both the UDHR and the CP Covenant (Article 27 in both). They were able to use the Nazis' persecution of Jews as a group to argue for some group protections.

In the prevention of discrimination, certain conflicts among Jewish NGOs cropped up. The WJC was active in drafting the provisions in the CP Covenant on the prohibition of incitement to racial or religious discrimination (Article 7). Based in London, the WJC's position grew out of postwar European legal thinking. As lawyers in the American legal tradition, however, the AJC's staff worried that a prohibition on incitement would infringe on the rights of free speech, press, and assembly. The same conflict was raised in the prohibition of racist incitement in CERD (Article 4): the WJC demanded a prohibition; the AJC demurred.[34]

Jewish NGOs not only participated in general standard-setting but advocated on behalf of particular vulnerable minorities. They exerted themselves on behalf of persecuted Jews in Iraq, Syria, Yemen, the USSR, and Ethiopia. While their activities on behalf of Soviet Jews were especially impressive, they did not neglect Jews from Iraq, Syria, Yemen, and Ethiopia who were persecuted by their governments between the 1950s and 1990s.[35] For example, on May 18, 1951, all the Jewish NGOs with consultative status (AIWO, CCJO, CBJO, WJC, ICJW, WUPJ) submitted a collective report to the Commission on Human Rights charging Iraq with violating the UN Charter and documenting its violations of Jews' human rights. These included the arrest of ten Jews in a synagogue sanctuary, the illegal search of their persons, their torture in Abu Ghraib prison, and the subsequent confiscation of all Jews' property and freezing of their bank accounts.[36] These petitions helped win international approval for the action by the Israeli government in Operation Magic Carpet to airlift the Jews of Iraq to Israel. That operation in turn would provide precedent for subsequent similar airlifts, including Operation Solomon, in which Israel transported almost the entire population of Ethiopian Jews to Israel in forty-eight hours in 1991, and Israel's subsequent efforts to win Soviet Jews their right to emigrate. They also tracked anti-Semitism that might affect smaller Jewish populations throughout Asia, Latin America, and Africa.[37]

Jewish NGOs' efforts did not stop at the borders of Jewishness but were often focused directly on oppressed non-Jewish populations. One of the constituent organizations of CBJO was the South African Board of Jewish Deputies, which provided the international NGO with first-hand accounts of the conditions of blacks under apartheid, leading the organization to call repeatedly for the end of legal segregation in South Africa.[38] As we will see in the chapter on Jewish responses to non-Jewish genocides (chapter 3), Jewish NGOs responded to human rights abuses in Indochina, Bosnia, Kosovo, Rwanda, and Sudan, among others.

Women, Children, and Families

The record of the substantial work of activists to promote and protect the rights of women, children, and parents eloquently testifies to the importance of family in Jewish tradition. This work was a part of the "Never Forget" ideology, inasmuch as families had been divided and decimated by the Nazis, and Jews wanted to ensure the stability of this essential unit of Jewish society in the future. It was also a testament to the traditional Jewish focus on the family, starting from the biblical commandments to protect widows and orphans. Concern for women and families also was expressed by feminists, among whom Jewish women worldwide, and especially in the United States, played significant leadership roles.

Jewish rights activists contributed to writing international protections for victims of domestic violence, reproductive rights, children's education, family contacts, family reunification, the prohibition of gender-specific war crimes, and the protection of civilians in wartime. From its inception in 1979, the ICJW and WJC also participated on the treaty body monitoring compliance with the Convention Committee on the Elimination of Discrimination against Women (CEDAW). Felice Gaer, director of AJC's Blaustein Institute, was the aide to Geraldine Ferraro, the head of the US delegation to the UN Conference on Women's Rights in Beijing, 1995. She was a principle actor at the conference, ensuring that its final program would declare, for the first time, that women's rights are human rights.[39]

Where children's rights were concerned, the ICJW, WJC, and Blaustein Institute made essential contributions to the UN Convention on the Rights of the Child. Norma U. Levitt of the WUPJ served on the United States Committee for UNICEF, working to ensure that the WUPJ's member synagogues created programming associated with the International Year of the Child (1979).[40]

At the same time, their efforts at the UN to condemn domestic violence, women's statelessness, and divorce had a reflexive effect, causing Jewish women's organizations to confront inequities toward women and children they perceived in Jewish law. Jewish human rights workers brought back demands for the human rights of women and children in their own communities. The ICJW worked for an end to domestic violence in Jewish families, and called for amelioration of the plight of *agunot*, or abandoned women. Jewish women's equality with respect to child custody, labor, and property were also objects of concern.[41]

Implementation

From early on in the UN's work, Jews recognized that the promise of universal human rights would be worthless unless there were means to ensure that states carried out their promises, and mechanisms for holding violators accountable. Regardless of the NGOs' particular area of specialization, they all had to work to secure the public legitimacy and enforceability of human rights norms per se. The attempt to give teeth to human rights has taken sixty years to date, with little end in sight, and it could not have succeeded even to the limited degree it has if it had not been for the contributions of Jews. In this area, UN history is especially inseparable from Jewish history.

Jewish NGOs' work on implementation took two concrete forms: they advocated for the rights of individual and group petition as well as for creation of an overall administrative position for the global human rights program. During the drafting phase of the CP Covenant, most human rights NGOs (Jewish and otherwise) took the view that the key to its effectiveness would be whether it included rights of petition. If it relied only on a complaint procedure initiated by states, they thought, it was sure to be powerless, since states are almost always unwilling to bring rights complaints against one another, which might compromise trade and military alliances.

Individual and group petitions would ensure that states would take complaints against them seriously, because states generally respond to public shame. However, because individuals only rarely have the capacity to investigate violations of their human rights, or present their evidence in an acceptable form, an intermediary was needed that could help shepherd their cases. Because fact-finding, evidence-gathering, and reporting were the strong suits of NGOs, these groups could intercede for abused individuals. Therefore a right of group petition was also indispensable.

Parallel to the idea of petition as the means of protecting human rights was the idea of a single official who could coordinate UN human rights activities.

As far back as 1947, René Cassin had argued for the creation of the position of attorney general, or, as it came to be called, High Commissioner for Human Rights (HCHR), a Secretariat-level position that would give a high profile to human rights within the UN system. The high commissioner would represent the UN human rights system to the world, receive complaints and determine their admissibility, refer admissible complaints to the relevant bodies, commission and circulate thematic and country reports, undertake site visits, and mediate disputes between individuals and their governments. Jewish activists believed that, together, the rights of individual and group petition and the HCHR would make rights enforceable.

They worked hard toward both goals, as it turned out, for the next fifty years. Throughout the Human Rights Commission's drafting of the CP Covenant, Jewish NGOs submitted numerous proposals arguing for the rights of petition.[42] A WJC memorandum on the draft covenant went so far as to declare that "the denial of this Right of Petition, at least to recognised Non-Governmental Organizations, defeats the purpose of the Covenant."[43] But states resisted inclusion of the right, since it might lead to international interference in sovereign state matters and open the states up to new kinds of liability. States also feared that giving legal standing to individuals or groups would result in the young commission being inundated with complaints. It is worth recalling that non-Western states, like the USSR, were not the only ones leading the resistance. US secretary of state John Foster Dulles tried his best to ensure that the CP Covenant would be shelved in the early 1950s. Dulles declared that the United States would not seek ratification of any human rights treaties, for reasons to be explored in chapter 3.

Frustration with the lack of progress on the rights of petition led Jewish NGOs to keep Cassin's idea for a high commissioner alive. Between 1947 and 1958, Moses Moskowitz, secretary of CCJO, continued to submit proposals for the position.[44] Moskowitz's proposal was defeated by the USSR, but he did not give up, continuing to promote it in various books.[45]

AJC's director of foreign affairs, Sidney Liskofsky, continued to promote Moskowitz's work. In 1962, in his role as chair of the broad-based NGO Committee on Human Rights Research, Liskofsky wrote that the high commissioner would be "the conscience of the covenanting States, [and] would have the rights and duty to institute, in response to petitions from individuals or groups of individuals (as well as from governments), or even on the basis of information derived from his own general super-visory activities, proceedings against States charged with human rights violations."[46]

In May 1963, Liskofsky coordinated the "Seminar on the International Protection of Human Rights" at AJC headquarters in New York. Participants included UN Secretariat staff, US government officials, Jewish and general human rights NGOs, and international law experts.[47] As a result of the seminar, John Humphrey, head of the UN Human Rights Division, agreed to draft a speech by AJC's executive director Jacob Blaustein. The speech, titled "Human Rights—A Challenge to the United Nations and to Our Generation," was delivered at Columbia University on December 4, 1963, as the first serious call for a high commissioner since Cassin's early advocacy.[48] In it Blaustein declared that "the time has come when the United Nations should face the immediate problem of transition from merely promotion of human rights, to implementation of human rights."[49] He recommended that individual and group petitions should be "sifted by a kind of International Attorney-General, who would be responsible for instituting proceedings before the Human Rights Committee."[50] The speech was well received by an audience of international dignitaries and succeeded in putting the HCHR back on the international agenda.[51]

Yet in 1963, the time for the HCHR had not yet come. In fact, states' resistance to serious implementation meant that the proposal would remain dormant for another thirty years.[52] Throughout the intervening period, Jewish NGOs never let the idea die, even when Cold War politics in the 1980s made it seem like a pipe dream.[53]

In the meantime, NGOs found other means to attain the objectives that the high commissioner position had been intended to fulfill. During the 1960s and 1970s, the UN human rights program took small strides in developing implementation measures. The CP Covenant had not included a right of petition (either individual or group), but the states agreed to include an optional protocol, which enabled states to declare themselves accountable to an individual petition procedure. The CERD treaty went further by incorporating a nonoptional petition procedure into the treaty itself. Even those treaties with no petition procedures require states to submit periodic reports on their compliance. The country reports are then subjected to intense scrutiny and questioning by oversight committees. In practice, in preparing questions for the states about their reports, the committee members rely heavily on information provided by human rights NGOs. So even though most treaties did not provide for the right of group petition, NGOs have still been able to get their complaints heard.

The commission also took steps to overturn its "self-denying rule." In 1967, the ECOSOC instituted a public procedure, and three years later, a secret procedure for investigating complaints.[54] The former permitted the commission to create working groups and special rapporteurs to study "patterns of gross and reliably attested violations" throughout the world. These entities began to issue thematic reports on various rights abuses (e.g., the Working Group on Disappearances, the special rapporteur on extrajudicial and summary executions) and country-specific reports (e.g., the special rapporteur on Chile). Thus, many of the functions for which the high commissioner had initially been desired were now being carried out by other bodies.

During the Reagan/Bush years, the State Department argued that there was no longer a need for the attorney general position because its function was already being filled by special rapporteurs. Even as late as spring 1993, State Department officials could be heard using this argument.[55] Besides, the Reagan and Bush administrations were deeply suspicious of the UN's human rights program, and looked unfavorably on expansions of it.[56]

Yet the Blaustein Institute and BBI never lost sight of the need for a human rights coordinator. By the early 1990s, with the massacres in Srebrenica and early warning signs of Hutu/Tutsi tensions in Rwanda, they believed that an office to coordinate UN human rights activities with peacekeeping and field missions remained a vital need. Their concerns were increasingly synchronized with those of US and UN officials. As the world human rights situation deteriorated during the first years of the Clinton administration, the UN decided to hold the World Conference on Human Rights in Vienna in 1993 to reinvigorate its program.

The continuing occurrences of mass murder and widespread abuse made clear the need for stronger measures of implementation. Amnesty International was joined by Blaustein's Felice Gaer and BBI's Harris Schoenberg in lobbying president Bill Clinton and secretary of state Madeline Albright.[57] In September 1993 the president publicly backed the proposal, which ensured it a prominent place on the agenda at Vienna.[58] Schoenberg, acting as chair of the UN NGO Human Rights Committee, organized numerous public and private meetings to build support for the position.[59] The delegates to the Vienna conference approved the position and the General Assembly formally established it on December 20, 1993. An Ecuadoran diplomat, José Ayala Lasso, was elected the first UN HCHR in April 1994.

After the position's establishment, Jewish NGOs continued to work to ensure it would be more than a paper tiger. The Blaustein Institute, in conjunction with the Carter Center's Human Rights Program in Atlanta, Georgia, held a series of four seminars with High Commissioner Ayala Lasso, beginning in June 1995.[60] These seminars sought to address perceived tensions between the high commissioner and the NGO community on field missions and country visits, monthly reports, the development of rapid response procedures for emergency situations, the procedures for fact-finding missions, and the incorporation of women's rights into the human rights program, among other things.[61] The result was better coordination and a more effective office.

The early and persistent efforts of Jewish NGOs to secure the rights of individual and group petition and to establish an effective human rights coordinator concretely demonstrate how much stock these activists put in building a strong UN system. They did so despite the fact that many of the UN bodies had demonstrated a strong tendency to criticize Israel, considering that any human rights protection was better than none.

DANCING AT THREE WEDDINGS IS HARD

Although Jews have continued to promote human rights throughout the past sixty years, the initial enthusiasm for and trust in the UN system they displayed in the 1940s and 1950s has eroded. As the UN majority changed, many of the treaties and enforcement mechanisms that Jews had built began to be used to discredit Jews and also Israel. The misuse of the human rights tools Jews had helped create led many to dismiss the claims of international human rights.

The relationship between the UN and Jewish NGOs began to sour in the early 1960s, in the wake of the UN's inadequate response to an international outbreak of swastika graffiti in 1959. Beginning in Copenhagen, a rash of swastika graffiti had appeared on synagogue walls and Jewish tombstones around the world, some 1,400 instances in all. When AIWO's Isaac Lewin brought these acts to the attention of Marrietta Tree, the US delegate to the Commission, she proposed that the draft CERD be amended to prohibit anti-Semitism.[62] The delegate from the USSR, seeking to prevent scrutiny of his country's anti-Semitic practices, responded that anti-Semitism could be outlawed as a form of racism only if other specific forms of racism were mentioned in the treaty, including apartheid, Nazism, and Zionism. This was the origin of what was to be General Assembly Resolution 3379, adopted on November 15, 1975, equating Zionism with racism.[63]

In the wake of the 1967 war, Arab states became increasingly unified against Jews and Israel by pan-Arabism and by support for the aims of the Palestine Liberation Organization. Arab states in turn found an ally in the USSR, which criticized Israel as an American proxy in the Cold War. Having abandoned its "self-denying rule" in 1970, the commission immediately began adopting resolutions against Israel. Israel was only the second country, after Pinochet's Chile, to be investigated under the secret procedure. The public procedure, which had been endorsed by Jewish NGOs, made Israel the direct object of more working groups, special rapporteurs, and thematic mechanisms than any other country.

The crisis of Israel's UN status deepened in response to the Arab/Israeli October War of 1973. No fewer than thirty-three African nations that had established earlier diplomatic ties with Israel severed them and joined the anti-Israel alliance.[64] This set the stage for the ritual annual condemnations in virtually everybody at the UN. Even conferences and specialized agencies with no ostensible connection to the Arab/Israeli conflict—UNESCO and the World Health Organization—were used as platforms for condemning Israel.[65] For example, during its Decade for Women (1975–1985), the UN held conferences in Mexico City (1975), Copenhagen (1980), and Nairobi (1985), on the human rights problems afflicting women throughout the world. At all these events, both the governmental forums and the parallel NGO forums were interrupted in almost every panel by Palestinians' and their allies' attempts to insert Zionism=Racism statements into the conferences' final programs of action.[66] Although criticism of Israel for its human rights practices was, in principle, no more outrageous than criticism of any other state, in practice, the anti-Israel alliance often brought charges with no evidentiary basis, introduced false or manipulated testimony into UN forums, and worked to prevent Israel from responding to the accusations.

As in other areas, the emergence of the anti-Israel alliance limited what Jews were able to accomplish at these conferences. Jewish NGOs sometimes decided to table their women's rights agenda in order to defend Israel from attack. The ICJW, which started as a humanitarian organization without a Zionist component, moved toward solidarity with Israel during the 1970s, especially in the wake of the Mexico City conference, which adopted a resolution equating Zionism with racism and apartheid.[67] The ICJW's representatives at the conference, Nettie Levy, Helaine Plaut, and Phyllis Rosenfeld, wrote to its president, Rosa S. de Herzceg, that "the fact that the ICJW is limiting its fields of vision and its commitment to the problems of Israel and the Jewish people, constitutes a handicap in our work and a risk to its status at the UN."[68] They worried that choosing solidarity with Israel would lose them credibility with other human rights NGOs.[69]

While Jewish NGOs were initially unprepared for these attacks at the women's rights conferences, WUPJ's Norma U. Levitt recounted that, by the time of the Nairobi conference in 1985, they had "prepared themselves through the last five years with training in parliamentary procedures and in dealing with the media, exchanges with government officials, meetings with non-Jewish organizations, and education about women round the world and ways to help them."[70] Their preparation paid off: after an all-night debate on the last day of the conference, the Palestinians' allies agreed to remove the language equating Zionism with racism from the "Forward-Looking Strategies" document, the conference program of action. Still, it was hard not to think that their success came at the expense of the conference goals themselves. Having to spend so much effort on what was really a side issue to the main work of the conference, the Jewish NGOs (and other conference participants) lost an opportunity to address the central issues facing women. The UN's self-destructive obsession with Israel was to compromise its work again and again, absorbing Jewish energies that might have been put to other uses.

The effort to ostracize Israel was not limited to the conferences or the Zionism=Racism resolution. Israel's behavior was the subject of emergency sessions of the General Assembly, a rare forum that was not even invoked to address genocide in Rwanda or Bosnia. Until May 2000, Israel was the only member state in the UN to be denied inclusion in a regional group, due to its rejection by Arab states for inclusion in the Asian Region. Of all the condemnations issued by the commission, a disproportionate 26 percent condemned Israel, while known violators such as Syria, Iran, Sudan, and Yemen were never criticized.[71]

One of the more recent confirmations of the UN's bias against Israel occurred in the controversy surrounding its World Conference against Racism, Racial Discrimination, Xenophobia, and Other Forms of Related Intolerance in Durban, South Africa, in August 2001. Even before the conference began, it was already embroiled in controversy. After the Asian Region met in Tehran in February 2001, it submitted its draft of the conference "Declaration and Programme of Action" to the second HCHR, Mary Robinson. Five of the declaration's forty-two points condemned Israel as a racist country and human rights violator. The declaration itself was in violation of the rules set out by the high commissioner's office, according to which no state was permitted to be singled out in the text. Point 34 of the Asian Region's draft, for instance, called for the international community to provide "protection for the Palestinian people under occupation against aggression, acts of racism, intimidation, and denial of fundamental human rights." Although the General Assembly had formally repealed Zionism=Racism in 1991, here the equation was placed back in the public discourse.[72]

This was disconcerting to many Jews, who blamed High Commissioner Robinson for refusing to excise the offensive language from the official conference program (while some Palestinians blamed her for refusing to accept the unofficial, NGO conference program's far more inflammatory language).[73] When Robinson was appointed to the position in 1997, Jewish activists had held high hopes for her. Yet Jewish NGOs expressed frequent disappointment, believing that she displayed bias in her reactions to the Israeli/Palestinian conflict that compromised her other efforts. In her first month in office, she refused to brief the Israeli ambassador, on the grounds that Israel was not in any of the UN's regional groups. She did not mention the reasons why Israel had been deprived of membership in its region. In October 1998, at a meeting on the Fourth Geneva Convention, Robinson's representative, John Pace, denounced Israel, a speech that was out of order since, by rule, no particular countries were permitted to be discussed in that forum. The high commissioner stood by Pace's statement. In 2000, Robinson issued a report criticizing Israel's imposition of curfews in the occupied territories as an example of collective punishment, yet she made no mention of the Palestinian suicide bombings that had prompted the curfews.[74]

Now, in preparation for the World Conference against Racism, Robinson refused to criticize the Asian Region's draft declaration. Her refusal dismayed Jews the world over, because they believed it demonstrated an unwillingness to abide by her own rules when it came to Israel. This was not the sort of behavior Jewish NGOs had hoped for from the position they had done so much to create.

Although the high commissioner did refuse to accept the inflammatory statements in the NGO conference program, the mood at the official intergovernmental conference in Durban was still tense. At the parallel NGO forum, a mêlée ensued that would have been ridiculous if it had not been so serious. Jews who attended the conference were greeted with Zionism=Racism signs. At the NGO forum, one pro-Palestinian group called the Arab Lawyers Union distributed pamphlets containing anti-Zionist propaganda cartoons. In one, Zionism was depicted as a tree, its branches snakes, its fruits stars of David and swastikas. In another, the star of David was simply superimposed on a swastika.[75] The Israeli and American delegates appealed to High Commissioner Robinson to put a stop to the anti-Zionist rhetoric, arguing that condemnations of Israel in many of the panels (for example, the panel on the rights of Inuits) were interfering with the delegates' ability to carry out their work. Still, the United States and Israel withdrew. The Jewish NGOs formed a caucus on the NGO process and issued a statement declaring that the final conference document was

> designed to delegitimize and have the effect, if accepted, of delegitimizing the State of Israel as a Jewish state and to deny to the Jewish people alone amongst the peoples of the world their right to self determination. . . . The accusations, singly and together, form a new anti-Semitism, directed against Jews around the world, and are, themselves, a form of racism, incitement to hatred and violence.[76]

Israel's allies in Europe and Canada chose to remain to try to salvage the conference but its final recommendations had been tainted politically and were largely ignored—another human rights opportunity misused.[77]

In a sense, the events of the Durban conference were old news for Jewish NGOs, merely the continuation of the sort of behavior they had come to expect from UN human rights bodies since the mid-1960s. Similar malfeasance had occurred at the UN's earlier world conferences to combat racism and racial discrimination in 1978 and 1983.[78] The honeymoon between Jews and international human rights had long since ended. Since the 1970s, Jews have found repeatedly that they have had to choose between commitments to human rights and Israel. After Israel's triumph during the Six-Day War (1967), the Jewish public was at no loss for how to decide, and its support for its leaders' international human rights work declined. Moreover, many American Jews—suburban, comfortable—began to move away from their traditional liberal stance toward conservatism, which tended to consider UN bodies ineffective tools and even dangerous to the extent that they became mouthpieces for anti-Zionism and Communism. These neo-conservative Jews began to experience political ambivalence.

International Jewish NGOs' declining interest in human rights after the mid-1960s can be measured in a number of ways. Most dedicated diminishing resources to their human rights programs. For example, while AJC has promoted civil rights since 1906 and human rights since 1942, in the mid-1980s, AJC removed its Jacob Blaustein Institute for the Advancement of Human Rights from the general budget and gave it its own board of directors, essentially putting the fund-raising onus on the institute itself and marginalizing the human rights program in relation to AJC's other activities. AJC's biweekly periodical on human rights issues, *Present Tense*, was established in 1973, the year after the Blaustein Institute was formed, but in 1989 the magazine was shut down, leaving the neo-conservative journal, *Commentary*, as AJC's major periodical.

Other NGOs have also dedicated declining resources to human rights. Whether measured quantitatively, by the sheer output of UN submissions, press releases, memoranda, and briefs; or qualitatively, by the increasingly defensive tone the NGOs adopted at human rights forums, the decline is evident. The ICJW presents a stark example of the change in tone. At the NGO's tenth Triennial Convention in April 1975, its human rights representative at the UN, Phyllis Rosenfeld, argued,

> We are interested in world problems, yet we are vitally concerned with Israel and the treatment accorded her at the UN, by the General Assembly and some of the Commissions and agencies. We are acutely aware of the use of a double standard, and the continued effort of recent years to isolate Israel. . . . We have mixed emotions as we sit at meetings. We see resolutions being adopted to combat many social evils, we see World Conferences convened to examine global problems. . . . Of course, we support all that is being done in these areas, and we cooperate in efforts for improvement here. Yet, recently, we have felt a growing concern about Israel, and have been talking about the wisdom of ICJW's continued service at

> the UN. . . . [Y]our UN representatives feel that we must remain . . . and present the Israeli point of view wherever possible (after all, if we do not, who will?).[79]

By the NGO's fourteenth Triennial Convention in May 1987, the delegates recommended that, with regard to Israel, "public statements by Jewish groups must be considered cohesive and supportive statements to avoid appearance of divisiveness in the diaspora." (55).[80]

But back in the heady 1950s and early 1960s, when the UN human rights program was still all before them, this kind of ambivalence was unforeseeable. During the years just after the Holocaust, the international community embraced rights for Jews as individuals, as members of a minority, and as members of a nation. For their part, Jewish activists exhibited a giddy optimism about the potential of the UN's human rights program, which they helped build with enthusiasm. Their extensive work toward standard-setting, public education, ratification, monitoring, and advocacy manifested their high hopes for universal justice.

They did not give up on these hopes even after it became evident that the UN system was weak and procedurally biased against Israel. As the next chapter will demonstrate, many of their efforts succeeded not only in achieving their goals but in strengthening the human rights system itself.

2

Freeing Soviet Jews—and After

THE PREEMINENT CASE OF JEWISH HUMAN RIGHTS ACTIVISM

By the mid-1960s, Jewish human rights activists had begun to question the ability of the international human rights system to protect vulnerable populations, especially Jews. How useful could the system be when it was frequently overtaken by anti-Zionists and anti-Semites? If the UN system were compromised, then activists would have to find some other way to defend Jews' rights. The attacks on Jewish nationalism by internationalists might cause Jews to invent entirely new steps so that they could continue the dance at both weddings.

This was no mere hypothetical question. Over two million Jews in the USSR were being deprived of their rights to emigrate, to move freely inside the country, to practice their religion freely, to transmit their cultural heritage to their children, to work, to make telephone and postal contacts, and to be reunified with their families abroad. They were detained for long periods without counsel, subjected to show trials, sent into exile, deprived of citizenship, and incarcerated in prisons, labor camps, and psychiatric hospitals. In the face of these abuses, the UN human rights system seemed powerless, and Jewish activists inside and outside the Soviet Union had to look to their other options. They had two. The first was to rely on the state of Israel to engage in international diplomacy, military operations, and economic bargaining to protect Soviet Jews. This was the option that had been chosen in the case of Operation Magic Carpet (1949) in which El Al transported forty-five thousand Jews of Iraq to Israel. This was the option world Jewry relied on in Operations Moses (1984), Joshua (1985), and Solomon (1991) in which El Al transported thirty-six thousand Jews from Ethiopia to Israel. But this strategy was unworkable in the case of the Soviet Union, one of the five permanent members of the UN Security Council, with power to veto any resolutions critical of its minorities policies. In the USSR, Jews confronted a superpower engaged in a Cold War against the United States and Israel, a Communist regime that, since Stalin, had mounted an official campaign of institutionalized anti-Semitism.

In this situation, the activists fell back on a second option: they created a global human rights network that could operate independently of the UN. An array of actors—Israeli, Dutch, and American officials; international Jewish NGOs with consultative status in global and regional human rights forums; state-based NGOs; and high-powered individuals ("lone rangers")—went to work.[1]

This chapter will investigate how the preeminent example of a global Jewish human rights network was structured, what kinds of initiatives were permitted, and how they were decided. The basic elements of the story have already been well canvassed in the academic literature, but rarely has it been placed in the overall context of human rights history. Here, therefore, I offer a synthesis of the narrative while supplementing it with some new archival discoveries and setting it in the broader context. The chapter will demonstrate that Jewish human rights activism on behalf of Soviet Jews was comprised of an informal web of private organizations, state agencies, and individuals, with multiple centers. These actors sometimes coordinated actions and sometimes competed with or even opposed one another. Each actor behaved according to its particular characteristics and on behalf of its constituents' interests. This general informality meant that the various actors could establish strategic alliances on particular objectives and tactics—when their interests overlapped—but also that, when the missions of the organizations differed, they were free to depart the coalition and pursue their own agendas. Their pressure was often successful in securing the release of Soviet Jews, but only when the Soviet leaders were prepared to make concessions for other reasons—to conclude trade and military accords with the US, to acquire US grain exports, to gain international recognition of its possession of the lands it controlled after World War II, and so on. The network was less successful—and did not try very hard, in any event—in securing Soviet Jews' "internal" rights of freedom of religion, culture, and association.

The emigration of over a million Jews from the Soviet Union to Israel, Germany, and the United States—approximately 970,000 to Israel alone between 1967 and 1990—represents one of the most important success stories of all human rights activism since World War II.[2] Yet it is striking that the UN system was paralyzed in the face of Soviet repressions of human rights—and in particular with regard to both Soviet Jewish emigration and the repression of

Soviet Jewish cultural and religious rights. The rights guaranteed by the UDHR, the Covenants, and the UNESCO Convention against Discrimination in Education were all powerless in the face of Soviet policies which restricted educational activities, suppressed first Yiddish and then Hebrew, and sought to abolish all forms of ethnic self-expression that deviated from official dogma.[3]

As far back as 1972, the international human rights expert Louis Henkin noted that protections for Soviet Jews and others were hampered by a lack of effective enforcement machinery.[4] The Soviets resisted attempts to create such machinery at every occasion. While the USSR ratified the Covenants, it called on the "internal affairs," "public order," and "national security" loopholes in those documents whenever its human rights record was called into question at UN meetings, and justified its behavior with reference to the USSR criminal code and other internal laws.[5] It used its Security Council veto to quash international criticism of its rights record and keep the focus on security matters like arms control and trade. It resisted the drafting of a convention to eliminate religious discrimination. After 1967, it frequently diverted attention from its own anti-Semitism to alleged Israeli human rights violations.[6] In addition, it effectively undermined Jewish NGOs' attempts to use UN human rights treaties as levers to criticize Soviet practices toward Jews by attacking the credentials of Jewish NGOs themselves and attempting to implicate their members as CIA spies.[7]

The USSR successfully manipulated not only the UN's human rights treaty and charter bodies, but even its specialized agencies. When in November 1972, a group of Moscow Jews wrote to the director general of UNESCO in Paris to request help in gaining Soviet permission to learn Hebrew, they received no reply other than a few exit permits for the letter's signatories, in an attempt to "decapitate" the group—detach it from its leadership.[8] The USSR routinely deprived Jews of the right to employment guaranteed by the International Labor Organization in 1958, and of the right of parents to choose their children's education, guaranteed by UNESCO in 1960, and neither agency condemned these violations.[9] Working with their Arab allies and others in the anti-Israel alliance, the Soviet representatives restrained the ability of the UN and its specialized agencies to monitor and compel the USSR's human rights compliance throughout the period 1948–1989.

Yet, although from the 1940s onward, the Soviet Union systematically tried to dismantle Jewish religious, cultural, and educational institutions; although it harassed those Jews who sought emigration visas with exit taxes and those who sought to assimilate with education taxes; although it required Jews to carry internal passports the fifth line of which branded them as members of the Jewish nationality; although it singled out Jews among the 108 recognized Soviet nationalities for discrimination—nonetheless, by the end of the Gorbachev era, the USSR had permitted most Soviet Jews to emigrate, while the restrictions on Jewish religious and cultural life inside Russia and the other successor states of the former Soviet Union (FSU) had been greatly eased.[10] Joshua Rubenstein, an Amnesty International observer, saw the success of the Jewish emigration movement as the second largest human rights success (after the release of millions of Stalin-era political prisoners) in Soviet history.[11] Given that the international human rights system at the UN was hamstrung in its attempts to compel Soviet compliance, how did these remarkable events come to take place?

The complex network of policymakers, operating largely outside of the purview of the UN, engaged in a broad range of activities, including the protests, letter-writing campaigns, monitoring efforts, and sacrifices of Soviet Jewish activists working with their fellow non-Jewish dissidents in the Soviet Union; the official diplomatic contributions to the development of a regional human rights system (the Conference for Security and Cooperation in Europe [CSCE]); the site visits and hearings undertaken by the US Helsinki Commission; the activities of state-based Jewish NGOs in the US and Western Europe; and the diplomatic, information-gathering, and immigration activities of the state of Israel.

How did this network come into being? How successful was it in circumventing Soviet efforts to undermine the UN human rights program? How successful was it in securing the rights of Soviet Jews? How unique was it? And to what extent has it persisted since the fall of the Berlin Wall?

This last question is of particular relevance today. Now that some 350,000 Jews remain in Russia and other republics of the FSU, to what extent do these Jews still experience human rights violations similar to those of a generation or two before? And what has happened to the Jewish human rights network that spent so much of its time in the 1970s and 1980s concentrating on the fate of Soviet Jews? Has the network continued to monitor the situation of FSU Jews and provide them with aid? Have the type and number of groups in the network changed, or changed their mission? Has the international Jewish community's responsibility to FSU Jews changed or dissolved now that most Jews have emigrated?

SOVIET JEWS AS SYMBOLS

Although numerous disparate groups became the victims of Soviet human rights abuse—the Crimean Tatars, Armenians, Ukrainians, Lithuanian Catholics, Chechens, Volga Germans, Greeks, writers, kulaks—it was Jews who came to symbolize the struggle for human rights in the Soviet Union.

The Soviet Jews came to fill a symbolic function for dissidents, for Soviet officials, and for the international community. Although in many ways they differed from other extraterritorial national minorities in the USSR, their struggle for human rights was held up as the model for all the other struggles.[12] It was their usefulness as symbols that drove the uneven development of the global Jewish human rights policy. So it is not surprising that, once Jews in the FSU lost their symbolic status, the global network that had focused on their human rights needs largely turned toward other issues.

Jews' symbolic status, above and beyond their suffering as activists or victims of persecution, was in some respects not particular to the Soviet period, but was rather a familiar response of European nation-states to Jews' struggle for liberalization from the start of the Enlightenment. One has only to think, at various periods, of Lessing's *Nathan the Wise*, Napoleon's Sanhedrin, Hegel's early theological writings, the Punch caricatures of Disraeli, Arnold's typology of "Hebraism and Hellenism," or Zola's defense of Dreyfus in *J'accuse*, to understand that Jews had been made to stand in for much about the liberalization process about which Europeans had been anxious—the stock market, journalism, Philistinism, racial pollution, the possibility of religious toleration, and the emergence of civil and political rights. Jews, Judaism, and Jewishness were, in other words, metaphors that could be put to a broad range of uses. These terms were extraordinarily flexible. This was because Jewish identity itself was an unstable composite of ethnic, religious, national, diasporic, linguistic, and genetic components, so that both Jews and non-Jews alike could choose to emphasize a particular mixture of these components at each given historical juncture. It was this category indeterminacy, combined with Jews' status as a visible and stateless minority in so many European states, which made Jews uniquely useful as symbols.

Within this broad European pattern, the Soviets could draw from a particular Marxist tradition, since Marx himself had published his famous essay "On the Jewish Question" (1856) in which he had called for the abolition of Judaism. In Marx's dialectic reading, Judaism becomes a symbol for capital, and like the bourgeois state itself, must ultimately wither away. Since Judaism has no world-historical role to play, there is no reason for its continuance. Note that it is Judaism as an ideology—not Jews—that is to disappear. Since Marx's solution to the Jewish question was coextensive with his solution to the question of capital, the fate of the Jews under Marxist-inspired socialism would henceforth be a measure of the worth of the socialist solution as a whole. Lenin knew this, and in the immediate aftermath of the Bolshevik revolution, he ensured that Jews were able to find high places within the Communist Party as long as they renounced their attachment to Judaism as a religious ideology and set of practices.

By the time Stalin came to power, however, the Marxist goal of abolishing Judaism had been transformed into the Stalinist goal of abolishing Jews, either by internal exile, deportation, forced labor, or outright murder. Stalin created and then abolished the Evsektsya, the Jewish section within the Communist Party. During the 1920s and 1930s, the state supported Jewish theater, schools, newspapers, films, synagogues, and publishing houses. But during the 1940s, Stalin shut almost all of these institutions down, and during his Black Years (1949–1953), the government purged Jewish writers and political figures through show trials, internal deportations, and murder. Stalin eventually accused a group of Jewish doctors of trying to murder Soviet political leaders. In response to the supposed Doctors' Plot, Stalin planned to deport all Soviet Jews to Siberia, but he died before he could carry out his plan.[13] For those in the Soviet dissident movement that emerged during the Khrushchev and Brezhnev eras following Stalin's death, and those in the international community, the Stalinist solution to the Jewish question became symbolic of the larger repressions that Stalin had undertaken—his forced collectivization of peasants, the gulag, and the show trials.

Once Nikita Khrushchev emerged as Stalin's successor, he gradually permitted a cultural "thaw," which enabled a degree of greater freedom of speech, and he abandoned Stalin's murderous tactics. This was not exactly a brave new world, however, because Khrushchev's openness was subject to arbitrary change. Historians speak of a first and second thaw, with a period of retrenchment in between, driven by deep anger even among loyal party members about the gulag and the forced collectivization of peasants, and by Cold War politics of seeming toleration. On the other hand, while the state's tactics against Jews seeking to emigrate or engage in cultural or religious practices were less severe, they remained harsh, which heightened the perception that Jews were exemplary victims. In fact, the symbolic value of Jewishness was not lost on any of the participants in the struggle for human rights in the Soviet Union. It was systematically put to use by Soviet officials, by dissidents, by Jewish refuseniks, Jewish NGOs outside of the Soviet Union, and governmental actors in the international community, each to advance their own agendas. As Petrus Buwalda, former head of the Dutch embassy in Moscow, has shown, the Central Committee lightened its tactics only at times when the interaction of external and internal factors seemed to promote Soviet national interests.[14]

DRAMATIS PERSONAE

To understand the complex dynamics of the struggle for the rights of Soviet Jewry, it is necessary to provide a brief catalogue of each of the actors, a glimpse of the typical activities in which each engaged, and the unique way in which each deployed Jews' symbolic status. How each chose to do so was usually determined by whether they favored internationalism, Zionism, or pluralism.

Soviet Officials

Official Soviet anti-Semitic propaganda often drew a symbolic connection between Jews and the broader dissident struggle for human rights in the Soviet Union. According to the World Conference on Soviet Jewry, "A favourite anti-Semitic theme is to tar human rights activists with a Jewish brush." The report goes on to explain that the Soviet government's "identification of dissidents with Jews or Zionism achieves two purposes simultaneously: the dissidents are discredited as Jews—i.e., basically aliens—and the Jews are discredited as 'dissidents'—i.e., enemies of the Soviet state and society."[15]

The linkage between Jews and dissidents often assumed absurd forms. When the Soviet Union marched on Prague in the spring of 1968, a number of dissidents, a majority of whom were not Jewish, participated in a demonstration in Red Square in which they held up banners that read, "For your freedom and ours." KGB agents ran toward them at once, shouting, "They're all Jews! Beat up the anti-Soviets!"[16] The KGB agents were simply expressing the equation, dissident=Jew=alien. When the USSR began permitting non-Jewish dissidents to emigrate in the mid-1970s, it often compelled them to emigrate on Israeli visas, in order to "humiliate political non-conformists and discredit the Zionist movement."[17] By insisting that even non-Jews emigrate to Israel, the regime increased the hostility of its non-Jewish victims who wished to emigrate but could not do so, and who now resented the Jews as recipients of special privileges.[18]

Soviet leaders used the Russian Criminal Code to harass Jews and dissidents in parallel under the cover of law. For example, dissidents reading poems in Moscow's Mayakovsky Square and Jews who gathered publicly outside the city's Choral Synagogue were often charged with violating the code's Article 70, which forbade "agitation or propaganda carried on for the purpose of subverting or weakening the Soviet regime."[19] Jews and dissidents could also be charged with "parasitism" once they were released from their jobs and unable to find any other, "hooliganism" when they engaged in public protest, or a range of other crimes. Jews who were refused emigration papers—refuseniks—were treated as enemies of the state.

In the interrogation scenes recorded in his memoir, Anatoly Sharansky illuminates the reasons behind official Soviet attitudes toward the symbolic status of Jews. If for the KGB, Jews were symbolic of the dissident struggle as a whole, Sharansky was the symbol of symbols. Not only did he act as a personal bridge between the Jewish emigration and dissident movements, but because of his skill in English and rapport with journalists, he also acted as the Jews' and dissidents' main medium of communication to the West. As a mark of his heightened status, he was arrested, not on the typical charges of "agitation and propaganda," or "slander against the state," or "parasitism," but on the charge of "treason," with a potential sentence of execution by firing squad. He avoided death thanks to an international outcry, but received three years in prison and ten years in a labor camp. He was the Soviet Jews' Nelson Mandela.

For the KGB, Sharansky was the emblem of a supposed worldwide Zionist conspiracy against the USSR. In a pretrial interrogation in Lefortovo Prison, Sharansky's interrogator accused him of entering into a conspiracy with American Zionists and Israel against the Soviet Union.[20] Specifically, Jewish dissidents like Sharansky were accused of transmitting state secrets abroad and of rendering aid to a foreign state carrying on hostile activity against the USSR.[21] To punish him was, symbolically at least, to strike a blow against his alleged fellow conspirators: the United States, Israel, world Jewry, and the dissident movement.

The Soviet regime's charge of conspiracy, which rested on the Zionists' symbolic status, widely overstated the case. While there were some coordinated activities on behalf of Soviet Jews and dissidents both inside and outside the USSR, most activities were largely ad hoc and short term, were typically done openly and not in secret, and were not directed against the USSR per se but only against its human rights policies. There were no "Elders of Zion."

Nonetheless, even after Gorbachev started his *perestroika* (reconstruction) and *glasnost* (openness) programs in the late 1980s, the KGB and some conservative elements of the party remained staunchly anti-emigration and, indeed, anti-Semitic. The KGB maintained a department the specific purpose of which was to spread anti-Zionist and anti-Semitic propaganda around the world and to harass refuseniks.

Soviet Dissidents

While Soviet officials mobilized the image of Jewishness in order to discredit the dissident movement, dissidents in the Khrushchev and Brezhnev periods mobilized the image in order to criticize the Soviet regime. In September 1961, the poet Yevgeny Yevtushenko read his poem "Babi Yar," focusing on the lack of memorials inside the Soviet Union to commemorate the Nazi massacre of Jews. The party rebuked the poet severely and Khrushchev himself denounced the poem.[22] The idea of memorializing the victims of Nazi terror was understood by his audience as a proxy for the more politically salient and dangerous idea that there should be a way to memorialize the victims of Stalin's terror.[23] Yevtushenko implicitly equated Jews' suffering with the suffering of all Soviet people under Communism. One of the first public acts of dissidence in the post-Stalin era thus began with this metaphorical equation.

Similarly, the equation of Jewishness with dissidence would receive publicity in the trial of the writer and editor Andrei Sinyavsky for spreading propaganda in 1965. The Doctors' Plot is the backdrop for Sinyavsky's novella *The Trial Begins*. He published the novella in the West under the pseudonym Abram Tertz in 1959, during the brief second cultural "thaw" of the Khrushchev era. But when Brezhnev's regime came to power in 1961, a new political and cultural freeze reigned, and Sinyavsky was arrested. His trial, which focused on his criticism of Stalin's anti-Semitism, was the occasion for the "awakening" of the human rights movement.[24] Here again the rise of the dissident movement was associated with reaction against Soviet anti-Semitism: dissidents equated their struggle with that of the Jewish minority.

Because they saw the Jews' struggle as symbolic of the larger human rights struggle, dissidents regularly advocated on behalf of Jews. The editors of the *Chronicle of Current Events*, the major dissident underground journal, included information about Jewish arrests, trials, and punishments in their publication. Non-Jewish dissidents often showed their support for the emigration movement by publishing in Jewish underground journals or engaging in letter-writing campaigns on behalf of the movement. Andrei Sakharov, the renowned physics professor, dissident, and Nobel laureate, allied himself with the Jewish emigration movement, convening a press conference in September 1973 to encourage the US Congress to pass the Jackson-Vanik Amendment to the Trade Act, linking the USSR's acquisition of Most Favored Nation status to Jewish emigration levels. "The abandonment of a policy of principle," he said, "would be a betrayal of the thousands of Jews and non-Jews who want to emigrate, of the hundreds in camps and mental hospitals, of the victims of the Berlin wall."[25]

One of the dissidents' first major successes in parlaying Jews' symbolic status into international notice for human rights in the Soviet Union was the case of the Jewish peasants of Ilynka, a village 400 miles south of Moscow.[26] The Moscow Helsinki Watch Group (HWG), the dissidents' most important NGO, received a complaint from an Ilynka Jew of ill-treatment by the local government. Anatoly Sharansky, a member of HWG, visited Ilynka and then recounted the story of the deprivation of their rights to *Los Angeles Times* reporter Robert Toth, who printed the story on June 27, 1976.

HWG published a number of documents claiming the Ilynka Jews had been turned into serfs—peasant slaves. These documents were carried by the *New York Times*, the *Washington Post*, and the *Baltimore Sun*. The Ilynka Jews' case was brought up in the trials of HWG members Sharansky, Yuri Orlov, and Alexandr Ginzburg. In this way, the Jewish case became symbolic of other human rights abuses and helped HWG gain public recognition for the democracy movement.

Soviet Jewish Activists

Some Soviet Jewish activists saw themselves as symbols of dissidence; others, as modern-day Israelites straining under Egypt's yoke; still others, as part of a persecuted religious minority.

Refuseniks—those Jews who had applied for exit visas and had been refused—sometimes claimed that being Jewish was intrinsically being an "otherwise-thinker," a dissident. To be a Jew, according to Aleksandr Voronel, the editor of a major Jewish unofficial journal in the 1970s, was to be the inheritor of the "freedom of will" which was exemplified by the Zealots at Masada.[27] Voronel argued that the dissident movement after Stalin's death was largely created by "rehabilitated Jews" who were bent on "improving, protesting, proposing, with the result that a feeling even arose of a broad democratic movement in Russia." Jews were the embodiment of freedom of thought and their "sense of freedom-with-responsibility" compelled them to act on behalf of others' freedom.[28] Emigration was a human right and it was symbolic of all of the other rights. One must therefore work to promote and protect all rights, which would ultimately be to Jews' advantage: even if 99 percent of Soviet Jews emigrated, the 1 percent that remained would need their rights.

Anatoly Sharansky was himself the embodiment of potential coordination between the dissident and Jewish emigration movements. As a young scientist, he was inspired to apply to leave by Israel's triumph during the 1967 war and by his disgust over the Soviet occupation of Czechoslovakia in 1968. As a refusenik who spoke fluent English, he became Andrei Sakharov's press secretary and a founding member of HWG. He drafted HWG documents on non-Jewish issues, specifically on Ukrainian refugees, and on the Meskhetians.[29] He participated in the "unlikely alliances" created by HWG among "Ukrainian nationalists and Orthodox believers, Zionist activists and Crimean Tatars."[30]

On the other hand, for Jewish activists, the symbolic connection between democrats and Zionists only went so far. For one thing, as Joshua Rubenstein has shown, the Jewish emigration movement went farther and was more radical in some respects than the dissident movement, relying on methods of civil disobedience that most dissidents refrained from using, and making contact with a broader ready-made constituency in the West by using their contacts among Jews in the United States and Israel who could carry their cause forward.[31] Not all refuseniks were willing to go this far—and some worried that being too noisy would only get them into further trouble with the state.

Moreover, not all refuseniks made the link between the dissidents' democracy movement and the Jewish emigration movement. In fact, some, like the Hebrew teacher David Khavkin, denied the connection at all, claiming instead that Jews' participation in the democracy movement would dilute their specific cause in a pool of other causes. Khavkin thought it futile for Jews to work for democratic changes within the USSR, and he claimed that 80 percent of the dissidents were Jews who, ironically, were working on behalf of Crimean Tatars.[32] For Khavkin, the Jewish emigration movement began soon after the October Revolution in 1917.[33] The destruction of Jewish institutions in the 1920s, the exiles and killings of Jews in the 1930s, and the Soviet invasion of Poland in the 1940s—all of these developments prepared the ground for the massive flowering of Zionism that succeeded the Six-Day War (1967), Prague Spring (1968), and the trial of the Leningrad Hijackers (1970).[34]

For many in the Jewish emigration movement, Soviet Jews were not symbols of dissidence; rather, they were the slaves in Egypt who needed to be freed to make their exodus to the Promised Land. Especially after the Soviets annulled the Trade Act on January 14, 1975, reneging on their promise to release more Jews, the emigration movement split into the democratic faction (e.g., Vladimir Slepak, Sharansky, Ginsburg) and the culturalist faction (e.g., Felix Dektor, Benjamin Fain, Iosif Begun). The latter sought the right of emigration, not rights per se. Vitaly Rubin, for example, a founding member of the Helsinki Watch Group, was nevertheless unconvinced by the democracy movement's broad claims. In his diary he wrote:

> I have never been a Russian democrat. With all my respect, even reverence, for those people, I have never felt any desire to join them, because from childhood I saw this as the country of slavery, I understood that from top to bottom it is permeated with anti-Semitism, and felt no desire to sacrifice myself for the enemies of my people."[35]

In her public appeals, Avital Sharansky also held to this position, stressing that her husband was "just a Jew trying to emigrate to Israel."[36] Much of Soviet Jewish culture in the 1960s and 1970s was inspired by Israel's triumph in 1967 and had a Zionist flavor. In place of the Yiddish culture which had been brutally suppressed, a Hebrew culture, which even in Stalin's days had existed clandestinely, now expanded exponentially.[37] The Hebrew circles led by refuseniks such as Iosif Begun and Lev Goradetsky relied on Hebrew dictionaries and underground translations of Zionist novels like Leon Uris's *Exodus*. A symbol of the transition of Yiddish to Hebrew culture was the Yiddish singer, Nehama Lifshitz, who switched to Hebrew in 1959 and emigrated to Israel a decade later.[38] Members of the Jewish emigration movement listened to radio broadcasts on the Voice of Israel, collected souvenirs from Israeli tourists, met with Israeli athletes at international sports tournaments, exchanged discussions with official Israeli delegations, and attended Israel Independence Day celebrations. At the few synagogues that the Soviets kept open as evidence of their religious tolerance, Jews, most of whom were not observant, met to celebrate Passover as an allegory of their own exodus from the USSR and their future emigration to the land of milk and honey. They used the synagogue for Israeli dancing, and, as Yaacov Ro'i put it, they emphasized "the undisguisedly nationalist features of the Jewish religion, its orientation toward Zion and Eretz Yisrael, its stress on the mutual responsibility of Jews everywhere and on the singularity of the Chosen People, and the Jewish-historical aspect of the festivals."[39]

One can trace the split between Zionists and democrats among Jewish activists through a study of Jewish samizdat, the unofficial, uncensored, laboriously copied literature that contained articles of Jewish interest and was circulated primarily to a Jewish readership.[40] From 1967 to the early 1970s, Jewish samizdat focused on the struggle for emigration. Exemplified by the journal *Iton*, this period's samizdat downplayed the potential of democracy and human rights to solve Jewish problems in the USSR.

From the early 1970s to 1979, however, Jewish samizdat began to identify the human rights movement and the Jewish emigration movement as one and the same. For example, the journal *Iskhod* (Exodus) appeared for four issues in 1970–1971. There were two epigraphs: "If I forget thee O Jerusalem" was one; a passage from the UDHR was another. The urge to emigrate to Israel and the passion for democractic universalism and the rule of law were seen as one and the same.[41]

During this period, Aleksandr Voronel established the samizdat journal, *Evrei v. SSR* (*Jews in the USSR*, 1972–1975).[42] Voronel and his contributors emphasized the legality of Jewish emigration, culture, and religion within the framework of the Helsinki Accords and other treaties and declarations that the USSR had signed.[43] When members of this group emigrated, they were more likely to emigrate to the United States than to Israel. By 1979, 68 percent of Soviet Jewish émigrés opted to "drop out" from their Israeli visas and go to the United States.[44]

While activists like Voronel placed their Jewish learning in the service of the struggle for democracy, others, like Eliahu Essas, began to claim a new form of Soviet Jewish identity: a religious identity. In December 1976, Essas organized a symposium on Jewish culture in the USSR. When this was shut down by the KGB, Essas led many Jews in a religious revival, learning Talmud, attending Torah study groups, and celebrating Simhat Torah, the Jewish holiday dedicated to the sacred text.[45] Those who followed Essas saw the Soviet Jews' struggle as symbolic of the search for religious pluralism in a Communist state.

Thus, during the Soviet period, three types of Jewish activism emerged, sometimes overlapping and sometimes competing: the universalist struggle for human rights, the nationalist struggle for exodus, and the pluralist struggle for religious freedom. While they saw themselves in differing symbolic terms, the international Jewish community saw them as symbolic of the Soviet Union's deprivation of human rights as a whole, and their suffering galvanized the global Jewish response.[46]

The United States Government

For the US government during the Cold War, the fate of Soviet Jews also operated on numerous symbolic and strategic levels. Congressional hearings on human rights and détente in the Soviet Union were often held in two parts, the first part taken up entirely with the question of Soviet Jewry, the second taken up with considerations of other groups that suffered discrimination (e.g., the Russian Orthodox, Ukrainian Catholics, Muslims, Pentecostals, Armenians, Crimean Tatars) even though the latter were far superior in numbers to the former.[47] After 1975, successive American administrations used the number of Jews permitted to emigrate as a proxy for Soviet action on a range of human rights issues under Basket III of the Helsinki Final Act.[48] The US government did place limits on Soviet Jewish immigration because of the limitations of its Immigration and Nationality Act (1965), and under President Reagan's secretary of state George Schultz the United States rejected linkage of trade with immigration, deciding instead to pursue each aim separately and vigorously.[49]

What explains this emphasis on a small minority among persecuted Soviet minorities? First, Jews in Eastern Europe had a special symbolic status for a majority of Americans, who saw these Jews as the primary victims of both Nazism and the Stalinist purges. Second, unlike the other human rights activists in the USSR, who sought to reshape the Soviet system from the inside out, the Jewish emigration movement's focus on the "right to leave" gave its struggle an explicitly international dimension, since it involved crossing borders. Third, US officials responded to a well-organized set of American Jewish NGOs (including the Union of Councils for Soviet Jews [UCSJ], the National Conference on Soviet Jewry [NCSJ], and others) that spoke on behalf of an important voting constituency.[50] Organized American Jewry served as an efficient source of information on what befell Soviet prisoners of conscience, refuseniks, and victims of religious persecution. They were able to provide this information because of their personal and familial contacts with Soviet Jews, and through official and unofficial delegations to the Soviet Union. Fourth, a number of elite American Jews served in multiple capacities, as members of American Jewish NGOs and of the American government. These elites could effectively argue the Jews' case.

An example of an elite with multiple hats was Morris Abram, who was not only the chair of the NCSJ, but also the US ambassador to the UN's Subcommission on the Prevention of Discrimination and the Protection of Minorities, as well as leader of an NGO called UN Watch, dedicated to reforming the organization. He later became the president of AJC. He had started work as an attorney for the National Association for the Advancement of Colored People (NAACP), learning from the US civil rights movement how to pursue international human rights. The several individuals who worked at the Jewish, American, and international levels were able to serve as personal bridges among the parties.

With all of these motivations, the United States supported a broad range of activities on behalf of Soviet Jews, emanating from both the legislative and executive branches. It sent a delegation to the Helsinki meetings, led in the early 1970s by ambassador Max Kampelman and then beginning in 1976 by ambassador Arthur J. Goldberg. The ambassadors promoted human rights at the Helsinki meetings.[51] They also worked with the US CSCE, which was created in 1976.

The congressional commission, chaired by Rep. Dante Fascell (D-FL), engaged in numerous activities relevant to Soviet Jews' human rights struggle. It staffed conferences to review the USSR's compliance with the Helsinki Final Act.[52] It convinced US delegations to include references to specific individuals, including Anatoly Sharansky, in their diplomatic efforts. It held public hearings on Soviet Jews' plight, engaged in casework to reunite thousands of refuseniks with their families, provided resources to members of Congress in the initiation and drafting of legislation, and exchanged samizdat documents and other information with both Jewish and mainstream NGOs.[53]

Congress, led by Senator Henry Jackson and Representative Charles Vanik, also endorsed the concept of "linkage" through the Jackson-Vanik Amendment to the Trade Act. The amendment was to become the source of a good deal of strain between Congress and the executive branch, particularly under the Nixon administration, in which Secretary of State Henry Kissinger wanted a freer hand to act. Yet although there were times when the amendment became a sticking point in US-Soviet negotiations and Jewish emigration suffered, overall the amendment probably did more than any other single US act to pressure the Soviets to meet their Helsinki and UDHR obligations.[54]

The executive branch also gave its time and effort on Soviet Jews' behalf. The US ambassador to the UN in the 1970s, Andrew Young, made prepared statements on behalf of Soviet Jewry, as did the US delegate to the Commission on Human Rights and State Department official, Rita Hauser. The White House's stance toward Jewish emigration shifted, depending on who was in the White House, between a realist attitude that placed Jews' plight secondary to other considerations such as arms control and trade with the USSR, and Wilsonian idealism that placed Jews' human rights higher on the agenda.[55]

After Gorbachev initiated the policy of restructuring, and the mass Jewish emigrations from the USSR in the early 1990s were completed, the congressional commission changed its focus to trade issues. Thereafter, the government agency that paid most attention to Jewish rights in the FSU was the US Commission on International Religious Freedom (USCIRF), established in 1999. It undertook fact-finding missions to monitor the state of religious rights in general in the FSU.[56] It did undertake at least one major initiative specifically on behalf of Jews. By 2004 it was working closely with the Organization for Security and Cooperation in Europe (OSCE) to make recommendations on combating discrimination, intolerance, and xenophobia, including anti-Semitism, in OSCE member states.[57] Led by vice chair Felice Gaer (also director of AJC's Blaustein Institute), USCIRF recommended creation of an OSCE special representative on anti-Semitism, regular public review of compliance with OSCE commitments on anti-Semitism, changing the perception of anti-Semitism from a minor form of hooliganism to human rights abuse, and doing away with the Russian legal requirement that religious groups register with the state.[58]

The Israeli Government

From the point of view of political Zionism, the Soviet Jews were symbols of what was wrong with the Diaspora. They were the poster case for *shlilat hagolah*, the Zionist concept of "negation of the Diaspora." In this point of view, Diaspora Jews' attempt to become integrated into majority non-Jewish societies would always fail. The Jewish state had to protect the rights that every non-Jewish state would eventually abrogate, if given enough time.

At various times during the Soviet period, Israeli officials staked a claim to speak on behalf of the human rights of Soviet Jews. Israel contended that the UN Charter's human rights provisions entitled it to speak on behalf of persecuted Jews who were not Israeli nationals, since no other government could be expected to speak with as much knowledge and effort on Jewish questions. While Israel could not claim to represent Jews in states where fair and competent authorities resided, it could urge Jews in Israel and the United States to cease to be "the Jews of silence," in Elie Wiesel's provocative phrase.[59] Standing by was not an option, especially after the Holocaust.

The Israeli government's Liaison Bureau in Jerusalem, called Lishka, had grown out of the secret ministry that helped Jews immigrate to Palestine illegally before the war, when the British had shut the doors.[60] Now it turned its sights on Soviet Jews. It collected information about refuseniks from successful émigrés who had reached the transit camp in Vienna and distributed that information to selected state-based and international NGOs. Its executive director, Nehemiah Levanon, lobbied American Jewish organizations and the US government to put the Soviet Jewry question on their agendas. The Liaison Bureau arranged state visits to the USSR, for example, by prime minister Golda Meir, or by Israeli athletes or musicians or diplomats. It prepared Israeli statements on the situation for press release or for communication in international bodies. It worked with NGOs to prepare statements for the CSCE and the US delegation to the Helsinki process. Perhaps most importantly, it offered generous immigration assistance and absorbed nearly a million Soviet Jews in a short span into Israeli society.[61]

The Israeli government tended to look on UN human rights bodies as ineffective and anti-Zionist. Besides, Israel favored another line of argument. Instead of arguing that restrictions on Soviet Jews' emigration were human rights violations, Israeli officials argued that such restrictions prevented family reunion and aliyah, decreasing the chances that the Zionist dream of the "ingathering of the exiles" would be fulfilled. From Israel's perspective, the right to leave was secondary to the right to leave for *Israel*. Some Israeli officials became alarmed when the impulse among most Soviet Jewish refuseniks ceased in the late 1970s to emanate solely from a Zionist desire to leave for Israel, and transformed into a universalist desire to leave for any freer place. The Liaison Bureau engaged in a protracted debate with American Jewish refugee support groups like the Hebrew Immigrant Aid Society and the Joint Distribution Society over whether these groups should support Soviet Jews who opted to "drop out" and leave instead for the United States. Although it eventually took a pragmatic approach to the issue, the Israeli government was generally disinclined to aid Jews who worked on behalf of the broader dissident movement rather than in a more focused way for aliyah.[62]

The Dutch Government

The Soviet Union broke off diplomatic relations with Israel in 1967, which made it impossible for Israel to process those Jews who did receive exit visas (after waiting for anywhere up to twenty years). In this situation, Israel asked The Netherlands embassy to represent its interests in the USSR, and The Netherlands agreed. This was a rare case of a formal, contractual agreement between actors in the process. From 1967 until the Jewish emigration was completed in 1990, The Netherlands embassy staffed a special section to represent official Israeli interests. Practically, this meant processing the Jews' exit visas, which began as a trickle in the late 1960s but turned into a flood in the late 1980s. The embassy issued nationality certificates, transmitted official letters of invitation by diplomatic pouch, and, on Israel's instructions, extended loans to those Jews who could not meet the stiff fees that Soviet officials attached to the application process.[63] It also undertook official démarches with the Soviet Foreign Ministry on behalf of specific cases.

International Jewish NGOs

NGOs with consultative status in UN human rights bodies—WJC, CBJO, CCJO, ICJW, and WUPJ—were permitted to submit reports and testimony to UN human rights bodies. They published reports on the status of refuseniks and political prisoners, engaged in quiet diplomacy to negotiate on behalf of political prisoners, held international symposia on the right to emigrate to stimulate the world community's moral concern, distributed information to relevant UN and regional bodies (e.g., CERD, the Commission on Human Rights, the Council of Europe, the OSCE), tied in with larger human rights NGOs on relevant press releases and statements, and raised awareness and funds among Jewish constituents.[64]

In some instances, Jewish NGOs sought to show that the Soviet Jews' situation was symbolic of the struggle for human rights in general. For example, in its report on the USSR's implementation of the Helsinki Final Act in 1986, the International Council of the World Conference on Soviet Jewry, a committee organized by WJC, wrote:

> The case of Soviet Jewry is a human rights case *par excellence* in so far as it encompasses virtually all aspects of human rights—the issues of non-discrimination, religious freedom, rights of national minorities, human contacts, freedom of movement, cultural exchanges, and so on. As such, the plight of Soviet Jews represents a microcosm of the human rights issue at large.[65]

The conference went on to trace Soviet violations of the UDHR, the covenants, UNESCO, the Helsinki Final Act, the Madrid follow-up meeting, and the USSR criminal code.[66]

Since Jewish NGOs were perceived by Soviet officials as part of an international conspiracy against the USSR, the NGOs were themselves often the object of Soviet attacks. After a series of swastika paintings appeared worldwide in 1959, the UN Commission on Human Rights requested that NGOs submit documentation on "manifestations of anti-Semitism and other forms of religious intolerance." The CBJO and the WJC responded by providing a memorandum on worldwide anti-Semitic activity, including instances of Soviet discrimination against Jews and Jewish culture. The CBJO also submitted a study to the subcommission, *Memorandum on Discrimination in the Matter of the Right of Everyone to Leave Any Country Including His Own and to Return to His Country,* in which it particularly named the Soviet Union as a violator of the right to leave (in contravention of the commission's own "self-denying rule" according to which no particular human rights situations were to be mentioned in its reports).[67] When the CBJO and the WJC subsequently gave oral testimony on their findings to the subcommission, they were excoriated by the Soviet representative, Boris Ivanov.[68] Ivanov tried to intimidate them, calling their documentation "slanderous," "tendentious," and "colored by cold war considerations," and warned that "by its provocative acts, 'B'nai B'rith' could only do a disservice to that population [i.e., Soviet Jews]."[69] Notwithstanding this intimidation, the CBJO's material was found convincing by special rapporteur José D. Ingles, who included it in his report on the right to leave.[70]

In response to these events, the USSR, with Arab allies, began to call for the removal of the consultative status of Jewish NGOs, arguing that they were funded by the CIA, and that they were the puppets of the state of Israel.[71] For the next thirty years, Jewish NGOs would simultaneously have to try to advocate for Soviet Jews while confronting the counterassault launched by the USSR and its allies against themselves.

State-based Jewish NGOs

Jewish NGOs housed in the United States, Britain, and South Africa also mobilized on behalf of Soviet Jews, whom they saw as symbols of the bonds linking all Jews together as brothers and sisters, co-religionists, and members of a people. These included both grassroots and elite organizations. The former engaged in symbolic actions, consciousness-raising efforts, letter-writing campaigns, and sending goods to refuseniks. Elite organizations, by contrast, specialized in policy advocacy at the national level, lobbying members of Congress and the executive branch, holding symposia of policymakers, and testifying on congressional committees. In the United States, the grassroots NGOs were most visibly represented by the UCSJ; the elite NGOs by the NCSJ. In the words of Irwin Cotler, these state-based NGOs became "major Jewish and human rights NGOs in their own right, helping to influence the course and conduct of both American foreign policy and the Helsinki process."[72]

The UCSJ was an umbrella organization that began in 1966 as the Cleveland Committee against Soviet Anti-Semitism, founded by Leo Rosenblum.[73] With local chapters throughout the United States, it distributed its newsletter with a "Refusenik Update," profiling individual Soviet Jews with information about their ages, occupations, education, types of harassment, arrests, trials, date of refused visas, sentences, and names of relatives living outside the Soviet Union. It compiled a refusenik databank with the profiles of more than three thousand individuals. It coordinated demonstrations by rabbis and ministers in front of the Soviet embassies in Washington, New York, and San Francisco. Its president, Morey Schapira, gave congressional testimony along with members of other major state-based Jewish NGOs, such as NCSJ, the Coalition to Free Soviet Jews, and the Executive Council of Australian Jewry. It engaged in local demonstrations. For example, in 1986 NCSJ's Colorado committee put on a demonstration in front of a hotel where a dinner was being held in honor of the Soviet Committee of Physicians for Prevention of Nuclear War. This group included scientists who had defended the Soviet misuse of psychiatry as a means to quell dissent. The Colorado Committee confronted the scientists as they left the hotel with signs, slogans, and chants. The UCSJ placed ads in newspapers on behalf of individual refuseniks, convinced synagogues to hold dinners in honor of them, held boycotts of businesses (e.g., Pepsi and Stolichnaya) that engaged in trade with the USSR, staged demonstrations at Soviet cultural events held in the United States, or had themselves arrested in front of the Soviet embassy for the cause.[74]

The NCSJ, chaired at first by Richard Maas and later by Morris Abram, was the more elite of the state-based NGOs, comprised in 1976 of thirty-eight major Jewish organizations and hundreds of local Jewish federations.[75] Along with delivering congressional testimony, the NCSJ engaged in private advocacy with senators and congressional representatives, and with the White House. In the early 1970s it played a key role in supporting Senator Henry Jackson's decision to draft his amendment to the Trade Act. It followed up with a massive letter-writing campaign to congressmen by its constituents. During the Carter years it argued for linkage between Jewish emigration and arms control and trade negotiations, and continued to argue for linkage even when the Reagan administration had rejected it. After perestroika, when Russian president Boris Yeltsin pressed the Clinton administration to revoke the Jackson-Vanik Amendment, the NCSJ urged him successfully to resist.[76]

Other American Jewish NGOs (HIAS, formerly the Hebrew Immigrant Aid Society, and the Joint Distribution Committee) provided social services and application assistance to emigrants in Vienna. The Council of Jewish

Federations, later the United Jewish Communities, provided funds for the absorption of émigrés arriving in the United States, numbering some 340,000 by 2002.[77] While not human rights organizations, these NGOs provided the assistance that made the human right of freedom of movement real for Soviet Jews.

Mainstream NGOs

While advocating on behalf of Soviet Jews, mainstream human rights NGOs perceived an intrinsic danger in Jews' symbolic status as the preeminent victims of Soviet persecution: the other victims might be forgotten. The International League for the Rights of Man, Amnesty International, and US Helsinki Watch published reports and calls for the amelioration of Soviet Jews' human rights, individually and collectively, but in testimony in congressional hearings, these groups also sought to place Jews alongside other persecuted Soviet minorities.

Lone Rangers

Well-placed individuals in the West also performed important tasks on behalf of Soviet Jews. Michael Sherbourne, a London schoolteacher, collected packets with refusenik data and lists of necessary items smuggled out by Sharansky, Aleksandr Lunts, and others, and distributed them to the grassroots network led by the USCJ.[78] Lawyers like Alan Dershowitz took up the cause and provided pro bono defense and public advocacy services.[79] Rabbis from the United States, athletes from Israel, and a multitude of individuals smuggled in Jewish ritual objects and books, blue jeans (a precious commodity), and hope to Jews in the USSR.[80]

Finally, some American Jews who struggled for the relief of Soviet Jews did so, not out of respect for civil or human rights, but out of a deeply entrenched anti-Communism that was part of their American identity. For neoconservative American Jews, like Elliott Abrams in Nixon's State Department and Richard Perle, the architect of the Jackson-Vanik Amendment, Soviet Jews were symbols, not of human rights in general, but of the larger struggle against totalitarian Stalinism. Thus, support for Soviet Jews' emigration and religious and cultural rights could come from both the left and the right in American Jewish politics.

This varied cast of characters includes some Jewish NGOs that were active at the international level—with consultative status at the UN—but others as well. Unlike the activities the NGOs undertook at the UN on principle (as described in chapter 1), the Soviet Jewry crisis was more urgent and Jews outside of the typical organizations became mobilized. Moreover, the crisis necessitated closer coordination with the American and Israeli governments than had been the case to date. All of this fancy footwork was required because Jewish human rights activists faced a unique situation: they had to figure out how to use the *norms* of human rights despite the fact that the *system* of human rights was broken.

INNER DYNAMICS

All of these actors coordinated activities on occasion, in ad hoc, unsystematic, and informal ways. The alliances they formed to work on particular projects were time-limited and strategic. This sort of structure is rather typical of international human rights action: public and private entities coalesce to work on a particular project, forming alliances that are unstable. In this respect human rights work is an expression of the latent anarchy always just under the surface of the global governance structure, where there are no permanent leaders and few effective decision-making bodies. For the most part, collective decisions are made through a push-pull process that can resemble either collaboration or coercion.

In this case the lack of structure was useful, insofar as it enabled the individuals and groups flexibility in their responses to the Soviet challenge. The alliances were easily dissolved when conflicts arose. The major conflicts were over the flow of information about refuseniks and where those who received permission to emigrate should go.[81] The underlying principle fueling the conflicts was whether their activism was in support of Zionism or human rights.

Jewish NGOs had already developed informal means of coordinating their activities on human rights in general, and so were able to apply their regular procedures to the special case of the Soviet Jews. As early as January 8, 1953, in reaction to the Doctors' Trial, WJC, CCJO, and CBJO met to assess the extent of persecution of Soviet Jews and to formulate a united program of action to present to the UN. They discussed the best way to proceed with the Israeli ambassador and issued a joint press statement. The Jewish agency then called a conference of major Jewish organizations to discuss the situation. The coordination was not limited to Jewish organizations. In 1971, the Ad Hoc Committee on Human Rights was established, comprised of international NGOs with consultative status on UN human rights bodies. Alongside members of the mainstream human rights movement, such as the International League for the Rights of Man and Amnesty International, several Jewish organizations were members, including CBJO,

WJC, ICJW, CCJO, the Women's International Zionist Organization (WIZO), and Agudas Israel. According to AJC's human rights director, Sidney Liskofsky, there existed among the Jewish members of the Ad Hoc Committee regular, albeit informal, consultation and coordination:

> Though the Jewish representatives . . . have no formal coordinating machinery, they consult informally, and often coordinate activities. . . .
>
> In our initiatives on matters of Jewish concern, without having made any formal decision to do so, we instinctively wait for, or encourage, one or another non-Jewish group to take the lead—and then hasten to offer our cooperation. The advantages of this are obvious.[82]

Conferences and symposia were another way that Jewish NGOs could engage in coordinated human rights activity on behalf of Soviet Jews. The best example here is the Uppsala Colloquium on "the right to leave," initiated by Sidney Liskofsky and organized in partnership with Karl Vasak of the Institute for Human Rights in Strasbourg. Planned as a general examination of the right of emigration, the conference included a broad range of organizations, while also giving attention to the specific plight of Soviet Jews. The conference contributed to influencing the US Congress to pass the Jackson-Vanik Amendment to the trade bill, which linked Soviet acquisition of Most Favored Nation status to improvements on Jewish emigration.

Coordination increased manyfold once Jimmy Carter came to office and committed the White House to an extensive human rights program that linked progress on trade and arms negotiations to progress on Soviet Jewish emigration. In January 1977, even before Carter was inaugurated, he was called on to respond to appeals by Yuri Orlov, the Helsinki Watch Group coordinator, and Nobel Prize laureate Andrei Sakharov to link progress on nuclear arms negotiations to the Soviets' "good faith efforts" toward progress on human rights, in particular Jewish emigration. The administration was further lobbied to make this linkage in a briefing held by the Union of Councils for Soviet Jews in the Rayburn House Office Building on Capitol Hill, January 13, 1977. The briefing brought together the high-profile attorney Alan Dershowitz, who was acting as Anatoly Sharansky's lawyer in the United States; Andrew Young, the newly appointed US ambassador to the UN; Congressman Dante Fascell, the chair of the CSCE; and Irene Manekofsky, chair of the UCSJ. On the other end of the phone, in Moscow, were Vladimir Slepak, a refusenik and founding member of the Moscow Helsinki Watch Group, and Sharansky. Here was a remarkable example of coordination. Inside the USSR, Jewish refuseniks teamed up with non-Jewish dissidents under the banner of Helsinki Watch, and then consulted with an array of representatives from US groups, including members of the legislative and executive branches, a grassroots Jewish NGO, and a high-powered lone ranger.

Questions over who should collect and distribute the data created conflict between Israel and the Diaspora, between elite and grassroots NGOs, and between activists inside and outside of the Soviet Union. The Israel Liaison Bureau was able to compile and distribute the most extensive and current database about refuseniks. The Israelis sought to develop a hierarchical strategy, by which the Jerusalem office would gather data from émigrés and then "assign" given refuseniks to a specific country's Jewish NGO, prohibiting other NGOs from campaigning for that refusenik's release. It refused to work with "grassroots" NGOs like the UCSJ, sharing its information only with "establishment" NGOs like the NCSJ. Israeli diplomats several times warned Moscow activists, including Sharansky, against sharing information by phone with London schoolteacher Michael Sherbourne for distribution to the grassroots Soviet Jewry network in Western Europe and the United States.

Because there was no formal international Jewish political framework for the protection of Jews in the Diaspora, Israel sought to assert control, maintaining that the state was the centerpiece of the Jewish political process. Israelis were also concerned that after an initial period in the mid-1960s to mid-1970s in which the Soviet Jewish emigration movement was led by Zionists who sought to make aliyah, many Soviet Jews in the 1980s were now opting to go to other places besides Israel (primarily the United States and Germany).[83] Called in Hebrew *noshrim* ("drop-outs"), the Jews choosing to go elsewhere outnumbered those opting for Israel by 2:1 by 1979.[84] In the 1970s, successive Israeli governments under Golda Meir, Yitzhak Rabin, and Menachem Begin perceived their interest to be, not only promoting emigration as an international human right, but promoting emigration as an expression of Zionism.

But as Fred Lazin has demonstrated, this stance brought Israel into conflict with some Jewish NGOs in the United States. Some American Jews disagreed with the Zionist focus of the Israelis' emigration efforts and sought "freedom of choice";[85] others began to perceive that emigration was not the only significant human rights issue for Jews in the Soviet Union. Grassroots organizations did not take kindly to their exclusion from the Israeli information network. Irene Manekofsky complained vociferously that the Israelis were exercising an unfair elitism by not sharing their information. For their part, the Moscow activists complained that Israelis often mocked Soviet Jews in Israel as "Jewish goyim" due to their lack of Jewish religious, cultural, and historical knowledge. Many appreciated the work done on their behalf by American Jewish NGOs and wished to immigrate to the United States.

Finally, the case of Sharansky generated intense tension within the network. Israeli officials initially distanced themselves from the case because they thought that Jewish activists' association with dissidents was dangerous. The Soviet Jewry office informed a Knesset member that the trial "is not an Israeli case."[86] On several occasions Avital Sharansky was prevented by Israeli government officials from attending a "grassroots" event—where support for the Soviet democracy movement was encouraged—and compelled to attend an "establishment" event arranged for the same evening, where only Jewish emigration within a Zionist context was discussed.

So was activism to free Soviet Jews based on Zionism, human rights, or Soviet civil rights? It depends on which actors, and when in the historical process, one chooses to emphasize.

SYMBOLS NO MORE

Despite its sometimes tense inner dynamics, the network was often successful in ameliorating Soviet Jews' suffering, and it played an important role in securing their right to leave—particularly when the combination of external factors (diplomacy, arms control) and internal factors (Jewish and human rights dissent) was favorable to Soviet interests. Whether the network has been successful at securing Jews' religious and cultural rights in the FSU is a more complex question. Even in periods of rising emigration, Jewish culture and Judaism remained insignificant and virtually nonexistent; the Soviets did little to foster it, and the American government did not push the issue very hard. When it came to the "internal rights" that had no international dimension, the Soviet regime remained indifferent to protests, and the protests themselves were few and far between.[87]

It was, after all, the right to leave, rather than human rights in general, that energized activity in the international community. Although legally the Soviet Union was not justified in using its sovereignty to quell international dissent from its restrictions on Jewish cultural and religious life, politically it was able to make the argument that these restrictions were "internal affairs" with which other states and organizations had no right to interfere. Once the major emigration was accomplished in 1990, many parts of the network considered that their human rights work in the FSU was done.

Almost as soon as FSU Jews' religious and cultural rights showed up on the international Jewish radar, the Jewish organizations' responsibility toward them became open to question. Once the Soviet Jews' mass emigration was accomplished in 1990–1991, the remaining Jews ceased to be useful to the international community as human rights symbols. As a result of the loss of their symbolic status, Jews remaining in the FSU have increasingly encountered an international community less attentive to their evolving human rights concerns.

The dissolution of the USSR, combined with progressive improvements in human rights protections through the Helsinki process and the mass emigration of Soviet Jews, make the rights picture of Jews in the FSU very different from that of Jews in the previous era. From the normative standpoint, Jews in the FSU are now guaranteed the rights of which they were routinely deprived during the Soviet period. The human rights protections offered by the Helsinki Final Act of 1975 and subsequent conference documents are at least as strong as, and in some cases stronger than, the protections offered by UN treaties.[88] To be sure, some of the reforms were equivocal. As the Lawyers Committee for Human Rights remarked, although the "anti-Soviet agitation and propaganda" and "slandering the Soviet system" laws that were used against Jewish activists were decriminalized, "'slander' against the 'honor and dignity' of the President was criminalized in May 1990." Similarly, "The law on freedom of association, adopted by the USSR Supreme Soviet in October 1991, gave legal protection to all kinds of public organizations, including independent political groups for the first time. But . . . it required prior registration with government agencies"[89]

Among the important rights now formally guaranteed Jews in the FSU are the rights to obtain religious objects and books, to train religious personnel, and to set up religious institutions. Freedom of movement within the country, the right to leave and return, freedom of thought, and the rights of national minorities are also protected.[90] The UDHR actually omits many religious rights that are listed in the documents emerging from the Helsinki process. The dreaded "fifth line" of the Soviets' internal passport, which stamped "Jewish" as the individual's nationality and guaranteed that the bearer would be the recipient of multiple forms of institutionalized anti-Semitism, has been removed. The internal passport itself has been abolished, preventing the state from restricting an individual's movement within the country. The charge of parasitism, which was used to apprehend many Soviet Jewish "criminals," has been removed from the Code of Criminal Procedure.[91] The government abolished the requirement that human rights NGOs register with the government—often a means of harassing their members—but has since reinstated it.

Although the documents of the Helsinki follow-up meetings (in Vienna, Madrid, Ottawa, and Stockholm) are not binding treaties; these documents combined have in practice had a much more profound effect on the protection of Jews' human rights than UN treaties or declarations. Because the

USSR initiated and participated in the Helsinki process, it could not subsequently complain, as it had with the UDHR and many of the UN's human rights treaties, that rights guaranteed by the process were Western inventions that had been foisted on it. Indeed, the regime published the full text of the Helsinki Final Act in its own newspaper, *Izvestia*. The Helsinki Watch groups, which adopted Jewish emigration rights as one of their causes, were able to seize on this circumstance to hold the USSR to its own word.[92]

The dissolution of the USSR, together with the formal guarantee of rights, changed the conversation about Jewish rights both within the FSU and abroad. The official anti-Semitism of the Soviet Union was quickly replaced with a grassroots variety, associated with nationalist political parties like Pamyat.[93] Nonetheless, by 1990 one could certainly perceive a change in the CSCE, the congressional committee charged with monitoring Russian compliance with the Helsinki process. Whereas earlier such meetings had focused exclusively on human rights issues, the 1990 meeting focused almost entirely on how the CSCE could work to help increase East-West trade, and one senses that both human rights itself, and Jews as symbols of human rights, fade into the background. The 1990 meeting of the commission was addressed, not by the secretary of state, who would normally have outlined Soviet progress on its human rights promises, but by the US commerce secretary, Robert Mosbacher. In his opening statement, Mosbacher remarked, "As we move into the nineties, the military threats fade, and the dialogue changes from specific human rights problems to the more generic issue of basic freedoms."[94] The vital role that he then outlined for the CSCE involved easing western trading practices into the USSR. When members of the committee raised human rights abuses for the secretary's consideration, these abuses concerned, not the rights of Jews, but the rights of Afghanis in the recent Soviet war, Chechens, and even, in one revealing aside, the Chinese dissidents in Tiananmen Square.[95]

Since the 1990 meeting of the commission, the US government agency that has advocated most for the human rights situation of Jews in the FSU has been the USCIRF. It has done substantial work on helping the OSCE to address anti-Semitism, but its work on behalf of FSU Jews has not had as high a public profile in the United States as did the CSCE. Indeed, it has reversed the emphasis of the CSCE, which highlighted the plight of Soviet Jews, and then only secondarily the plight of other groups. By contrast, apart from its focus on anti-Semitism as a specific form of religious intolerance, USCIRF has mainly discussed Jews as one group among others whose religious freedoms need to be protected. This is not necessarily an indication that FSU Jews have ceased to require special human rights protections, only that for the international community they have ceased to serve as symbols.

For their part, the international Jewish NGOs have in many cases redirected their efforts in the region away from the immediate human rights concerns of FSU Jews. Much of the international Jewish community's effort in the region since 1989 has been on resolving Jewish material claims in Central and Eastern Europe to property that had been stolen by the Nazis.[96] As early as 1944, the WJC published a study on claims restitution by Dr. Nehemiah Robinson. Nahum Goldmann, cofounder of WJC, raised the issue at the War Emergency Conference in Atlantic City, in November 1944.[97] The obstacles were many, but after the Cold War ended, restitution efforts were renewed by WJC, B'nai B'rith, the Joint Distribution Committee, the Jewish Agency, and survivors' groups. Together they created the World Jewish Restitution Organization (WJRO), chaired by Edgar Bronfman in 1991. Bronfman and Israeli finance minister Avraham Shohat signed a memorandum of agreement between the WJRO and the Government of Israel in November 1992.

The WJRO has met with East European governments and the US secretary of state to try to secure agreements on restitution of private property.[98] Laurence Weinbaum, in a study of the restitution effort, remarked that "the response of new governments in the former Soviet bloc to the present challenge will be seen as a test of their respect for basic human rights and the rule of law."[99]

Yet other human rights concerns have received less attention and resources, in particular the work of repairing the damage done to FSU Jews from three generations of rights violations. After initial enthusiasm for aiding in the revitalization effort, some international Jewish NGOs have diminished operations in this regard. In his introduction to the volume of essays *Jewish Culture and Identity in the Soviet Union*, edited by Yaacov Ro'i and Avi Becker, WJC president Edgar M. Bronfman called for a massive influx of printed books, educational materials, and funding by world Jewry to help sustain the newly free Jewish communities in the FSU.[100] After 1988, WJC's International Council of the World Conference on Soviet Jewry, led by Simcha Dinitz, "decided to move toward a major emphasis on developing Jewish culture, on a long-term basis, in the Soviet Union."[101] The WJC's concern quickly became less about the formal legal rights of Jews in the FSU, and more about the practical issues involved with maintaining, growing, and transmitting FSU Jews' religious and cultural identity. Twenty-five American Jewish organizations participated in the October 3, 1989, National Meeting on the Revitalization of Jewish Life in the Soviet Union, sponsored by the National Conference on Soviet Jewry.[102] Other NGOs, particularly the WUPJ, perceived this change as well. Its International Committee on Soviet Jewry spent about $250,000 on various programs in 1992, $500,000 in 1993, and $320,000 in 1994. It has continued to sponsor mission trips to Russia to investigate conditions and bring potential funders to meet FSU Jews, build and subsidize some forty Reform schools and synagogues across the region, implement leadership training seminars, build an Institute for Modern Jewish Studies to train Jewish rabbis and educators, provide humanitarian aid to elderly Jews, produce Russian translations of religious texts, raise funds for FSU bar/bat mitzvah students by matching them to their American peers, and promote progressive Judaism in the FSU. The Lubavitch movement also established footholds in every major FSU city as part of the religious revitalization effort, and Berel Lazar, the chief rabbi of the Chabad movement in Russia, became the chief rabbi of Russia.[103]

Yet, worthy as these endeavors are, it is far from clear that rebuilding Jewish religious life was what FSU Jews either wanted or needed. In the Soviet Union, all religion was ruthlessly stamped out for seventy years and has only regained a small foothold. In the 1980s, when emigration was restricted, there was a small bloom of religious activity, but the vast majority of FSU Jews did not participate.[104] On the other hand, because most cultural institutions had also been degraded, few other forms of affiliation were available.[105] Since then, support for cultural institutions—schools, day care facilities, community centers, nursing homes, libraries and collections, theaters, and newspapers—have come from Chabad, the WUPJ, and the American Jewish World Service's development fund. For its part, while the state of Israel has worked with local governments to set up day schools, and Sunday schools sent *shlichim* (liaisons) to bring books and audio-visual materials and hold festivals, its main purpose has been to encourage continuing emigration.[106]

Still, many of the community's cultural treasures are inaccessible or dilapidated, and participation in the new institutions is lax.[107] The essays by the scholars in Zvi Gitelman's collection, *Jewish Life after the USSR*, present a picture of life in the FSU that is uniformly pessimistic as to the future prospects of the community. Although Jews do not face the same level or kind of official discrimination, freedom of movement restrictions, or religious persecution, they do face the long-term consequences of seventy years of restrictions on Soviet Jewish life. They lack leadership, stable fund-raising mechanisms, religious institutions, and in some cases support for academic studies.[108] A delegation of Jewish studies professionals on a 2005 trip to Moscow and St. Petersburg led by Association for Jewish Studies president Judith Baskin found the conditions for a resurgence of Jewish cultural life bleak.[109]

Although cultural rights are often considered less significant than civil, political, economic, or social rights, their enjoyment is often essential to the "dignity" promised to individuals by the UDHR. Such rights also serve to protect individuals as members of a minority community from both the state and the majority.[110] On the other hand, in many ways the weakened state of FSU Jews' cultural heritage is the least of their problems. Grassroots anti-Semitism has been mobilized by Russian political leaders and leaders of the Russian Orthodox Church in the face of economic and political crises at convenient moments.[111] Jews are aging, with high intermarriage rates, high death rates, and low fertility rates. Demographer Mark Tolts characterizes this as the "terminal stage" of the demographic evolution of the FSU Jews and forecasts their "demographic collapse."[112]

Russian Jews' survival may, at first glance, no longer appear to be related to their human rights, which are no longer formally denied them. Rather, as the sociologist of FSU Jews, Zvi Gitelman, asks, the question appears to be whether there can be "a viable, transferable secular Jewish life" in these areas.[113] This may seem to be a question with which Jewish human rights activists can have little concern. Having advocated for Soviet Jews when they were being thrown in prison, deprived of jobs, and rejected for visas, human rights activists might well think that the FSU Jews' struggle to regain a cultural and religious foothold in Russia is not part of their purview.

Yet cultural and religious rights on paper are worth little if they cannot be exercised. The internal challenges of structure, leadership, affiliation, institutions, and demographics that Jews in the FSU face, alongside grassroots anti-Semitism and the decimation of their cultural and religious heritage, present significant obstacles against the implementation of their rights. The Soviet struggle to eliminate the Jewish presence has not succeeded, but the quality of Jewish life in Russia is thin. The question is whether Jewish human rights activity ought to include repairing communities and institutions damaged from systematic human rights abuse.

At least one part of the American Jewish NGO network that struggled to free Soviet Jews still continues to work on behalf of living FSU Jews, though in a somewhat different form. In 1990, the UCSJ established the Bay Area Council for Jewish Rescue and Renewal. Based in San Francisco, the BACJRR publishes a periodic newsletter, *Outcry*, with information about the status of Jews in the FSU. It has funded educational and other institutions in St. Petersburg, including a Jewish community center and a Jewish school. Working with Leonid Stonov, UCSJ's International Director for Human Rights Bureaux, it has funded a bureau to fight anti-Semitism in Moscow and similar ones in Kiev, Ukraine; Almaty, Kazakhstan; and Bishkek,

Kyrgyzstan. The small organizations have three to five workers each, and are aided by volunteers. Their mission is to promote human rights education and help those at risk of hate crimes.

Since the end of the USSR, two new Jewish human rights organizations have emerged in Russia: the Moscow Bureau on Human Rights of UCSJ, and the Harold and Selma Light Center for Human Rights Advocacy in St. Petersburg. The Moscow Bureau on Human Rights is funded by a grant from the European Commission rather than Jewish NGOs and, together with the Moscow Helsinki Watch Group and UCSJ, has mounted a three-year project, "The Public Campaign to Combat Racism, Xenophobia, Antisemitism, and Ethnic Discrimination in the Multi-National Russian Federation." The group works with Russian NGOs, the government's federal human rights ombudsman, its Presidential Commission on Human Rights, the Ministries of Education and Justice, and others. It deploys monitors across Russia's regions and mounts annual conferences in Moscow. It offers political advice and legal intervention to victims of hate crimes, as well as educational programs.[114]

The Light Center sponsors some similar programs and offers others with a different emphasis. Leonid Lvov formed the Light Center at the end of the 1980s with a group of refuseniks who had been unable to emigrate due to their so-called work in secret spheres. The Light Center has been supported almost entirely by American organizations: the Jewish Community Development Fund, based in New York, and the Bay Area Council for Jewish Rescue and Renewal. The Russian Jewish Congress, the Russian Jews' central community organization, funded it briefly.

Since 1994, the Light Center has concentrated on protecting the rights of national minorities—not Jews alone, but all minorities. As Leonid Lvov remarked in an interview, "We realized that in a country where we suppress the rights of the majority, to speak of the rights of a minority like the Jews is not only senseless but counterproductive." In 1996, the center started a series of public discussions with journalists, educators, policymakers, and national minorities on the rights of national minorities that led to its major effort, the "Climate of Trust" program. A nucleus of fifteen to twenty people who, as Mr. Lvov put it, "professionally or by the call of life or will were interested in these issues" was developed. They set up regional centers in St. Petersburg, Ryazan, Kazan, and Stavropol Territory to promote cooperation in the fields of prevention of xenophobia, chauvinism, and extremism. The regional centers invited members of law enforcement agencies, educators, and human rights NGOs to join them in cooperative efforts.

With minimal financing and only two paid staff in its central office, the work of the Light Center is necessarily modest, but it nonetheless contributes a vital Jewish presence to the embryonic Russian civil society. Under Vladimir

Putin, the hard-won rights of Jews and other minorities and Russian civil society itself have been eroding. In 2005, Putin reinstated the requirement that NGOs register with the state, which has had a chilling effect on freedom of association and speech. If the course of human rights protections in Russia turns sour, organizations like Mr. Lvov's will be well placed to receive the "crisis dollars" that will surely flow in their direction from the international community. Yet one would think that the international NGOs would have an interest in growing these groups preventively. A strong, vigorous Russian Jewish NGO could defend Jews against encroachments on their rights.

THE RESPONSIBILITY TO REPAIR

The struggle for Soviet Jewry was the preeminent example of Jewish activism to protect the human rights of an embattled Jewish community. While the Soviet case is not the only example of such work—advocacy on behalf of Iraqi and Ethiopian Jews comes to mind—it represents the apogee of Jewish human rights activism. It bound together in time-limited strategic coalitions the homeland and the Diaspora, elite and grassroots NGOs, Jewish and non-Jewish organizations, private and governmental partners, and left and right wing ideologues as never before or since. The network largely skirted the official UN human rights process, which its members recognized was too dysfunctional to be used in this case.

The grassroots character of this network was striking and new. While from the 1940s to the early 1960s, Jewish enthusiasm for human rights was much in evidence, it flowed mostly from the top down, through the efforts of elite NGOs, which engaged in human rights standard-setting and enforcement efforts at the UN, and education efforts in the form of radio broadcasts, cartoons, synagogue dinners, and school curricula. Partly because of the UN's failure to act—due to its anti-Semitism and anti-Zionism—the movement to help Soviet Jews from the 1960s to the 1980s took a more bottom-up form, one that has rarely if ever been repeated. The emerging network had to devise ways outside of the UN framework to achieve its aims. The use of candlelight vigils, public protests, and letter-writing campaigns—many of which were learned by American Jews from their experience in the US civil rights movement—was made necessary by the inability of the elite NGOs to protect Soviet Jews through official diplomacy. The ingenious use of regional mechanisms like the CSCE in Europe and the Helsinki Accords would surely also have been unnecessary if the global human rights system sponsored by the UN had been functioning properly.

Jewish activists successfully created short-term, informal, alliances in an evolving network with multiple power centers. Whether this type of human rights network has survived the specific nature of the Soviet challenge seems doubtful. The web of Jewish human rights actors has diminished its activity on other issues, Jewish or non-Jewish. Partly this is because, at least symbolically, the Jewish question in Russia has been "solved" through emigration. Partly it is because the major human rights issues of the past fifteen years have not been about Jews, but about ethnic Albanians in Kosovo, Tutsis in Rwanda, and Darfuris in Sudan.

The Jewish issues that do exist in the FSU—such as ensuring the implementation of the cultural and religious rights of FSU Jews—do not have crisis hallmarks like long prison terms and state-sponsored anti-Semitism that inspire fund-raising campaigns. Jewish human rights activists working on the Soviet case recognized their responsibility to document abuses, raise international awareness, and participate in standard setting and enforcement of standards. It is less clear that they have since recognized a long-term responsibility to help repair the damage to communities that resulted from over a century of czarist and Communist rights violations.

When called on to protect a vulnerable community, Jewish activists proved they could coalesce to work in effective if informal alliances with government officials and high-powered individuals. However, when the task was transformed from rescuing Jews to rebuilding their devastated communities, the Jewish human rights network has not coalesced to as much effect. Now that FSU Jews have been guaranteed their human rights, Jews outside of the region face the sustained challenge of helping to make these rights real.

3

Jewish Responses to Non-Jewish Genocides

We thought it was "Never Again," but it has been again and again—over and over again—ever since.

—Benjamin Ferencz, chief prosecutor at the trial of the Einsatzgrüppen at Nuremberg.[1]

I have never doubted the uniqueness of the Holocaust. But neither have I doubted its universal meaning, and its challenge to all people on behalf of all peoples.

—Hyman Bookbinder, Washington Bureau, American Jewish Committee.[2]

As Jews, we have a particular moral responsibility to speak out and take action against genocide. We must respond and save as many lives as we can.

—American Jewish World Service, Darfur Action Campaign.[3]

THE HOLOCAUST, ISRAEL, AND GENOCIDE

If the previous chapter showed how Jews were able to employ the language, strategies, and institutions of international human rights for the particular defense of their own group, this chapter asks to what extent Jews have been involved in human rights struggles on behalf of other groups—in a nonparochial, universal sense. The chapter analyzes the contributions made by Jews, in the wake of World War II, to the establishment of international criminal justice, and in particular in the prevention of and intervention in genocide. From the International Military Tribunal at Nuremberg to the Genocide Convention to the establishment of the ICC, Jews have been active in trying to ensure that the Holocaust never happens again. At the same time, the three-wedding dance has placed certain constraints on their efforts, which this chapter will explore.

Judging from the most recent genocide in the Darfur region of Sudan, it might seem that Jews have been among the most vocal of antigenocide activists. Since 2000, state-sponsored Arab militias from the north have been carrying out a coordinated mass slaughter of Sudanese Africans in the south. The militias have killed over two hundred thousand people to date, forced children to join their ranks, and engaged in a systematic program of rape, often with rifle barrels. Two and a half million people have fled to refugee camps across the border in Chad, where tens of thousands have already died of wounds, starvation, and disease. Although the killings were formally identified as genocide in 2003 by the UN Security Council and the US government, neither has done much to stop the catastrophe. Instead, the charge for intervention has been led by international NGOs. While Jewish NGOs were initially slow to respond to the killings, it is not too much to claim that, since 2004, they have led the world's activist response to the tragedy. In June 2004, the American Jewish World Service (AJWS), led by Ruth Messinger, established the Save Darfur Coalition, the major umbrella organization dedicated to the issue, comprised of 170 NGOs. Inspired by the activities of the AJWS, American Jews have mounted their own separate grassroots effort to stop the genocide.

Are Jews' activities on behalf of the Darfuris typical of their historical responses to genocides? One might assume that after the Holocaust Jews had a special sensitivity to the issue. Does that assumption hold up? To find out, we must look at an array of tragedies and Jews' response. Sadly, in the past sixty years there has been no shortage of examples. Has "Never Again" always meant that Jews have been committed to universal genocide protection for victims who do not share their religion, nationality, or ethnicity? I think we will see that, while Jews have made important contributions here, the level of their antigenocide activism is one indication, among others, that Jewish NGOs' commitment to human rights has declined since the mid-1960s.

Relatively few studies have investigated responses to genocide, let alone Jewish responses. While scholarship on the Holocaust and responses to it would fill up a large room in a university's research library, scholarship on genocides and antigenocide activism would take up several bookcases. Although the UN Genocide Convention was adopted in 1948, little credible scholarly work assessing genocide as a general phenomenon was published until Helen Fein's *Accounting for Genocide* (1979) and Leo Kuper's *Genocide: Its Political Use in the Twentieth Century* (1981). Israel W. Charny consolidated the state of the field when, in 1984, he published the proceedings of the first International Conference on the Holocaust and Genocide, held in Tel Aviv, in *Toward the Understanding and Prevention of Genocide*.[4] Thereafter, Charny served as the founding editor of the periodic *The Widening Circle of Genocide: A Critical Bibliographic Review*, a series of essay collections by a wide variety of scholars published in five volumes to date.

The study of antigenocide activism began only during the 1990s, when Samuel Totten published the first of two essays on antigenocide NGOs.[5] In order to map out this unknown territory, Totten paid attention to broadly focused antigenocide NGOs, two of the most prominent being International Alert and Genocide Watch, rather than to the particular antigenocide work of Jewish organizations. Since then, scholars and activists have focused on NGO efforts to elaborate early warning detection systems to anticipate genocides in the making.[6] While, to date, the efforts of Jewish NGOs and individuals to prevent and intervene in genocide have been studied tangentially as part of larger inquiries, the study of such efforts for their own sake is in its infancy. In a general-purpose book of this nature, such a study can hope only to establish a preliminary map, and to indicate avenues for future research.

The study of genocide as a human rights violation has also been impaired by the crime's treatment by the international community. As we will see, the sole enforcement mechanism envisioned by the Genocide Convention is an international court. That is, the world community would only assign accountability after the fact. The convention did not establish the type of supervisory body that became common with later human rights treaties. Hence, genocide has largely been treated outside the regulative UN human rights system. The Commission on Human Rights did not see genocide as part of its mission. On the other hand, the destruction of a group entails the gross and systematic violation of virtually every right to which its members are entitled.

I will begin with a caveat: Jews, by themselves, either individually or as a group, cannot be expected to have averted genocide in any or all cases. There are many good reasons why Jews' influence as a group was profoundly limited. Jewish NGOs often lacked access to political power because of the small size of their constituent community; they almost always lacked sufficient staff, money, and other resources to devote their energies exclusively to genocide monitoring and prevention; and because of the lack of resources they were frequently unable to gather timely information about developments on the ground. Coming by reliable information about genocides in progress has been difficult for even the largest NGOs, the UN human rights monitors, and state officials, let alone small Jewish NGOs.[7] During a genocide in progress, events move quickly, and hallmarks include severe restrictions on free movement of fact-finders and quashing of the free press. For its part, the state of Israel's ability to respond to non-Jewish genocides has been limited by a continuing national security threat, which has functioned as a constant drain on its resources and attention. Its exclusion from UN committees also frustrated its attempts to participate in this work. The point here is not that Jewish activists should have been able to prevent or stop genocides, but to examine, through Jews' antigenocide work, the extent of their commitment to universal human rights.

Since the nineteenth century, Jews have been drawn to the effort to prevent and intervene in genocides and other mass killings, having been sensitized by their own historical persecution. The names tell the horrific tale of death, torture, starvation, forced marches, rapes, and other atrocities Jews have endured: Babylonia, Rome, Lincoln and York, Inquisition Spain, Damascus, Romania, Ukraine, Soviet Union, and Nazi Germany. It is no accident that some of the earliest advocates on behalf of international intervention to rescue threatened minority communities were Jews. The humanist arguments Jews advanced for state interventions on behalf of members of their community could easily be extended (and Jews did extend them) to other groups, such as Roma.

Of course, not all Jews have acted on behalf of other Jews, let alone on behalf of non-Jews. During the Holocaust, US Supreme Court justice Felix Frankfurter, philosopher Isaiah Berlin, and Israeli prime minister David Ben-Gurion were among those Jews who, in the early 1940s, did not believe the Nazi "pogrom" was intended to destroy European Jewry, despite the massive evidence collected by Rabbi Stephen Wise, president of the AJCongress.[8]

Nor did Jews always treat their people's experience of victimization as the basis for a universal antigenocide policy. One group of Jews who rejected such a policy was comprised of some survivors and Jewish activists, who maintained that the Holocaust was a unique, incomparable event. This group refused the linkage between the distinctively horrific experiences of the Holocaust and other mass killings, on the ground that doing so would dilute or distort the Holocaust's meaning. This attitude probably originated as a reaction against the tendency by many commentators, in the immediate wake of the Holocaust, to compare Jews' suffering to that of other populations enslaved and killed by the Nazis (e.g., Poles, Roma, Catholics, political dissenters, people with disabilities, homosexuals). For example, in 1946, after the WJC commissioned a group of scholars to write *The Black Book*, an early attempt to produce a historical record of the Holocaust, a number of staff members of the WJC's Institute for Jewish Affairs criticized their NGO's own book for failing to distinguish the Jews' fate under the Nazis from that of other groups. The staff maintained that

> The true character of Jewish martyrdom at the hands of the Nazis expresses itself in the *peculiarity of the Jewish tragedy* which is completely different and much larger in scope than the plight of any of the other nations enslaved by Nazi Germany. Jewry represented a separate, segregated target for Nazi bestiality. . . . The destruction of the Jewish people had been one of the main aims of the Nazi program. The editors of *The Black Book* tried to merge this tragedy into the broader one.[9]

Insisting on the uniqueness of the Nazis' efforts to eradicate Jews was, and remains, a means to call attention to the special virulence of Nazi anti-Semitism, to combat Holocaust-denial, and to honor the memory of the dead.

Zionists also often interpreted "Never Again" in a nonuniversalist sense. For leaders of the new state of Israel in the late 1940s, the lesson of the Holocaust was that Jews should never again allow themselves to be the victims of mass slaughter. To prevent it, they would build a Jewish state with its own powerful military that would defend Jews' rights. Once the state was actually established, Israeli officials sometimes engaged in realpolitik that prevented them from taking a universalist stance on genocide. During the 1980s, for example, Israel was attempting to build an alliance with Turkey, one of the few primarily Muslim states in Israel's neighborhood willing to engage in economic and military trade with it. So valuable was this alliance that in 1982, the Israeli government refused to condemn the Turkish genocide of Armenians, despite the existence of a sizable Israeli Armenian minority, and it acted to prevent an international genocide conference in Tel Aviv from going forward because the conference contained a panel on the Armenian genocide. Here was a particularly stark example of Jewish national interests colliding with international human rights.

Yet for many Jews and scholars of Jewish history, "Never Again" *has* meant that the lessons of the Holocaust ought to be applied to any situation where a state engages in the deliberate killing and/or cultural decimation of an ethnic, religious, or racial group. Those who embrace the comparative perspective often recall that, as Hitler prepared his officers to undertake "the final solution," he asserted: "Who, after all, speaks today of the annihilation of the Armenians?"[10] Here and elsewhere, perpetrators have participated in a genocide history, of which the Holocaust was the terrible zenith but by no means the only instance, before or since. (For a partial list of genocides and mass killings perpetrated during the past century, see appendix A.)

As the incidence of genocide and mass killings has evolved during the twentieth century, scholars and activists have begun to identify certain distinctions in the types of genocide. In some cases, as in Turkey, Nazi Germany, Bangladesh, Biafra, Iraq, Yugoslavia, Burundi, and Rwanda, the motivation of the perpetrators was ethnic, racial, and/or religious domination; in others, as in the Soviet Union, Cambodia, Guatemala, and China, the motivation was primarily political or economic domination. Some genocides or mass killings took place as part of international conflicts; others as part of civil wars; others during peace time.

The killings in each case constituted only part of the victims' suffering. As in the Holocaust, many of the victims were tortured, degraded, or humiliated. Often before or during the mass killings, the perpetrators also systematically destroyed the people's cultural inheritance and educational institutions and banned their use of ancestral languages. The victims were demonized and excluded from what scholars call "the universe of obligation of the collective conscience" through official statements, media propaganda, and discriminatory legislation and law enforcement.[11] Typically, at least as many people—and often far more—were internally displaced or forced to flee to other countries as were killed. Perpetrators have used ethnic cleansing to clear towns and villages of the targeted group in order to "purify" the area for their own civilians. Many of those who fled were permanently displaced and/or subjected to forced marches; many died of starvation, disease, or wounds. In several cases—in Cambodia, Biafra, Ukraine, and the Soviet Union—enforced starvation was employed as a systematic policy of genocide.[12] Rape and other sex crimes have often been employed as a means of destroying a people. During the partition of India from Pakistan, Hindu forces often cut off the circumcised penises of Muslim men and stuffed them in their mouths. In Bosnia-Herzegovina, Serbian forces systematically raped Bosnian Muslim women, in some cases tying them up as sex slaves until they became pregnant, then holding them in captivity until an abortion was no longer possible. The children of the rapes would take on their Serbian father's ethnicity, their Bosnian identity erased.[13]

The world understood after the Nazis' defeat that such atrocities cried out for international intervention. International attempts to respond to genocide have historically developed in four phases:

1. Naming, defining, and prohibiting the crime
2. Monitoring genocidal outbreaks and early warning signs; educating the public toward intervention
3. State and intergovernmental intervention
4. Punishing the perpetrators

Jewish activists have made contributions at three of these stages (except for intervention, which is the preserve of states). They have been more active at some stages than others, due to the vicissitudes of the three-wedding dance. Specifically, they have made more significant contributions to defining and punishing than to monitoring and advocacy. In what follows, I pay special attention to the activities of those Jews who have participated explicitly *as* Jews in a politics founded on Jewish values, history, and/or ethnic commitments.

PHASE ONE: NAMING, DEFINING, AND PROHIBITING GENOCIDE

The initial phase—naming, defining, and prohibiting the crime—was fundamental to any international effort to prevent and intervene in genocide. It was also the most abstract, dealing with the crime in general rather than specific manifestations of it. Here UN officials, member state governments, lawyers, NGOs, and individuals sought the appropriate words to name and define the crime, to draft a treaty outlawing it, and to persuade UN member states to become parties to the treaty.

At this stage special mention must be made of Raphael Lemkin, a Polish-Jewish legal scholar, who coined the term "genocide" in *Axis Rule in Occupied Europe* (1944) and called for the world to outlaw genocide as an international crime. Even as a child in Poland, Lemkin had drawn up lists of historical examples of what was then called "barbarity" going back to antiquity. As early as 1933, he had already begun to define aspects of genocide for a conference presentation in Madrid.[14] According to William Korey, the author of a respected study of NGOs, Lemkin was "an NGO in the form of a single person."[15] As a staff member of associate supreme justice Robert K. Jackson at the Nuremberg Tribunal, he tried but failed to persuade the prosecutor to use the term *genocide* in prosecuting the Nazis, and to include under this rubric both the "racial" genocides against Jews and Gypsies and the plans for the "national" genocide of Poles, Serbs, Russians, and French for the purposes of colonization.[16] The prosecutor did not want to introduce such a new legal concept at the trials.

Although this initial effort failed, Lemkin succeeded after Nuremberg in introducing the genocide concept into international law. On October 31, 1946, he persuaded US ambassador to the UN, Warren Austin, to support a genocide treaty. He then persuaded Panama to be his sponsor, followed by Cuba and India. With three sponsors, he was able to put the idea for a genocide treaty on the General Assembly agenda. He followed up this achievement by carrying on an endless correspondence in five languages (English, Spanish, German, French, and Yiddish) for support from government delegates and NGOs, and composing supporting speeches for as many as thirty delegations. The General Assembly adopted Resolution 96 (I) on December 11, 1946, formally declaring that "genocide is a crime under international law which the civilized world condemns and for the commission of which principals and accomplices are punishable." The UN adopted the Genocide Convention on December 9, 1948.[17]

The special nature of his achievement was described by John W. Davis, US ambassador to Great Britain and a Democratic candidate for the presidency, in a letter of May 8, 1947. "I . . . congratulate you," he wrote, "on being one of the few men in history who has been able to define a crime, give it a name, and have the definition accepted by the world at large. Your name will always be associated with this achievement."[18]

Although Lemkin was the principle figure in defining and codifying the crime of genocide, he did not work alone: Along with the United States Committee for a United Nations Genocide Convention, Jewish NGOs gave Lemkin substantial support in this effort.[19] In 1947 the WJC submitted an influential memorandum to the UN Economic and Social Council (ECOSOC) urging it to outlaw genocide, but proposing a narrower definition than Lemkin's in order to increase the treaty's chances of passage.[20] The draft was circulated and largely incorporated by the council. In 1948, the WJC added urgency to the effort by submitting a claim to the council that an anti-Jewish genocide was currently taking place in Pakistan.[21] In April 1948, when the council appointed an Ad Hoc Committee to draft the Genocide Convention, the WJC's acting political director, Robert S. Marcus, gave an oral submission arguing that human rights are meaningless without protection from genocide.[22] Moreover, the WJC urged that the convention do more than criminalize genocide, which would accomplish nothing more than to create accountability after the fact; rather, the convention should create a mechanism for international intervention to prevent genocides and stop genocides in progress. Responding to the claim of a delegate from Lebanon that the destruction of a group is sometimes necessary for national defense, Marcus argued that the admission of such a justification would make the Genocide Convention a travesty.[23]

The WJC's national chapters also were involved in the effort to ensure passage of the treaty. In August 1947, Rabbi Stephen S. Wise, president of the AJCongress, sent letters to WJC affiliates throughout the world, as well as to the American delegation of the UN, with the signatures of the Federal Council of Churches, the AFL and CIO, and other American NGOs, urging the delegation to support passage. In 1964, Louis E. Shechter, chair of AJCongress's National Committee on Ratification of the Genocide Convention, exchanged letters with president Lyndon B. Johnson and myriad members of the House and Senate, urging their support.[24] The Canadian Jewish Congress lobbied Canadian officials as well.[25]

During the drafting years, the CCJO took care of planning and conducting the public relations campaign, with Professor Lemkin as the principal advisor and liaison with the United Nations. The CCJO published press releases such as the one on July 29, 1947, titled: "Consultative Council of Jewish Organizations Urges U.N. to Tighten Punishment Clause in Draft Convention on Genocide."[26] It circulated a letter signed by Nobel Prize winners, members of parliaments, and national presidents to the UN General Assembly's Sixth Committee (Legal), to which the question was referred. Each of CCJO's constituent organizations—the Alliance Israélite Universelle, the AJC, and the Anglo-Jewish Association—lobbied its own government's UN delegation. Along with conducting a public campaign, CCJO sought, like the WJC, to intervene in the legislative process. From May 1947 to December 1948, the CCJO submitted numerous formal briefs and informal papers to the UN, particularly the ECOSOC and its commission's Ad Hoc Committee on Genocide.[27] Its proposals sought to strengthen the convention's definition of individual liability.[28]

Unfortunately, the challenge of defining genocide properly did not end with the UN's adoption of the Genocide Convention. Article II of the convention defines genocide as

> acts committed with intent to destroy, in whole or in part, a national, ethnical, racial, or religious group, as such.[29]

Of the eight fields Lemkin had identified in which genocide could be carried out (political, social, cultural, economic, biological, physical, religious, and moral) only two, physical and biological, were protected by the convention.[30] The convention's definition has proved problematic and has often rendered the treaty ineffective as an instrument to prevent and punish mass killings. For one thing, the requirement that there be demonstrable *intent* to destroy has often made prosecuting perpetrators difficult, although recently the International Criminal Tribunal for the former Yugoslavia (ICTY) has interpreted *intent* in the broadest way possible. The definition's focus on "national, ethnical, racial or religious groups" excludes political, economic, gender and/or sexual groups targeted as such. The exclusion of political groups was a particular sticking point during the drafting stage. The WJC argued for the exclusion for pragmatic reasons—to ensure the convention's adoption.[31] Yet this exclusion has meant that many mass killings (e.g., in the USSR, Cambodia, and China) could not be covered under the convention. The definition also excludes the systematic destruction of a group's culture and language.

Furthermore, by defining genocide as the destruction of a group "in whole or in part," the convention raised a complicated set of moral and political questions that it did not resolve, such as: How large a proportion of the population of the targeted group would have to be destroyed for the destruction to count as genocide? Can the moral repugnance of genocide be measured in mere numbers? If one person were murdered as part of a larger (yet unsuccessful) intention to commit genocide, could the perpetrator be held responsible for genocide?

Jewish activists and scholars have participated in largely unsuccessful efforts since Lemkin to refine the definition of genocide. The first scholarly attempt appeared in the proceedings of the aborted International Conference on the Holocaust and Genocide (Tel Aviv, 1982), sponsored by the Jerusalem-based International Institute on the Holocaust and Genocide.[32] Numerous other scholarly efforts followed, but the convention has proven resistant to amendment.[33]

Still, Jewish NGOs have tried to work around the convention's flaws by building safeguards against types of killing not covered under the treaty into the broader framework of international law. In 1949, when the General Assembly asked the International Law Commission (ILC) to codify the principles of international criminal law derived from the judgment of the Nuremberg Tribunal, the WJC pressed for prohibition of a general category of "crimes against humanity" in the code, which would ensure accountability for perpetrators of many specific crimes not addressed in the convention, including the destruction of a group's culture and language.[34] The WJC's suggestions were largely incorporated into the ILC's recommendations.[35] More recently, Blaustein's Felice Gaer helped craft a joint statement signed by twenty women leaders and activists regarding "Women and the Bosnian Peace Process: Preliminary Questions on Ten Issues of Concern," which was circulated by Secretary of State Madeline Albright, and influenced the NATO commander in Sarajevo and the Office of the High Representative of the Peace Implementation Conference in Sarajevo. The statement argued, among other things, that rape and other gender-specific crimes must be treated as war crimes by international tribunals and that in some cases these crimes can rise to the level of genocide. These statements helped bring about a substantial rethinking of international humanitarian law, and in 1998 the changes Gaer promoted were incorporated in the treaty establishing the ICC, the permanent war crimes tribunal.[36]

Definitional questions aside, the Genocide Convention's adoption in 1948 seemed to give states a powerful new tool to protect some vulnerable minorities. Yet it was surprisingly difficult to persuade some UN member states to ratify the treaty. Lemkin and the Jewish NGOs worked unceasingly for ratification in multiple countries.[37] The WJC's activities were typical: it published pamphlets and books on the subject, tracked state ratifications, engaged in advocacy through its national affiliates, and passed resolutions urging ratification at its plenary meetings.[38] Nehemiah Robinson, WJC's coordinator of activities on the convention, published *The Genocide Convention: Its Origin and Interpretation* (1949) and *The Genocide Convention: A Commentary* (1960).[39] Likewise, the CBJO and its constitutive organizations B'nai B'rith (US), the Board of Deputies of British Jews (UK), and the South African Board of Jewish Deputies (South Africa), worked with Lemkin and the Conference of Consultative Organizations in 1949 to secure a resolution endorsing the convention. The British Board of Deputies initiated a debate in the British parliament on the treaty.[40]

In their work toward ratification, neither Lemkin nor the Jewish NGOs had as much influence as they had had in drafting the treaty. Communist states, including the USSR, Belorussia, Ukraine, Czechoslovakia, and China, adopted the treaty but attached a series of reservations essentially immunizing them from its demands. Western powers, including Britain, France, and the United States, refused to adopt the treaty at all. For Britain and France, the fear was that Communists would misuse it to charge them with genocide during their colonial rule (e.g., in French Algeria and British India).

In the United States, the reasons for resistance were somewhat different. The internationalist enthusiasm of the late 1940s was swept away in the 1950s by a wave of isolationism, due to the Cold War. The Korean conflict and McCarthyism both gave rise to fears that Communists could use the international order to undermine US sovereignty and interfere in its domestic affairs. In this spirit, Nehemiah Robinson's book on the Genocide Convention provoked a refutation by the American Bar Association (ABA), which claimed that human rights treaties would undermine civil rights laws at home.[41] Once ratified, the ABA argued, human rights treaties would be incorporated into federal law. The treaties would negate states' power to determine the civil and political rights of their inhabitants. Foreign ideas would be foisted on Southern states, forcing them to discard their discriminatory racial laws. State officials might even be tried for genocide with regard to lynchings. Starting with the Genocide Convention, international human rights treaties would be used as part of a Communist attempt to undermine the American way of life, which included Jim Crow.[42]

In reaction against these prospects, Senator John W. Bricker (R-Ohio) introduced a series of amendments to the Constitution between 1951 and 1955, seeking to prevent all US participation in international human rights treaties.[43] The amendments failed, but the suspicion of international human rights as part of a world Communist plot to undermine US sovereignty gained widespread bipartisan support. President Eisenhower and his secretary of state, John Foster Dulles, promised never to be a party to an international human rights treaty. This meant that the United States refused to participate in any of the early UN treaties of the 1950s and 1960s, including those widely considered fundamental to the International Bill of Human Rights: the Convention on the Elimination of Racial Discrimination (CERD), the International Covenant on Civil and Political Rights (CP Covenant), and the International Covenant on Economic, Social, and Cultural Rights (ESC Covenant). The American distrust of entanglement in international treaties came to be called "Brickeritis."[44]

This was a high-stakes wedding dance between international human rights and national civil rights, but American Jewish organizations did not succumb to the Brickeritis of their government. Predominantly liberal on civil rights issues, and linking these to the international treaties, Jewish NGOs between 1950 and 1988 not only supported Lemkin and his lobbying efforts on behalf of US ratification of the Genocide Convention, they also contributed drafts to the two human rights covenants in which they successfully urged that prohibition of genocide be classified as a human right.[45] They also refuted the attacks on ratification by the ABA.[46] Still, Brickeritis continued well into the 1980s. To combat it, the AJC, AJCongress, B'nai B'rith, the Jewish Labor Committee, and the National Community Relations Advisory Council together created the Ad Hoc Committee on Human Rights and Genocide Treaties in 1960. Arthur J. Goldberg, the US ambassador to the UN and former Supreme Court justice, agreed to serve as chair, and the Jewish NGOs were joined ultimately by forty-seven NGOs, comprising church, labor, civic, ethnic, and women's rights advocates, as well as civil rights and liberties advocates.[47] The Ad Hoc Committee engaged in extensive and often ingenious public campaigns, educational programs, and political advocacy from the 1960s through the 1980s.[48] The committee worked closely with members of the Senate Foreign Relations Committee, among others, Senators J. K. Fulbright, Claiborne Pell, William Proxmire, and Thomas J. Dodd, who were staunch supporters of ratification. It was joined by the United States Committee for a United Nations Genocide Convention, the general secretary of which was Willard Johnson, who was also president of the National Conference of Christians and Jews.[49] The Ad Hoc Committee's activities would make a fascinating subject for a separate study on the gap between US rhetoric and behavior on human rights.

In the beginning, the Ad Hoc Committee worked broadly to convince the US Congress to ratify many treaties, both major and minor, but over the years its work became more and more focused on the Genocide Convention. Its lack of success on the covenants, CERD, and treaties on forced labor, statelessness, and asylum, led its members to realize that the Genocide Convention was "the cork in the human rights bottle."[50] Once the US Congress was persuaded to ratify this treaty, it would be much easier to persuade it to ratify many of the others. As the initial strategic plan of the AJC's human rights program noted in 1972, "the focus is on the Genocide Convention, because of its symbolic importance and also because if the Senate does not act favorably on this fundamental measure, it is not likely to approve more far-reaching treaties."[51]

The committee's approach to advocacy was to clothe its support for the convention quite deliberately in terms of American values. In the first draft of the February 23, 1967, testimony of the committee's chair, Arthur Goldberg, to the Senate Foreign Relations Subcommittee dealing with ratification, AJC's Sidney Liskofsky had written: "we are directly and immediately concerned with the international human rights treaties if for no other reason than that the Jewish people have been classical victims of violations of human rights, including slavery, forced labor, and of course, genocide." The final testimony includes no such statement. Instead, it offers perspectives on why ratification was the natural outgrowth of American tradition and history.[52]

Still, the committee's extensive activity over a quarter of a century produced few results. Even President Carter, the US leader most supportive of human rights, proved unable to cure the Senate of Brickeritis, hampered as he was by the OPEC oil embargo, the Tehran hostage crisis, and rampant inflation. His successor, Ronald Reagan, did not seem the type to break the impasse. During Reagan's first term, B'nai B'rith tried to keep the pressure on to ratify the treaty by arranging an exhibit at the New York Public Library on the life of Raphael Lemkin, but Jewish NGOs were not optimistic that progress would come anytime soon.

At this point, the NGOs received some limited help from a cultural quarter. The US Holocaust Memorial Museum was chartered by Congress in 1980, Reagan's first year in office. One of the first acts of the museum's founding Holocaust Memorial Council, presided over by survivor and Nobel laureate, Elie Wiesel, was to establish a Committee on Conscience. The idea for such a committee had been initiated by Hyman Bookbinder, the head of AJC's Washington office, in 1979.[53] The Carter administration's President's Commission on the Holocaust had incorporated the committee into its recommendations for the museum. The committee would

> receive reports of genocide (actual or potential) anywhere in the world. In the event of any outbreak, it would have access to the President, the Congress, and the public in order to alert the national conscience, influence policy makers, and stimulate worldwide action to bring such acts to a halt.[54]

After its establishment in 1980, however, the committee was permitted to meet only twice before being disbanded. In the words of Holocaust Memorial Council member Ruth Mandel, the White House was concerned about "the appropriateness and feasibility of empowering a voice to speak with the aura of government authority but with no real portfolio."[55] The Committee on Conscience was stillborn.

Still, the committee's parent body, the Holocaust Memorial Council, could serve as a platform: Wiesel and his successors, Harvey Meyerhoff and Miles Lerman, used the council as a bully pulpit to speak out about the plight of newly threatened groups around the world, including Vietnamese, Cambodians, Kurds, and Roma.[56] Through these means they were able to raise public awareness about genocides and mass killings and put pressure on the government to act.

The turning points that led to US ratification of the convention occurred during Reagan's second term. His visit in 1985 to the Bitburg Cemetery, forty years after the end of World War II, was intended to honor the victims of the war and the Holocaust, and to celebrate the reconciliation between the United States and West Germany. However, a great deal of controversy arose because the cemetery contained the graves of Nazi soldiers of the Waffen SS. On national television, Elie Wiesel castigated Reagan: "That place is not your place. Your place is with the victims of the SS."[57] When Reagan persisted in going to Bitburg, he lost a good deal of support in the American Jewish community. The Holocaust anniversary, the new museum, and the desire to reestablish good relations with American Jews combined to persuade Reagan to support ratification, even against his own right wing. Thanks to behind-the-scenes lobbying by William Korey, a member of both the Ad Hoc Committee and B'nai B'rith's UN affairs department, a State Department spokesman announced at the 1984 B'nai Brith annual convention that the president would support ratification.[58] Four years later, on December 9, 1988—forty years to the day after the UN General Assembly adopted the Genocide Convention—the treaty became part of US law.

Brickeritis did not end there, however; it persisted in a nuanced form. When the United States ratified the convention, it attached numerous "signing statements" and reservations, the cumulative effect of which was to ensure that no United States citizen could be charged with genocide. The Reagan administration won the symbolic victory of signing a treaty it never planned to enforce, continuing the United States' "hypocritical double standard" in which it "talk[s] about human rights but appear[s] reluctant to act."[59] President Clinton sought, to some extent, to soften Brickeritis by signing the statute of the ICC, which would have made it technically possible (although highly improbable) for an American citizen to be tried in an international tribunal for committing genocide. However, president George W. Bush's first act as president was to unsign the treaty, citing concerns familiar from the supporters of Bricker.

Hence, even after ratification, there was still a need for human rights supporters to ensure that the convention could be enforced. Jewish NGOs continued to weigh in. In "Finish the Job," an article in *Washington Jewish Week* on June 16, 1988, David Harris, AJC's executive director, praised Congress for considering ratification.[60] In 1993, an ad hoc committee was convened to study the desirability of reviving the US Holocaust Memorial Museum's Committee on Conscience. The ad hoc group determined that the committee should be reconstituted, and it was formally established in April 1996, under the leadership of Ruth Mandel. It immediately began the process of establishing relations with Congress, ironing out its relations with the State Department, mounting temporary exhibitions on genocides in progress, and gathering information on particular situations through hearings.[61] The museum's first exhibition on a mass killing in progress was "Faces of Sorrow: Agony in the Former Yugoslavia," which opened on September 22, 1994. The Committee on Conscience put its information-gathering apparatus to use for the first time in February 2003, to sound the alarm on the genocide in Darfur.

PHASE TWO: MONITORING OUTBREAKS, EDUCATING THE PUBLIC

In the monitoring arena, Jews have also made important contributions, although without as much fervor and without expending nearly as much of their resources as they have used on the other stages of antigenocide, or on campaigns on behalf of vulnerable Jewish communities. The level of their response has probably been about on par—in some cases more or less robust—with the level of human rights activists in general in the West. Of the thirty thousand to forty thousand human rights NGOs operating today, only a small number have made monitoring and intervention in genocides a key element of their work. As genocide scholars Samuel Totten, William S. Parsons, and Israel W. Charny noted in their influential *Century of Genocide*: "As it now stands, most individuals and organizations dealing with the issue of genocide are putting more time into working on the scholarly examination of genocide . . . than the actual prevention of or intervention in genocide" (9). Certainly the Jerusalem-based Institute for Holocaust and Genocide Studies and the International Association of Genocide Scholars, attest to international activity by Jewish scholars in this area. As early as 1973, Charny began to develop one of the first early warning systems to enable the assessment of the potential outbreak of genocides around the world.[62]

To some extent, the relatively small amount of nongovernmental work in this arena reflects the low priority that the international community—and in particular the US government—has ceded to preventing and intervening in genocides. The first Bush administration, for example, refused to use the term "genocide" to describe the killings in Bosnia, and the Clinton administration would only describe the Rwanda murders as "acts of genocide" rather than "genocide"—in both cases so that the United States would not be legally bound to act.[63] The Clinton administration did eventually become active in the former Yugoslavia, but diplomatic disagreements with the European community over whether to use military solutions were protracted over a two-year period. By the time NATO air strikes finally stopped the Serbian ethnic cleansing campaign in Bosnia, 250,000 people had been killed and over one million displaced.[64] When the genocide in Rwanda broke out, the Clinton administration determined that the country was not central to US national interests, and that, in the wake of the American failure in Somalia, little political will existed to act in Africa. It therefore did little to stop the slaughter of eight hundred thousand people. The administration did not even complain when Rwanda took its turn in the UN Security Council during the very months the genocide was taking place. President Clinton later admitted that "the failure to try to stop Rwanda's tragedies became one of the greatest regrets of my presidency."[65]

The American public, too, was not tremendously interested in genocides occurring overseas in countries that had no obvious links to US national interests. Political scientists have long noted that American citizens are generally uninterested in foreign affairs. They have usually tuned out genocides as well. For example, as Herbert Hirsch has shown, in opinion polls, only about 10–12 percent of the American public reported following the news about Bosnia and Rwanda—as opposed to 80 percent who followed the Challenger space shuttle story, and 25 percent who followed the O. J. Simpson trial.[66] Following Clinton's lead, the leaders of the civil society also did not stir on Rwanda's behalf. In the words of journalist Samantha Power, in her influential book, *"A Problem from Hell,"* "No group or groups in the United States made Clinton administration decision-makers feel or fear that they would pay a political price for doing nothing to save Rwandans."[67] Even if they had, it is often the case in foreign affairs that public opinion has little impact on the decisions of policymakers.

Jews' organizational responses to recent genocides must be understood in this context. Since the 1970s, Jews have reacted to genocides and mass killings with mixed intensity: very little activity on Cambodia, relatively more on Bosnia, relatively little again on Rwanda (until after the fact), more again on Kosovo—all unsystematic, all ad hoc. Their response was about typical of that of other groups. Although Jews responded to each genocide with outrage, until the recent Darfur genocide they did not mount the full-scale effort of which the Soviet Jewry campaign had proved them capable.

One measure of the extent of Jewish activity on genocide might be the *American Jewish Yearbook*, the annual encyclopedic publication of Jewish world activities compiled by the AJC. The yearbook lists no Jewish responses to any of the genocides of the past half-century. We know from other sources that this picture is inaccurate, but there is a kernel of truth here. Jewish NGOs have tended to track events in areas of the world where there are at least minimal Jewish populations—where their self-interest has been engaged. Indeed, their responses to non-Jewish genocides have themselves showed a measure of self-interest inasmuch as they contributed more to areas where the genocide resonates with Jewish history (e.g., Eastern Europe), and less to areas where historically there has been little or no Jewish presence (e.g., Rwanda). So, in the regions of the world the *Yearbook* covers, it leaves out Africa almost entirely (with the exception of South Africa), and thus has paid no attention to the various genocides and mass killings in Rwanda, Burundi, Namibia, Uganda, Congo, and Nigeria.

Of the small percentage of human rights NGOs whose mission is primarily to respond to genocide, the London-based International Alert: Standing International Forum on Ethnic Conflict, Genocide and Human Rights, was largely established by Jews. Its founder, Leo Kuper, was raised in a South African Orthodox family, his early scholarly studies in the apartheid system leading to his later groundbreaking analyses of systematic mass killings around the world. In 1985, he enlisted Martin Ennals, the former secretary general of Amnesty International, to lead the effort to intervene in and prevent genocides.[68] While International Alert's mission has expanded to include broader peace-building efforts in Asia and Africa, the organization remains a member of the International Campaign to End Genocide, an international coalition of NGOs. Kuper himself went on to design a curriculum for teaching human rights and genocide for the state of California.[69]

Various Jewish defense and interfaith groups with broader missions than genocide, mainly in the United States and Europe, have also engaged in antigenocide campaigns, albeit sporadically. Israeli officials, too, have sometimes attempted to place a particular genocide on the public agenda. For these groups, the very breadth of their missions has presented an obstacle to undertaking substantial antigenocide work, because the latter requires an enormous investment of targeted resources and energy, often more than the NGO has or is willing to lay out for causes not directly related to Jews. Charny's proposal for an early warning system estimated that, to be carried out properly, the task would require the resources and staff of the CIA. This has posed a challenge not just for Jews but for all NGOs.

The consequence has been that Jewish NGOs have often devoted resources to monitoring genocides and massacres that were, at least in a small way, associated with Jews. I. Schwartzbart, a member of the WJC Executive, remarked that the NGO's interest in Indochina, for example, was mainly to establish "contact with the remoter outposts of the Jewish people in dispersion."[70]

The interest in Jewish communities throughout the Diaspora could, however, lead to a broader Jewish concern for non-Jews threatened with genocides and mass killings. For example, since the 1940s, the WJC had been in close contact with its Chilean affiliate, the Comité Representativo de la Collectividad Israelita de Chile (Representative Committee of the Jewish Community of Chile), which was in a position to report on general developments throughout the country. Chile boasted a sizable Jewish community of thirty-five thousand (about .4 percent of the total Chilean population, most living in the capital city, Santiago). When Chile's democratically elected president, Salvadore Allende, was ousted in a coup led by General Augusto Pinochet, the Santiago chapter served as the WJC's eyes and ears, enabling it to track the events leading to mass disappearances and torture of Allende supporters.[71]

Jewish NGOs, together with the state of Israel, did mount responses to non-Jewish genocides where no Jewish victims were involved. The AJC responded to the crisis of the Cambodian refugees in the 1970s by working with the National Coalition for Refugee Resettlement to advocate for increased Cambodian immigration quotas to the Ford and Carter administrations. Quotas, it argued, carried a "special message" for Jews because the United States had closed the doors of immigration during the Holocaust.[72] The AJC sponsored a full-page advertisement in the *New York Times* ("Do a Mitzvah—Save a Life"), mobilized synagogues to join Catholic and Protestant churches in relief efforts, and created a Cambodia Relief Fund through which its members could donate aid for refugees. In an essay in the *Forward* on the refugees known as "boat people," the AJC's executive director, David Harris, sought to increase Jewish public support for the victims by appealing to the Jews' own history of persecution:

> As Jews, we understand very well the motivations of refugees. We understand that fear, threats, persecution, and violence based on fanatical and misguided religious, national, ethnic, and political beliefs force people to flee their homelands in the hope of a more secure life for themselves and their children.[73]

Rabbi Marc H. Tanenbaum, AJC's national interreligious affairs director, testified before the US House of Representatives Subcommittee on Asian and

Pacific Affairs of the Committee on Foreign Affairs that the only parallels he could think of when making a site visit to the killing fields were "Belsen and Dachau."[74]

During the massacres in Bosnia in 1992–1995, and the genocides in Burundi and Rwanda in 1993–1994, Jewish individuals and human rights and defense organizations also reacted. At the dedication of the US Holocaust Memorial Museum, Eli Wiesel, who chaired the museum's planning council, used his remarks to plead with President Clinton directly: "I have been in the former Yugoslavia last fall," he said. "I cannot sleep since, for what I have seen. As a Jew, I am saying that we must do something to stop the bloodshed in that country!"[75] The genocides in Bosnia and Rwanda together convinced the Holocaust Museum's board of directors to revive the Committee of Conscience.

Other individual Jews whose Jewish identity was a factor in their decision to become active in the campaign to stop genocide in Yugoslavia include Jonathan Fine, the first executive director of Physicians for Human Rights, who directed the exhumation of bodies in the mass graves of Srebrenica, providing evidence for genocide at trials in the ICTY. Aryeh Neier, director of Human Rights Watch/Helsinki Watch, edited the NGO's influential report on the systematic slaughters perpetrated by Serbian forces in Kosovo in 1992 that called the slaughters a "genocide."[76] Numerous Jews served on the board of advisors of Genocide Watch, one of the leading NGOs with a mission to monitor and prevent outbreaks of genocide.[77]

Jewish NGOs, too, put aside the Jewish/Muslim conflict in the Middle East to make efforts on behalf of Bosnian Muslims. The AJC, the AJCongress, and the Anti-Defamation League pressed Brent Scowcroft, president George H. W. Bush's national security advisor, to intervene, and took out a full-page advertisement in the *New York Times* titled, "Stop the Death Camps."[78] They were joined by Israeli prime minister Yitzhak Rabin, who in an August 1992 meeting with President Bush also compared the Serbian camps to Nazi death camps.[79] The AJC urged President Clinton to invoke the emergency provisions of the Refugee Act and open immigration quotas to twenty-five thousand. In July 1995, after the Srebrenica massacre of eight thousand Muslims, Kenneth Roth, director of Human Rights Watch, organized a coalition of twenty-seven NGOs, seven of which were Jewish organizations, to call for military intervention and safeguard Bosnian civilians. Felice Gaer largely drafted the coalition's joint statement, released on July 31, and she subsequently met with Alija Izetbegovic, the president of Bosnia, to discuss ways to protect human rights during the conflict.[80] On June 26, 2006, Simon Wiesenthal and a number of American Jewish NGOs (AJC, AJCongress, B'nai B'rith, Anti-Defamation League) tied in with a coalition of 211 international NGOs and high-profile individuals to send a letter to the G7 summit of world leaders calling on them to consent to use force to apprehend the major Yugoslavian war criminals and extradite them to the ICTY in The Hague.[81]

Such responses were significant, although largely reactive and unsystematic. They were also usually ineffective. On February 23, 1994, Michael Berenbaum, chair of the US Holocaust Memorial Museum, gave a confidential briefing to members of the Committee on Conscience in which he recounted an attempt made by Elie Wiesel to persuade Clinton's undersecretary of state for political sffairs, Peter Tarnoff, that "whether or not genocide was underway in Bosnia, the Serb concentration camps and mass murders there constituted a moral imperative for decisive outside intervention." Tarnoff replied that failure in Bosnia "would destroy the Clinton Presidency."[82] Politics won the day.

Yet, effective or not, these acts were evidence of Jewish concern over the crisis. Concern was more than Jewish NGOs were able to muster in response to the situation in Rwanda. Hutus in Rwanda prior to the genocide spoke of "the Tutsi question"—with its parallel to the Nazis' Judenfrage. Like the Nazis' victims, Tutsis were made the objects of dehumanizing policies and propaganda—referred to by Hutu radio announcers as "cockroaches." During the slaughter, carried out in a mere two months, largely with machetes, numerous commentators in the Western media referred to the Tutsis as the "Jews of Africa."[83] A memorial to the victims built on a hill in Kigali, the Rwandan capital, made explicit links to the fate of Jews as well as Armenians.[84] Yet the organized Jewish community did not distinguish itself by its activity during these mass killings. Jewish NGOs like the AJC and WJC did provide aid and assistance in the *aftermath* of the genocide.[85] However, they were not out front calling for intervention during the killing, as they had been in the case of Bosnia. Here, their response was entirely typical of that of the US government and of most US citizens—which is to say, not nearly enough.

The official US and European reaction to the most recent genocide in Darfur, Sudan has consisted of delays, circumlocutions, and inaction. European leaders declared the slaughters of two hundred thousand civilians were "tantamount to genocide" rather than "genocide," ensuring that the Genocide Convention would not compel them to mount a military response. The Bush administration occasionally wrung its hands but did little other than to support a relatively small African Union force. The United Nations Security Council dithered.[86] The US media has done only marginally better. One of the few writers consistently concerned with the situation has been Nicholas D. Kristof, a *New York Times* columnist, who has published a series of pleas and reports on the situation, the title of one being "If Not Now, When?" after the famous question of Rabbi Hillel.[87]

In this case Jews have not succumbed to the inaction of their national and international leaders. Perhaps partly as a self-reflex against their silence on Rwanda, Jews have reacted to the Darfur genocide with a wide range of grassroots and elite responses. It is not too much to assert that Jews have led the movement for government and UN action against the Sudanese government and the *janjaweed* militias it has supported.

Still, the history of the recent mass Jewish organization against the genocide in Sudan tells us a good deal about the state of contemporary Jewish human rights activism. While Jews have developed a full-throated grassroots effort on Darfur, it would be difficult to claim this response resulted from the leadership of Jewish human rights activists, or that it demonstrated Jews' commitment to universal genocide protection. In the first place, although the atrocities began in 2000, and the US Holocaust Memorial Museum determined in February 2003 that the killings amounted to genocide, it was not until April 2004 that the AJWS began providing food and medicines to Darfur refugees. It was not until June 2004 that Ruth Messinger formed the Save Darfur Coalition. And only in November 2004 did the AJC issue its first Human Rights Discussion Paper calling for international intervention to stop the genocide.[88] Thus, Jewish human rights NGOs did not play a vanguard role on the issue.

The Jewish World Service's leadership in this effort reveals a good deal about how Jewish human rights activism has declined since the mid-1960s. Although there are many Jewish NGOs with explicit human rights platforms, AJWS is not one of them. It was established in 1985 to fight global poverty, hunger, and disease—it is what is known in the NGO world as a humanitarian aid organization, not a human rights NGO. Its Save Darfur Campaign is really outside of its mission—a testament to the courage and vision of its leader. By contrast, the human rights NGOs lagged behind.

Still, by 2006 the coalition had grown to over 170 member organizations. AJWS has led the entire Jewish NGO network in its response to the issue, and has worked with the Holocaust Museum throughout the effort.[89] Jewish NGOs on Save Darfur's executive committee include the Jewish Council for Public Affairs and the Union for Reform Judaism. In a measure of how widespread the Jewish community's concern for Darfur has been, the constituent NGOs of Save Darfur have included Jewish defense, human rights, diplomatic, denominational, student, federation, and interfaith groups.[90] Among other activities, the coalition launched a "Million Voices for Darfur" campaign, collecting over one million postcards urging President Bush to support intervention with a strong multinational force in Sudan. By the end of 2006, the coalition had raised over $4 million, approximately 80 percent of which has gone to humanitarian relief.[91] Independently, the AJWS has held rallies in cities throughout the United States, compiled educational resources, tracked the congressional legislative agenda on the issue, and sold "Save Darfur" wristbands, yarmulkes, CDs, and DVDs to raise funds for humanitarian relief projects in southern Sudan.

The Save Darfur coalition is only the Jews' most visible effort to stop the genocide. The WJC has tacitly used the inaction of Western governments and NGOs on Rwanda as a means of educating Jews about Darfur. In April 2006, the WJC, together with the Belgian *Fondation pour la Mémoire de la Shoah*, sponsored a "Shared Memories—Collective Action" trip for two dozen Jewish students and eight Rwandan students to Rwanda. According to Peleg Reshef, the WJC's trip coordinator, "We have to learn about the unique place of the Holocaust in the context of genocide. We must understand we have a vital role to play, including what is happening today in Darfur and other dark corners of the world."[92] Various rabbinical groups, Jewish community centers, and student groups have mobilized rallies in the name of the Jewish tradition of social justice.[93] Led by Rabbi Harold Schulweiss of Valley Beth Shalom synagogue in Los Angeles, Southern California rabbis from every denomination formed Jewish World Watch in October 2004, in order to "challenge the Jewish people to begin to honor the promise made following the Holocaust—that "Never Again" would we be silent in the face of genocide."[94] Mark Hanis, a Jewish student at Swarthmore, all four of whose grandparents survived the Holocaust, led a group of his peers in raising $250,000 to help pay for African Union peacekeepers in Darfur.[95]

Jewish newspapers across the country called for Jews to mobilize, and museums like the William Breman Jewish Heritage Museum in Atlanta, Georgia, have contracted with Human Rights Watch to mount an exhibit of drawings by Darfur children depicting the acts of violence they have witnessed.[96] Many of the Darfur activists have made explicit links between the history of American Jews' participation in the black civil rights movement and their antigenocide work. In the struggle against genocide and Darfur, two weddings—the commitments to human rights and pluralism—once again seemed to be aligned.

The activism has been motivated not only by reflections on Jewish history but also by values drawn from Jewish tradition. Ruth Messinger herself has frequently made the link between her work and the tradition. For example, in a letter to the *New York Times* she wrote: "We put into action the biblical maxim to not stand idly by when another's blood is being shed."[97] As a guest speaker one Saturday morning at Ahavath Achim, a conservative synagogue in Atlanta, Messinger also called attention to the holiday of Sukkot, when Jews traditionally live in temporary shelters, pointing out that for Darfurian refugees in Chad "the sukkah is not temporary, but a permanent way of life."[98] These appeals underscore the universal human rights lessons she draws from Jewish theology and practice.

That such linkages were often missing in Jews' reactions to earlier genocides suggests that the social justice sources in Jewish history and tradition are not ever-present in the community's collective consciousness: like the golem, Jews require the proper messenger to awaken them. While American Jewish organizations have played a key role in the US and international response to Darfur, one can ask whether, if it had not been for a single passionate and well-placed individual, a Jewish movement would have emerged. It would be difficult to claim that their response resulted, in the first instance, from a broader commitment to international human rights or even universal genocide protection. By the turn of the century, the energetic Jewish human rights presence of the post-Holocaust period had lost a good deal of ground.

As we have seen, since the 1960s when the anti-Israel alliance arose at the UN, the Jewish NGOs have undergone parochial retrenchment. They have felt increasingly compelled to tend to family, religious community, Diaspora, and nation-state as a result of the international community's ceaseless attacks on Israel and Jews. They no longer trusted the UN's human rights institutions to work toward justice. The founding statement of UN Watch, established by US ambassador and former AJC president, Morris Abram, asserts that the UN's "obsessive, unidimensional preoccupation with Israel has resulted in exculpatory immunity being granted at the same time to the real violators of religious human rights—including even the perpetrators of genocide."[99] Having lost faith in the UN human rights system, many Jews shied away from interacting with it. No doubt this situation reduced their effectiveness at using international tools to confront genocide.

It is possible, of course, that the massive grassroots support for a Jewish communal response to Darfur may become the basis for a renewed commitment to antigenocide work, and perhaps, to international human rights work in the broad sense. This seems to be the long-term aim of Jewish World Watch, an NGO founded to respond to Darfur, whose mission statement asserts that "as other global crises emerge in other countries, Jewish World Watch will expand its focus, and be a call to conscience to respond to human rights abuses wherever and whenever they occur."[100] Whether the NGO's American Jewish constituents will continue to fund it and volunteer on behalf of the general cause of human rights will now be put to the test.

PHASE THREE: ENSURING ACCOUNTABILITY

While the initial stage of naming and prohibiting genocide was fairly successful, many believed that for half a century after the adoption of the convention, the effort to prevent genocide had nonetheless failed. The problem was not just definitional, and it was not just in the tendency of states to avert their eyes from mass killings. The problem was that one of the convention's main goals, ensuring accountability, had not yet been achieved. States that commit or permit genocide on their territory are unlikely to be willing or able to bring the perpetrators to justice. Hence, the Genocide Convention's Article VI called for the establishment of an "international penal tribunal" to ensure that perpetrators of genocide would be punished.[101] For fifty years this call remained unheeded. Benjamin Ferencz called the lack of such a tribunal "the missing link in the world order."[102] As José Ayala Lasso, the first UN HCHR, remarked: "A person stands a better chance of being tried and judged for killing one human being than for killing 100,000."[103] Finally, at a diplomatic conference in Rome in 1998, a treaty was adopted to establish the ICC with jurisdiction over genocide, war crimes, and crimes against humanity.

The road to enforcement has been long. An international criminal tribunal was first discussed during negotiations over the Versailles Treaty at the end of World War I. The first experiments with such a court were the International Military Tribunals (IMTs) in Tokyo and Nuremberg after World War II. They established a precedent for holding individuals accountable for war crimes and crimes against humanity, regardless of whether these individuals had been ordered by superior officers to commit these crimes. The IMTs also established that states that permit or direct individuals to commit such crime can have no expectation of sovereign control over the fate of their own culpable citizens. These tribunals did not result in the establishment of a permanent international criminal court, however. Although most states were willing to ratify the Genocide Convention, many fewer were willing to cede to an international court the power to put their own citizens in the dock.

In 1947, the General Assembly had instructed the ILC to draw up a draft statute for an international criminal court. Accordingly, between 1947 and 1957, the WJC submitted one recommendation after another to the commission. It distributed a memorandum to numerous UN delegations promoting the extension of the Nuremberg principles to include "international criminal jurisdiction."[104] However, the UN's enthusiasm for the court soon waned. The delegate from India, Mr. Pal, expressed the feeling of many member states when he argued that the court would mete out Nuremberg-style victors' justice and that the justice would only have limited use since it could be exercised only after the genocide. He objected that the court's procedures displayed a Western European and Anglo-Saxon bias, that there were insufficient fair trial guarantees, and that the court was hamstrung by the absence of an agreed definition of "aggression." In its memorandum, the WJC countered that it was necessary to establish the court so that individual officials, and not a given state in the abstract, could be held accountable for the most heinous crimes. It applauded the ILC for its decision that "crimes against humanity" could be punished whether perpetrated during times of war or peace.[105]

During the 1950s, UN action on the court stagnated, having been caught up in Cold War politics: neither West nor East was willing to subject itself to the risk of politically fueled claims by the other.[106] Jewish NGOs' attempts to persuade the UN to draft a statute for the court were mostly futile.[107] Nonetheless, in the midst of this impasse, there were incremental steps toward a permanent court. The Israeli kidnapping and trial of Adolph Eichmann in Jerusalem in 1961 represented a proactive step toward the establishment of a principle of "universal jurisdiction." This legal concept maintains that any state can hold *genocidaires* accountable regardless of whether the crime was committed in that state or against that state's nationals, as long as the state has written legislation criminalizing genocide into its domestic law. This controversial principle has lately been tested again, first, in the trial of former Chilean dictator Augusto Pinochet by the British Law Lords for massacres and disappearances during his reign, second, in the attempt by Belgium to try a Congolese foreign minister for war crimes allegedly committed in Congo. In the latter case, the president of the International Court of Justice, Judge Guillaume, denied that individual states could exercise universal jurisdiction unless the alleged perpetrator or the victim was a national of that state; otherwise, he asserted, universal jurisdiction could be rightfully exercised only by properly constituted multilateral tribunals.[108] Even after a multilateral court was established, however, (i.e., the ICC), prominent commentators, including Henry Kissinger, continued to argue against universal jurisdiction, on the grounds that it violated national sovereignty.[109]

The first step toward a permanent court was made by the UN Security Council on August 13, 1992, when it called upon states and human rights NGOs to collect evidence of grave human rights violations, including genocide, in Bosnia. This was the first time the council had directed NGOs to collect such evidence. Although the resolution did not promise to establish a tribunal to adjudicate the evidence once collected, the implication was that a resolution to establish a court would follow.[110] Building on this step, the Commission on Human Rights called for a special rapporteur on Bosnia-Herzegovina, and eventually formed a Commission of Experts to investigate potential crimes there; both reported that "genocide" was taking place in Bosnia.

NGOs then began to weigh in with reams of documentation. Aryeh Neier, director of Human Rights Watch/Helsinki Watch, published an influential report on Bosnia calling for an international tribunal.[111] In his introduction, Neier reminded his audience that he had lived as an infant in Berlin until his family fled to England in 1939, thus establishing a parallel between victims of the Holocaust and victims in Rwanda and the former Yugoslavia. In May 1993, in part as a response to Neier, the Security Council established the ICTY, with jurisdiction over genocide, war crimes, and crimes against humanity. Two years later, it established a parallel tribunal in Rwanda (ICTR). Together these courts would serve as evidence that a permanent ICC could be effective.[112]

Jewish NGOs have generally supported the ICC, but in one respect they have greeted it with ambivalence. Although Israel's diplomats contributed to the drafting of the ICC statute in the late 1990s, Israel was one of only seven states to refuse to sign the statute, and is one of a minority of states (including the United States) that have refused to ratify it. Israel's refusal to join the court rests on a single paragraph in the section of the statute on war crimes that criminalizes

> the transfer, directly or indirectly, by the Occupying Power of parts of its own civilian population into the territory it occupies.[113]

Israel interpreted this section of the treaty as the international community's effort to restrain the West Bank settlement enterprise. The paragraph has become an obstacle to Israel's participation in a court designed to enforce the prohibition of genocide. As a state born out of the ashes of the Holocaust, Israel clearly has an interest in struggling to end genocide, and it was one of the first states to ratify the Genocide Convention. Yet, in Israel's refusal to join the ICC we find a stark example of international law and national policy failing to dance together. Moreover, Israel's decision not to join the ICC has created a tension with at least some Diaspora Jewish NGOs, like the AJC, which has supported US ratification of the ICC statute. AJC's support is an acknowledgment that Diaspora Jews may not always be able to count on Israel's military to defend them from future genocidal threats, that they identify with those minorities more vulnerable than they are, and that they support the universalist principles codified in the court's statute.

The attempt to hold perpetrators of genocide accountable is inseparable from the broader twentieth-century effort to develop international law. Numerous Jewish lawyers and jurists have demonstrated the linkage between genocide as a specific field within international law and the concerns of the broader domain. Profiles of three individuals illuminate how their work on genocide has been linked both to their Jewish identity and to their passion for other areas of international human rights and humanitarian law: For these individuals and many others whom they represent, work to determine the responsibility for genocides has Jewish roots, but many branches.

Benjamin Ferencz, the US chief prosecutor at the Einsatzgrüppen trial at Nuremberg, went on to become a tireless advocate for the ICC. He also worked for the particular justice of Jewish victims of the Nazis. In the early 1990s, Ferencz worked with the WJC to launch a public campaign on behalf of the Nazis' victims and survivors with respect to funds and property still held by Swiss banks. In 1992, Ferencz helped the WJC, B'nai B'rith, the Joint Distribution Committee, the Jewish Agency, and survivors' groups form the World Jewish Restitution Organization (WJRO). As a result, in 1996, many Swiss banks agreed to an audit of their records, which eventually resulted in a $4.7 billion survivor fund. Later the WJRO was able to win a similar restitution agreement for Jewish survivors from Sweden.

Judge Richard Goldstone has also mixed work on issues of particular importance to Jews along with more general work toward international criminal justice. He served as a member of the South African Constitutional Court for nine years, where he worked to defuse the tensions arising from apartheid and its dismantlement. He then served as chief prosecutor of both the tribunals for the former Yugoslavia and Rwanda in 1994–1996 and in August 1997, became a member of an international panel established by the government of Argentina to monitor the inquiry into Nazi activity there since 1938. After a brief stint as a governor of the Hebrew University in Jerusalem, in August 1999 he was appointed chairperson of the International Independent Inquiry in Kosovo. Throughout the course of his efforts, Judge Goldstone has strived to keep Jews informed of why they need to support international criminal justice.[114]

Like Ferencz and Goldstone, Thomas Buergenthal has worked on a wide range of Jewish and more general issues. He has been motivated in part by direct experience with the Holocaust, his mother having survived Auschwitz. Among other accomplishments, Beurgenthal has been a member of the United States Holocaust Memorial Council since its founding in 1996 and the chair of its Committee of Conscience. He participated as a member of US delegations to meetings of the Conference on Security and Cooperation in Europe, where the Helsinki Accords were drawn up, helping to construct a major tool that Soviet Jews would put to good use in their struggle for freedom. He has served as president of the Inter-American Court of Human Rights in Costa Rica, a member of the UN Human Rights Committee in Geneva, and, since 2000, has sat on the International Court of Justice in The Hague.

Surveying the history of Jewish efforts on behalf of international justice for the victims of genocide, a fair assessment is that their contributions have been considerable. As in the first stage of genocide work (naming, defining, and prohibiting the crime), the accountability phase has been concerned with creating a general system of law, rather than with any given case. The establishment of a permanent ICC will, however, provide the means of punishing *genocidaires* in specific cases in the future.

EVALUATING JEWISH RESPONSES TO NON-JEWISH GENOCIDES

The content of the phrase "Never Again" has always been open. Jews the world over have interpreted it in a variety of ways. They have heard it as a call to build memorials to the victims of the Holocaust, or to compose and recite prayers over their ancestors' and the Jewish people's fate. They have given oral histories, published documentary histories, compiled "memory books," and written autobiographies by the thousands. They have heard the phrase as a clarion cry to establish, build up, and preserve the Jewish state. They have responded to it by tracking down Nazi war criminals and bringing them to justice. In all these ways, Jews have made the Holocaust an object of familiar concern, a catastrophe of their family and religious community, their people and nation.

To some extent, "Never Again" has motivated Jews to look beyond their own community. Until recently, Jewish NGOs have allocated far fewer resources toward monitoring and advocating than defining and punishing. Jews have contributed to the naming and prohibition of genocide and the establishment of institutions to hold perpetrators to account. Jews have built Holocaust and genocide museums and academic programs for remembering past atrocities and calling attention to genocides in progress. Yet, Jews have applied the command to work toward the relief of specific victims of genocide only sporadically. The lack of sustained efforts has had many causes: scarcity of resources, the belief that comparing the Holocaust to any other event is impossible and undesirable, and paralysis borne of the conflict between Jews' passion for justice and their skepticism about the human rights system's capacity to mete it out. No doubt the most important reason for the episodic nature of Jews' approach, however, has been the most mundane: most Diaspora Jews shared a lack of interest in foreign affairs with the governments and people among whom they lived. They had achieved assimilation.

With the exception of Darfur, their responses to specific genocides have been similar to those of other groups—reactive rather than proactive. Israel, too, has acted in this arena more like a nation among nations than a light unto the nations. When its national interests clashed with an idealistic commitment to antigenocide, national interests prevailed. Perhaps the energy Jews have displayed to stop the killing in Sudan will mark a new effort to establish a permanent Jewish antigenocide organization.

4

American Jews and Violations in Zion: A Case Study

THE DIASPORA AND ISRAELI DOMESTIC AFFAIRS

We have seen that, at the international level, the three-wedding dance has sometimes witnessed a convergence between Jewish enthusiasm for human rights abroad, civil rights at home, and Israeli national projects and Zionist ideals. At other times, these political commitments have not merged but existed in tension, sometimes even in opposition. The result has been profound political ambivalence. Nowhere does such ambivalence emerge more clearly than when Israel is accused of committing, or actually commits, human rights violations. How have Diaspora Jews reacted when such tensions arise?

For decades, American Jews have engaged in formal, public contacts with Israeli officials through their NGOs. These quasi-diplomatic summits usually feature the Diaspora in a supporting role, helping forward the state's aims by offering monetary, political, and moral support. In fact, many Israeli leaders have expressed the opinion that Diaspora Jews should not attempt to intervene in state affairs.[1] But in the late 1970s, one American Jewish NGO played a leading role in attempting to alter the Israeli political landscape. According to memoranda and letters that have recently been made available to scholars by the AJC archives in New York, in 1977 the AJC's Foreign Affairs Department initiated an informal, private meeting with members of a nascent Israeli NGO to intervene in the Jewish state's human rights practices toward Palestinians.

This chapter describes the external contexts, and the internal conflicts, that motivated the AJC to help establish the Association for Civil Rights in Israel (ACRI). It evaluates the significance of the AJC staff's funding and technical support for ACRI's development. It speculates on how the AJC's action affected the Israeli human rights movement as a whole. Finally, it analyzes what this episode says about American Jewry's attitudes toward Israeli human rights practices. This compelling episode in the history of human rights monitoring highlights the dilemmas faced by ethnic minority NGOs, and raises questions about their willingness and ability to monitor the human rights practices of their own identity groups. It explores the complex transnational relations existing between a diaspora and its homeland.

During the 1970s, the emergent anti-Israel alliance acted in concert to condemn Israel's alleged violations of Palestinian human rights in the occupied territories at a wide variety of venues, ranging from UNESCO; the International Labor Organization; the World Health Organization; the Economic and Social Council, the Commission on Human Rights and its Subcommission; the treaty bodies monitoring the Covenants; the Special Committee to Investigate Israeli Practices Affecting the Human Rights of the Palestinian People and Other Arabs of the Occupied Territories; the World Conference on Human Rights (Teheran, 1968); the Human Settlements Preparatory Conference (Teheran, 1975); and the International Women's Year Conference (Mexico City, 1975).[2] The conference and committee resolutions criticizing Israel served as warm-ups for the General Assembly's "Zionism=Racism" resolution of November 10, 1975, which in turn led to further investigations of purported Israeli rights violations by Amnesty International, the London *Sunday Times*, and many others in the late 1970s.

Anti-Zionism was often linked to, or used as a screen for, anti-Semitism. Canadian minister of justice Irwin Cotler has described the "New Anti-Semitism" that emerged during this period as "the discrimination against, or denial of, the right of the Jewish people to live as an equal member of the family of nations." Whereas nineteenth-century anti-Semitism discriminated against Jews either as individuals or as a minority within a given state, the new anti-Semitism was an attempt by an intergovernmental body, "the very body created to combat racial and religious discrimination—the United Nations"—to discriminate "against Jews as a People."[3] As John and Henry F. Carey define it, UN anti-Semitism consisted of "hostility in UN bodies to Judaism, the Jewish People, and Jews as such."[4] While "anti-Zionism" might have several meanings and its adherents are fond of denying that it was equated with anti-Semitism, the tendencies just described were demonstrably part of an overall determination to deny Jews fundamental legitimacy as a people with the right of self-determination. They could thus be properly described as both anti-Zionism and anti-Semitism.

Not every criticism of Israeli practices with regard to Palestinians and the Arab world could be construed as anti-Zionist or anti-Semitic. First, as in every democratic country, some of Israel's fiercest critics in the 1970s were its profoundest patriots, who neither denied the legitimacy of the Jews as a people nor the state as the culmination of the people's national self-determination project. These included highly placed individuals, political parties, peace organizations, and human rights NGOs. Second, charges that Israel violated Palestinians' human rights could not easily be dismissed if they attended to specific situations or individual cases, were accompanied by verifiable evidence and testimony regarding the alleged violations, and were investigated by a properly constituted body that permitted the accused to respond to the charges—for example the Human Rights Committee overseeing the Civil and Political Rights Covenant.

Reports by credible human rights NGOs documented Israel's violation of the Fourth Geneva Convention prohibition on the settlement of its civilian population in the occupied territories beginning in the late 1960s. As we saw in the introduction, human rights NGOs, the Israeli Supreme Court, and UN treaty and charter bodies have documented numerous violations by the Israel Defense Forces or the Israeli government. More recently, Reporters without Borders, in association with Amnesty International, Human Rights Watch, B'Tselem, and the Palestinian Centre for Human Rights, provided a complete dossier of credible, reliably attested violations in the occupied territories after the second intifada began in 2000.[5] These included extrajudicial executions, ill-treatment and torture of prisoners, and excessive use of force. International law experts have documented Israel's illegal approach to land use in the occupied territories, and the uneven application of international law by the Israeli Supreme Court.[6]

Even in cases where abuses in the 1970s could be confirmed, however, the proper international response would have been to call for alterations of particular policies or practices, not the wholesale delegitimation of the state. Unfortunately, in the 1970s, neither international nor Israeli national bodies were capable of handling such allegations responsibly, and the various nonjuridical UN human rights forums were usurped and put to use for a great deal of political grandstanding.

How did one Jewish NGO, the AJC, respond to the anti-Zionist and anti-Semitic campaign at the UN in the 1970s? The AJC took a double course: in public it stood in solidarity with Israel, at some cost to its perceived credibility as a proponent of international human rights and domestic civil rights. But in private, and then later only to a select public, it devoted considerable effort to the formation of a credible, liberal, human rights organization in Israel. In particular, the AJC provided funds and technical assistance to build the capacity of the Association for Civil Rights in Israel while working to diminish the capacity of the Israel League for Human Rights. The AJC's involvement marked a new moment in the transnational relations between Israelis and Diaspora Jews. For the first time, Diaspora Jews intervened in Israeli domestic affairs to bring about political change in the human rights arena. In this intervention, the AJC had to balance its triple commitments: to internationalism, nationalism, and a secure Diaspora. The AJC staff's motivations for undertaking their course of action were ambivalent and complex.

THE ZIONISM=RACISM DECADE

In May 1968, the UN was already adopting the first of many resolutions condemning Israel's administration of the territories occupied during the Six-Day War, and by December the General Assembly had, in a rare move, created a special committee to launch an investigation, composed of three members from states that did not recognize Israel's right to exist. By 1975, the world body would be entertaining a proposal by the Arab League for Israel's expulsion from the UN, the implication being that Israel was comparable to apartheid South Africa, which had recently been forced to withdraw.[7]

Contrary to the claim of the anti-Israel alliance that it emerged in protest against Israel's handling of its occupation in the West and Gaza, the alliance had in fact formed well before the Six-Day War. By 1964, the alliance had already begun trying to undermine Israel's legitimacy by introducing language equating Zionism with racism into the draft Convention on the Elimination of Racial Discrimination (CERD) (see chapter 1 for details). Despite this, the AJC had been deeply supportive of CERD. In fact, as the basis for its work on the treaty, the UN's Subcommission on the Prevention of Discrimination and the Protection of Minorities adopted a draft by former AJC president and US ambassador Morris Abram. The ensuing struggle over the treaty language of CERD—between the USSR and its allies and the United States and its allies—was a Cold War hot spot, surfacing East/West tensions that could then be mobilized in a variety of other arenas.[8]

In this state of siege, all international Jewish NGOs felt compelled to stand in solidarity with the Jewish state. For some NGOs, like the AJC, solidarity was a relatively new position. The AJC was founded in 1906 by members of the German-Jewish community in the United States "to prevent infringement of the civil and religious rights of Jews, and to alleviate the consequences of persecution."[9] As an NGO concerned with protecting Diaspora Jews' civil rights, it did not see Zionism as part of its mission. In its early years it classified itself as a "non-Zionist organization," although it nonetheless worked to help reorganize the Jewish Agency in pre-state Palestine.[10] The AJC's immediate reaction to the Holocaust was not to embrace Zionism. Instead, the AJC members believed that in order to safeguard the rights of Jews, Jews must work to safeguard the rights of all human beings. If as an ethnic, religious, and linguistic minority Jews wanted justice, they must work for justice for all minorities, a stance that informed their domestic civil rights work in the United States as well as their international human rights approach.

Even during the difficult 1970s, when Israel was under attack, the AJC maintained its historic character as a human rights organization. During the Zionism=Racism decade, the director of the AJC's Foreign Affairs Department was Sidney Liskofsky, a graduate of City College of New York and New York University School of Law, and chair of the Subcommittee on Basic Human Rights of the American Bar Association. In 1970 Liskofsky convened the Ad Hoc Committee on Human Rights and Genocide Treaties to advocate for US ratification of international human rights treaties.[11] He was a leading force in the effort to compel the USSR to recognize Soviet Jews' right to emigrate. He sat on the board of the International League for the Rights of Man. He served as the founding director of the AJC's Jacob Blaustein Institute for the Advancement of Human Rights, established in 1972. And he drafted substantial portions of what ultimately became the UN Declaration on the Elimination of All Forms of Religious Intolerance, adopted in 1981.

Under Liskofsky, the AJC's human rights program developed unusual characteristics for an NGO based in the United States. Henry J. Steiner, director of the Harvard Law School Human Rights Program, has argued that most US-based NGOs and international NGOs with American headquarters take the view "that neither NGOs nor the American polity have much to learn from an international human rights movement designed for less fortunate peoples."[12] They "follow a nationalist path to enforcement of international human rights" by lobbying the US government to put diplomatic pressure on offending nations rather than by using international organs.[13]

Yet the AJC has differed from other US NGOs in advocating for US ratification of international treaties and citation of international law in domestic cases. Unlike many NGOs based in the developed world, it has advocated for group as well as individual rights. And like many NGOs in the developing world, it has articulated in many instances a structuralist analysis of rights violations by identifying patterns of discrimination involving race, ethnicity, and gender. While Liskofsky formed the Ad Hoc Committee on Human Rights and Genocide Treaties that worked with senators Proxmire, Pell, and Javits in the Senate Foreign Relations Committee, he also extended his work into the international machinery of the UN itself. In all these ways the AJC behaved more like NGOs in the developing world than those in the developed world. These differences are likely due to its character as a representative of a diaspora with a strong ethnic minority group affiliation. Its foundation as a diaspora/ethnic minority NGO helps to account for why, although many more mainstream US NGOs did not at first have a strong presence at the global level, the AJC sought from the beginning to be successful there.

Liskofsky believed that human rights were universal, and that Jews should pursue their particular aims through universal channels. For example, when he sought to address the USSR's refusal to permit Soviet Jews to emigrate, he worked with Karel Vasak at the Institute for Human Rights in Strasbourg to put together an international conference of lawyers, government representatives, and activists on the "right of everyone to leave his own country," rooted in Article 13(2) of the UDHR. He declared in a memorandum to the AJC president Bert Gold that, to be successful, Jews must place their particular concerns about the plight of Soviet Jews in a broader field:

> Since the conference would be concerned with the right in general and not alone with the Soviet Jewish situation, it has, presumably, a better chance, than a project concerned solely with Jews, of eliciting the interest and participation of "experts" (loosely defined) from a variety of interest groups (religious, legal, human rights, civic) from as many geographic regions as possible.[14]

Liskofsky thought that by couching Jewish wrongs in the language of human rights, Jews would be able to secure broader alliances than if they sought redress through isolated special claims. Human rights activism was, for him, a means of coalition building.

Held in Uppsala, Sweden, the colloquium on the "right to leave" produced a declaration and proceedings that are still considered to be the standards in the field.[15] The Uppsala declaration played a significant role in persuading Congress to pass the Jackson-Vanik Amendment linking Soviet acquisition of Most Favored Nation trade status to Jewish emigration. Jackson-Vanik in turn helped convince the Soviet Union to engage in the Helsinki process, resulting in its pledge in the Helsinki Final Act (1975) to permit both freedom of movement within its territory and family reunification.[16] This episode seemed an affirmation of Liskofsky's belief that particular ends were best achieved through universal means.

While Liskofsky operated through a universalist perspective, he was genuinely proud of Israel's victories in the Six-Day War and repulsed by the UN's subsequent unfair treatment of Israel. He looked on the Zionism=Racism resolution as a threat, not only to the legitimacy of the state, but to the legitimacy of the UN itself. Under Liskofsky's direction, the AJC's press statements publicly challenged UN condemnations of Israel as anti-Semitic and anti-Zionist. The AJC endorsed Senator Daniel Patrick Moynihan's call for reform of the United Nations, and the NGO spawned its own UN watchdog organization, UN Watch, led by its former president, Morris Abram.[17] The AJC called constant attention to the practice in the Commission on Human Rights of holding Israel to a higher standard than it did states with far worse human rights records. The NGO engaged, both behind the scenes and in the press, in a multipronged attack on the first Arab League resolution to expel Israel in 1975 that included writing petitions and open letters, using high-level private contacts and friendly US and UN officials, influencing and tracking UN member votes abroad (especially in Latin America), contributing draft language to House and Senate resolutions, supporting efforts by international law experts to respond to abuse charges, and lobbying officials like the president of the United Nations Association.[18]

The increasing attacks on Israel eventually did begin to have an impact on the NGO's sense of its mission. In reaction to the Arab League's attempt to get Israel expelled from the UN, the AJC began to include Zionist declarations in its mission statements. Since 1975, the NGO has sought not only to advance the cause of human rights, but also "to interpret the position of Israel to the American public."[19] For the first time, the organization reflected its members' growing commitment to a *vicarious nationalism* on behalf of Israel.

The question would be how well the new nationalist and the older internationalist platforms would sit side by side.[20] Although the AJC staffers had begun to express public solidarity with Israel, they maintained their skeptical attitude toward nationalist ideology, even when the state in question was Israel and the ideology was Zionism. To be sure, they publicly expressed their great pride in Israel's victory in the Six-Day War, and their outrage at the unfair treatment Israel received at the UN. Yet in private, in their letters and memos, the AJC staffers worried that Israel's new status as an occupier could undermine its willingness and ability to abide by human rights norms, and they wrung their hands over whether there was any substance to charges of abuse.

Such charges accumulated with increasing rapidity and force in the late 1970s, and while many of the charges remained speculative and were driven by politics and hatred, even these nonetheless began to take on a veneer of credibility for some observers in the international community once the Likud government came to power in May 1977. Menachem Begin's rise from Irgun terrorist to excoriated Herut politician to leader of a newly respectable conservative political party in Israel has been chronicled by historians Ilan Peleg and Sasson Sofer.[21] These scholars emphasize that Begin's government brought a radical, ultranationalist program into the mainstream, a program that included an expansionist "territorial imperative" to annex the West Bank and Gaza through settlement, a belief in the eternal anti-Semitism of the Arab world, and what Peleg calls a "fundamental negation of the outside world."[22] One could understand why, faced with an international community intent on negating Israel's existence, the Israeli electorate would in turn choose a leader who espoused a negation of the world. Yet such a stance could not comfort those Jews, both in Israel and in the Diaspora, who still identified with the goal of international human rights.

From 1977 to 1978 the anti-Israel alliance at the UN was aided by prominent NGOs, including the International Commission of Jurists, the Swiss League of Human Rights, the National Lawyers' Guild, the International Association of Catholic Jurists, and even the International League for the Rights of Man, with which the AJC was closely aligned.[23] These human rights NGOs cited Israel for torture, arbitrary detentions and ill-treatment of prisoners, and for the construction of illegal West Bank settlements.[24] While Amnesty International's monitoring of Israel was consistent with its human rights program, many Israelis and Diaspora Jews objected that it did not at this stage also engage in parallel monitoring of Palestinian Liberation Organization (PLO) activities.

In these cases, the damage was still more or less limited to Israel's standing in the diplomatic and NGO communities, but several issues took on higher prominence. American civil rights groups began refusing to work with the AJC due to *its* refusal to criticize Israel for engaging in commercial and military trade with apartheid South Africa. The World Conference on Religion and Peace, for example, warned that the AJC's silence on Israeli-South African trade risked bearing out the charge that Zionism was an endorsement of racism. A Liskofsky memorandum, "Backgrounder on South Africa," suggests that after the 1973 war, the African countries broke relations with Israel, which left it "isolated and unable to get resources," causing an increase in trade with South Africa.[25] Then it began trading light arms in return for coal, steel, power plants, and the right of South African Jews to emigrate to Israel. Liskofsky remarked:

> This offer was one that the Israelis could hardly refuse. However, it has caused disastrous international repercussions including: The UN Zionism-Racism equation, Third World rejection of Israel, further split between American Jews and Blacks, loss of support for Israel in the mass media, and hostility towards Jews by American Church organizations opposed to Apartheid, Arab propaganda success amongst radicals and third-worlders.[26]

Liskofsky was painfully aware that questions regarding Israel's commitment to international human rights were causing some potential allies among US groups (some African-American and church NGOs) to question American Jews' commitment to civil rights at home. An AJC staff meeting on March 15, 1975 on "AJC Policies Re. South African Issues" lays out the difficulties for Jewish NGOs:

> Apartheid is clearly an evil system, which Jews abhor. At the same time, they are concerned about the implications of various proposals for change for the Jewish community in South Africa and for relations between Israel and South Africa. The resulting inaction is a source of friction in the area of intergroup relations and is often used to support the charge that AJC's human rights concerns are ethnocentric.[27]

The staff decided to pass out policy statements condemning apartheid and have members of the NAACP Legal Defense and Education Fund and the Legal Action Center address an AJC luncheon on the theory that "so long as we are not yet ready to act, we should at least expose ourselves to more learning and insight."[28] They also decided to sponsor a speaking tour by a South African Jew actively involved in the anti-apartheid struggle. With regard to this issue, the NGO seemed nearly paralyzed by ambivalence.

Then on June 19, 1977, the London *Sunday Times* printed a story claiming that Israeli torture of Palestinians was "widespread and systematic" and was "sanctioned as deliberate policy" in the occupied territories. The story was followed by Noam Chomsky's August 30, 1977, open letter to the International League for the Rights of Man, alleging fifteen separate charges of Israeli human rights violations.[29] The next year Amnesty International weighed in, issuing the first of several reports criticizing Israel for unlawful detentions, ill-treatment and torture of prisoners, and unfair military tribunals.[30] These high-profile condemnations threatened to leave the public with the impression that there was more to Zionism=Racism than a decade of Cold War geopolitics and Arab propaganda.

The crowning challenge was the second campaign to eject Israel from the UN in 1979–1980.[31] In September 1979, the ninety-two–member Non-Aligned Movement, meeting in Havana, Cuba, resolved to achieve Israel's exclusion from the international community. Following the nonaligned bloc's lead, the UN General Assembly set a deadline of November 15 of the following year for Israeli withdrawal from the West Bank, Gaza, and Jerusalem, or else it would bring the expulsion resolution to a vote.

AMBIVALENT INTERVENTION

The AJC staff responded to these attacks in contradictory ways. Publicly, they offered vociferous defenses of Israel. In 1979, Liskofsky arranged for the publication of a volume of essays that included polemics by Senator Moynihan and International League president, Jerome Shestack, applauding Israel's rights record and excoriating the UN.[32] Privately, however, the AJC staff was engaging in a remarkable series of internal discussions over what Liskofsky called "the

Jewish ambivalence re: the Israel-human rights question."[33] In a letter marked "confidential" and dated October 18, 1977, Abraham Karlikow, the AJC's European director in Paris, had put what he called the "fundamental underlying issue" before the AJC staff with the greatest starkness and clarity. "How valid are the charges leveled by Israel's enemies?" he asked. He continued:

> Distasteful as these may be, one cannot ignore them simply because they come from enemies or those, like the *Sunday Times*, who may be convinced by Israel's opponents. . . . If there are such abuses (even after taking into consideration all the special difficulties Israel faces and after making allowance for them) then I think that we help, not hurt, Israel by calling attention to them, and seeking to get government action for change. Which of course makes it all the more important that we should have an informed, human rights–impartial body inside Israel to which one could go for knowledge and evaluation. I readily can see that this stance is not easy for the AJC to take, will not be popular, and [will be] open to misunderstanding in both Israel and the American Jewish communities. It would be the kind of stance, though, I should hope AJC would undertake, consonant with its history and ideals, and, I am convinced, in Israel's own best interest.[34]

This was an extraordinary statement, coming from a "Cold Warrior" who had cut his teeth on anti-Communism and had criticized the New Left for its anti-Zionist and anti-Semitic statements.[35] For Karlikow, the Jewish ambivalence generated by Israel's military occupation required some kind of response. Yet how could these Diaspora Jews help bring into existence "an informed, human rights–impartial body inside Israel"?

For these activists, even asking how valid the charges were implied a particular course of action. Human rights NGOs like the AJC assumed that the most powerful force NGOs could mobilize on behalf of human rights was public shame.[36] In fact, some NGOs had begun refusing to work with the AJC, charging that, where Israel was concerned, the AJC had abandoned public shame in order to protect parochial Jewish interests. From the perspective of an NGO like the World Conference on Religion and Peace, to act consistently as a human rights organization, the AJC needed to do more to let the sunshine in on Israel's human rights activities. It needed to urge Israel publicly to ratify human rights treaties, to monitor the state's faithfulness to its treaty obligations, to release press statements condemning particular, well-attested violations, to pressure government officials with letter-writing campaigns, to lobby US State Department officials to use economic aid as an incentive or punishment, and so on.

The AJC staffers nonetheless believed that if they used the standard shaming tactics in this case, Israel's enemies in the Arab world would only co-opt the criticism for their advantage. That in turn would enable the Israeli government to shrug off the AJC's concerns, both as the product of a self-hating Diaspora nosing itself improperly into sovereign state business, and as the product of enemy hostility. Such tactics might also cause the AJC to lose support among its own membership, since many American Jews after 1967 saw Israel as the symbol of Jewish rebirth and redemption, to be supported almost no matter what it did. Despite these constraints, AJC staffers did not give up on public shame, even in this case. But they did come to think that shame would be much more effective if it originated—or at least could be made to *seem* to originate—from Israeli citizens themselves.

The result of these debates among the AJC staff was a momentous, confidential meeting, held in Jerusalem on October 30, 1977. M. Bernard Resnikoff, the director of the AJC's Israel office, issued an invitation for a "one-time consultation, over coffee and cake, in the Conference Room of the Moriah Hotel" to a "small number of non-governmental Israelis with demonstrated competence in and concern for human rights and civil liberties."[37]

In preparation for the meeting, Resnikoff met with Israeli Supreme Court Justice Haim Cohn for consultation on various legal matters relating to the charges.[38] One can only imagine the substance of their conversation. Were Palestinian affidavits accepted in the Israeli High Court of Justice? How lawful was the government's justification for denying international inquiries? Were General Security Service (GSS) interrogators actually torturing Palestinian detainees? Was the Israeli Defense Force's (IDF) practice of demolishing the homes of suspected terrorists in violation of international law? Was its detention of Palestinian suspects for long periods without charge, counsel, or trial permissible?

The select group of invitees included three members of the Hebrew University law faculty, two staff members of the Ministry of Justice, and officers of what Resnikoff called the "alive but non-kicking" ACRI.[39] Founded in 1972, ACRI's first president was Professor H. Klinghoffer, a former MP for the Liberal party and the controller of the Hebrew University. Ruth Gavison, then a law professor at Hebrew University with a visiting appointment at Yale, was active on behalf of ACRI beginning in 1978, helping with fund-raising in the United States and advisory matters. The chair of the executive committee was Joseph Dueck, a Jerusalem attorney, and the committee included Claude Klein, dean of the Faculty of Law of Hebrew University.[40] By 1978 ACRI had about one hundred dues-paying members but was run on an entirely voluntary basis, and was nearly ready to self-destruct due to its members' sheer exhaustion. According to a fund-raising letter, it had "no office, no staff, no administration. Its activities are carried out by volunteers helped by a part-time secretary whose salary is financed out of a grant from the American Jewish committee."[41]

In short order, the participants in the Moriah meeting reached a historic agreement: in Resnikoff's words, there should be a "proper beefed-up civil-rights organization in this country."[42]

Actually, this was not the first time the AJC had tried to help Israelis develop a human rights organization. Starting in the early 1970s, the NGO had discretely helped the nascent Israel League for Human Rights, led since August 1970 by Israel Shahak, to become affiliated with the International League for the Rights of Man. But by 1975 the AJC had become disaffected with Shahak. A Holocaust survivor and chemistry professor at Hebrew University, Shahak wrote articles and gave speeches at US universities in the mid-1970s in which he claimed that Israel was like apartheid South Africa, and that the occupation was a cruel and repressive regime. He compared the Israeli government to the Nazi regime.[43] He went on to become associated with Noam Chomsky and the Third World radicalism popular among American university students, and was investigated by the Israeli government for treason. When on January 12, 1976, the Israel League's members nonetheless voted to follow Shahak's recommendation and affiliate with the Communist movement, the AJC and the International League both removed their support.[44] For the AJC, Shahak's affiliation with the Communists was the last straw, for reasons that we now need to explore.

It was as much in reaction against Shahak as to the continuing international outcry that the AJC decided to intervene in Israeli human rights politics in a bolder way.[45] Abraham Karlikow wrote to Yoram Dinstein, who had become disillusioned by what he perceived to be the imbalanced approach to Palestinian human rights issues taken by Amnesty International's London headquarters. Karlikow encouraged Dinstein to establish an alternative organization to both Amnesty International and the Israel League, saying, "we on the outside need a credible instrument in which we have confidence and to which we can turn in order effectively to counter those exaggerations or inaccuracies as may be found in the charges of [Israel League attorney Felicia] Langer or Shahak."[46]

As an American secular-liberal NGO, the AJC's tactics were, in part, driven by Cold War anti-Communist ideology. The AJC sought to oppose the Communist-leaning League by incubating ACRI as a new, liberal, human rights organization. Liskofsky wrote to Jerome Shestack of the International League that "our interest in encouraging . . . the Israel Civil Rights Association stems in large part from unhappiness with the role of Shahak, Leah Tsemel, Felicia Langer, and other extremist Israeli critics" from the Israel League of Human Rights. He quoted Midrash Isaiah: "Thy ravagers and destroyers shall issue forth from thee."[47] A centrist liberal American organization like the AJC could neither align itself with an organization that employed the leftist shock tactics of Shahak, nor with what seemed to them to be increasingly anti-Zionist human rights advocacy at Amnesty International. Cold War anti-Communism dictated a break with the Israel League; vicarious nationalism dictated a break with knee-jerk international human rights organizations.

Thus, for the AJC staff, ACRI came to be seen as the solution to the dilemmas presented by both indigenous Israeli and international human rights developments. Resnikoff seemed sanguine about the prospects of creating a liberal-centrist human rights organization in Israel. He wrote, "This could easily be done by strengthening the Association. All this would take is manpower and budget."[48] When Liskofsky nonetheless dragged his feet in providing aid, Resnikoff urged him again the following year to help ACRI become "a proper, non-political organization for the protection of the civil rights of all citizens of the country, in accordance with *US models*" (emphasis added).[49] We will come back to these words.

By January 1979, Liskofsky was still deliberating about whether to act. He wrote to Jerome Shestack with a memorandum that he wished to send to a "small AJC group with an invitation to meet" to discuss supporting ACRI (Liskofsky [1979b]).[50] The invitees included Morris Abram, Rita Hauser, Philip Hoffman, and Bert Gold. After laying out Jews' concern with the Arab propaganda and the UN's bias against Israel, the memorandum states: "At the same time, many [Jews] have retained long-standing Jewish identification with human rights causes, domestic and international." It goes on to explain why the AJC wishes to support an Israeli organization that would be "both friendlier to Israel, and more objective" than the Israel League for Human Rights, and why the criticisms by Amnesty International "have incurred the displeasure of the Israeli authorities as well as of American Jewish organizations." The memorandum wonders whether an International League for Human Rights mission—supported by ACRI from inside Israel—would be a strong alternative to both Amnesty International and Israel League criticisms. (Ultimately, this mission was not carried out, because it seemed to the League just to throw fire on the situation.) But the depth of Liskofsky's ambivalence becomes clear in four questions he lays out for the group to discuss:

1. Is the Israel Civil Rights Association capable of functioning as an informed and honest critic of its country's human rights practices and would the Israeli authorities permit it to do so? Is it capable of combining this role with that of counteracting politically motivated, anti-Israel propaganda, whether emanating from the UN or from nongovernmental sources?

2. Assuming the Israeli authorities agreed to admit an International League inquiry mission, would they give it free access to prisons and other sensitive facilities it requires? Suppose the Mission found, and felt obliged to report, genuine violations—lesser ones, say—could the media be relied on to report or comment on it with proper perspective? Would the Mission—and the International League—risk attack by some for pro-Israel bias and by others for anti-Israel bias?
3. Are there other ways to defend Israel against politically motivated attacks based on human rights criteria, while not seeming to absolve her from accountability for her improper practices?
4. Is the Arab propaganda threat to Israeli security so overriding and our confidence in the essential morality of the Israeli people and government so strong, that we should give priority to the antipropaganda objective while adopting a neutral and passive stance with regard to the human rights issue?[51]

This list of questions is fascinating for two reasons. First, Liskofsky's struggle to articulate the delicate balancing act required of the AJC among its commitments to solidarity with Israel, international human rights, and the rule of law, is palpable. Second, Liskofsky explicitly asks the group to consider whether to adopt a "neutral and passive stance" on the human rights question: apparently the group decided not to do so. For them, supporting an Israeli human rights NGO was a way to help strengthen Israel in the long run, and avoid seeming hypocritical in its dedication to both universalism and particularism.

In March 1979, after six months of deliberation, Liskofsky acted. He informed Bert Gold that he intended to honor ACRI's request to use the AJC as a conduit for receipt of charitable funds to help build the capacity of the organization.[52] Up to now, the AJC had been able to use behind-the-scenes maneuvers to help ACRI along. This new commitment would require a measure of publicity. Liskofsky arranged for a fund-raising appeal to go out from ACRI's Jerusalem letterhead; the signatories included, among others, Ruth Bader Ginsburg, then a law professor at Columbia, Alan Dershowitz at Harvard, and Norman Dorsen at New York University. According to the fund-raising appeal, contributors could make out checks to the "American Jewish Committee—Human Rights in Israel."[53] These would then be sent to Resnikoff with instructions to "contribute equivalent amounts in Israeli currency" to ACRI.[54] The public to which this appeal was addressed was quite limited compared to the public addressed by the AJC press statements or the book of essays Liskofsky had arranged to defend Israel: only those on the mailing list received the appeal. Although the archives are silent about the names on the list, one can assume it was composed primarily of the AJC members, or perhaps an even more select group than that. Thus although there was some risk of exposure, at this point, the campaign could only be considered public in a limited sense.

Having committed himself, Liskofsky did all he could to support the fledgling Israeli NGO. In April 1979 he urged Jerome Shestack of the International League to persuade his board to accept ACRI as an affiliate, which it did on Israel Independence Day, May 14, 1979. The next month, Liskofsky persuaded his own board to approve $2,400 in seed money for ACRI.[55] From that point forward, he sent a monthly stream of correspondence keeping ACRI current about UN attacks on Israeli human rights practices and relevant international conferences.[56]

IMPACT

The funds and technical assistance the AJC provided helped ACRI at a critical moment to build its organizational capacity.[57] With the AJC's help, ACRI hired a staff, doubled its membership in two years, sponsored a celebration of the UDHR, and issued its first statements and reports.[58] On the other hand, the amount of funding was probably not significant enough to ensure its ultimate success: the most significant source of ongoing support would ultimately be provided by the New Israel Fund beginning in 1982.

By the time of the first intifada in 1987, ACRI was the most well-established human rights NGO in Israel. The high profile of its members and its reputation for accurate reporting cleared the way for a new generation of Israeli human rights NGOs, led by B'Tselem, that formed in reaction to the intifada. To be sure, numerous individuals like Uri Avneri, Mattityahu Peled, Amos Oz, and Yeshayahu Leibowitz; peace organizations like Peace Now; and political parties like Mapam had also been agitating for the Israeli government to uphold its human rights obligations since the Six-Day War.[59] But for the human rights movement as a distinct strand within the Israeli political scene, a movement based mainly in NGOs advocating human rights as their primary mission, ACRI served as a model. Because ACRI received an important push from the AJC a decade before the intifada, the Israeli human rights movement as a whole owed a good deal to the AJC's well-timed intervention.

The aftershocks of Zionism=Racism clearly triggered the development of complex new relations between at least some Diaspora Jews and Israelis. In working toward an Israel that would be proof against international calumny, the AJC staffers strove to help Israel look more like their own country of citizenship—more like a first world democracy operating under the rule of law. (Recall Resnikoff's insistence that ACRI be based on "US models.") Here, in a reversal of the received paradigm, the *Diaspora* was to be the ideal to which *Zion* should aspire. For these Jews, Homeland/Diaspora relations were shifting from a traditional model to a transnational one, from a center/periphery model to a model of co-equal, interdependent centers exchanging a constant flow of contract and influence.[60] They believed that Jews outside the state had the right to intervene in Israeli affairs, because Israel's actions could have harmful repercussions for *them*, because unlawful IDF or government actions could undermine Israel's nascent democracy, and because the pursuit of universal justice, then being realized through the framework of international human rights, was at the core of Jewish traditions and historical experience. Their intervention may provide a yardstick by which to compare the approach of other diaspora or ethnic minority NGOs to the human rights practices of their own identity groups.

Liskofsky knew that, even if the AJC helped establish a strong, credible Israeli human rights NGO, his own NGO would continue to face a terrible dilemma. He wrote:

> [O]ur interest is defensive and apologetic, as perhaps it should be, given the nature and scope of the Arab propaganda apparatus. The problem is that, along with this motivation, we also accept the need for genuine human rights activity with what this implies. This inclination to "dance at two weddings" is bound to lead to problems. . . .[61]

Liskofsky thought that both "weddings"—the Jewish people's national liberation and the development of international human rights—were thrilling achievements, worthy of celebration. He might have added a third "wedding," American pluralism, as well. Yet at times he must have diminished the wine in his cup when he realized that he could only celebrate one of these weddings at the expense of the other.

It is difficult to tell whether these political elites were acting in step with the American Jewish community as a whole. The National Jewish Population Survey (NJPS), a representative survey of the Jewish population in the United States sponsored by the United Jewish Communities and the Jewish federation system, was given in 1971, 1990, and 2000; that is, it was not given in 1980, the year that would have been closest to the relevant dates of these events. Had it been given then, it is not clear how useful its questions about American Jewish attitudes toward Israel would have been in helping to determine if American Jews (or even AJC's own members) would have supported the AJC staff's actions. The NJPS asks whether American Jews feel they have an "emotional attachment" to Israel, or a "shared destiny" with Israel. Typically, the responses to these questions are 75 percent or higher. But the survey does not ask about American Jews' attitudes toward specific Israeli policies or practices, for example human rights practices in the occupied territories. Thus, from a social science perspective, there is no sure way of knowing what the American Jewish public thought in 1979 about the Begin government's settlement expansion policy.[62]

The confidential nature of the AJC staff's deliberations may suggest, however, that they believed that, while they were operating within the terms of their organization's mission, they may have been operating beyond the bounds of some of their own members' sense of what was appropriate. That is, after 1967, and especially in the wake of Zionism=Racism, some of their members' sense of the mission may have been changing, emphasizing defense of Israel over defense of human rights. If so, this would have placed the staff in an excruciating position, caught between their organization's historical mission and its evolving membership.

In such a fraught context, the AJC staff's own ambivalence was both inevitable and irresolvable. In fact this state of endless self-conflict, rooted in these Jews' tripartite identity as internationalists, vicarious nationalists, and pluralists at home, was the ground condition for an enormous amount of activism. These American Jews had a measure of courage, the courage to act in the face of their internal struggles, if sometimes only in private, and the courage to permit each of their commitments to exercise a check upon the others. In their own way, they sought out answers to the ancient questions of Rabbi Hillel: "If I am not for myself, who will be for me? And if I am only for myself, what am I? And if not now, when?"[63]

5

Israeli, Jewish, Human

When we turn from human rights activism in the international arena to its manifestations in a specific state, we immediately notice a shift in the "weddings" at which human rights workers have had to dance. Israeli Jewish activists have still attempted to balance the tensions they experience among Zionism, internationalism, and pluralism, but now each of these relationships has had to be configured in a different way.

Nationalism for Israeli activists has not meant the vicarious Zionism of the international Jewish human rights activists, most of whom have been situated in the United States or other Western democracies. Israeli human rights activists have been impelled to engage with their state's ideology and practices in a much more direct and concrete manner. This encounter has resulted in a painful amalgam of various attitudes toward the state: Zionist, post-Zionist, non-Zionist, and/or anti-Zionist.

While many Israeli activists have identified international treaties as the source of universal rights norms, they have also been impeded in their work by the international community's ongoing attempts to delegitimize the Jewish state. These attempts have given ammunition to Israeli critics of domestic human rights NGOs. The NGO Monitor, founded jointly by the Jerusalem Center for Public Affairs and the Wechsner Family Foundation, keeps track of funding by grantors like the New Israel Fund (NIF) of what it calls "radical NGOs," including those that, in its estimation, use "the rhetoric of demonization to propagate an extremist anti-Israel agenda."[1] Amnon Lord, a newspaper columnist and former leftist, claimed in *Yediot Aharonot* in 1999 that activists calling for Israel's withdrawal from Lebanon were "defeatist voices" who were "enemies . . . within Israel's domestic political system."[2] Jessica Montell, executive director of the human rights NGO, B'Tselem, tells the story of speaking with a group of generals at a training course for officers. One of the officers commented, "You're harming Israel in its propaganda war." She responded, "The propaganda war is not the real war; it is metaphorical," but he replied, "The latter affects the former. If the United States won't sell Israel Apache helicopters because of human rights violations, the propaganda war is harming the real war."[3] In other words, human rights activists were traitors, aiding and abetting the enemy. During the 2006 Lebanon war, Uri Orbach, an opinion writer on *Yediot Aharonot*'s website, *ynetnews.com*, suggested that intellectuals in favor of human rights were "supported by the European Union, directors and critics who preach against Israel and are fans of Palestinian rights."[4] The implication was that Israeli critics of their government were foreign anti-Zionists. In this way, international anti-Zionism has damaged Israeli rights work by discrediting the source of rights norms.

Perhaps a more broadly held criticism of domestic human rights activists is that they are not Israeli enough, their opinions inauthentic expressions of Israeli beliefs. When the first rights NGOs began to emerge in Israel in the 1980s, most of the activists were what Israelis call "Anglo-Saxim"—Jewish immigrants from English-speaking countries. In the cultural context in which Middle Eastern Jews are the majority, the human rights commitments of Anglo-Saxim appeared to many native Israelis to be foreign imports, naïve, overly optimistic, and incapable of being transplanted to the harsh Israeli soil. For example, the NIF was established in 1979 by a wealthy couple from San Francisco, and its seed grants were themselves made possible through American Jewish philanthropy.[5] The Israel Women's Network, which NIF began to fund in 1985 as the first women's rights advocacy and litigation NGO in Israel, was formed by the AJC, and its director, Alice Shalvi, was from the United States. By contrast, the founders of B'Tselem were generally sabras. B'Tselem's funds have largely come from the Ford Foundation, a primary funder of human rights organizations around the world, as well as Protestant development agencies channeling European government funds, like EZE (Germany), and Dan ChurchAid (Denmark).[6] These circumstances have led some Israelis to accuse human rights workers of working on behalf of foreigners to influence internal Israeli affairs.

Such accusations are based more on politics than evidence. There is little difference here between Israeli activists and their counterparts in other states in the developing world, many of whom could not persist without first world donors and support.[7] There is no logical reason why such an organization should be incapable of contributing to Israeli civil society, provided that it is able to establish the reliability of its reports. Some of the Israeli NGOs have indisputably achieved this.[8] The employees of these NGOs are Israelis, steeped in the Israeli context and reacting to it. To claim that because human rights activists draw on norms promulgated outside the state, their claims are un-Israeli, is to misunderstand entirely the nature of human rights; such rights are, by definition, universal norms, not national ones, the express aims of which are to limit a state's sovereign power over its inhabitants. Such rights certainly are imposed on the state by a supranational order. But they are imposed on it by its own consent—through its adoption of the UN Charter, the UDHR, and international treaties—and Israel is no exception. Moreover, as rights theorist Jack Donnelly has explained, as the central actor in contemporary politics, the state may be the "principal violator," but it can also be the "principal protector" of human rights.[9] Hence it is perhaps the most important object of human rights activism.

Perhaps a more substantive difficulty for Israeli NGOs is that, unlike international Jewish human rights NGOs, they have not been free to focus exclusively on the global source of rights norms emanating from the United Nations and other international and regional organizations. As Israeli NGOs, they have had to confront a variety of legal traditions, each of which has approached human rights using its own principles: international law has existed in an uneasy relation with Israeli law and, in some cases, with Jewish law (halakhah). Each of these legal systems has carved out its own formal jurisdiction in Israel, yet each has also occasionally poached on the domain of the other. The tensions arising among these various legal sources have engendered activists with profoundly complicated political identities, and have created the conditions for the development of a wide variety of specializations and tactics.

Just as Israeli activists' commitments to Jewish nationalism and internationalism have differed from those of the Jewish international activists, so pluralism also has had a different history and meaning. For Jewish human rights activists in the United States, pluralism has been deeply associated with their historic action during the American civil rights movement on behalf of African Americans, and on behalf of women, gays and lesbians, and people with disabilities. In Israel, the idea of equality and justice for all citizens has had to be applied to different religious and ethnic minorities, including Jews from Arab countries, Ethiopian Jews, Russian Jews, Palestinian Israelis, Christians, Druze, and Bedouin.

Before we can analyze how effective Israeli human rights activists have been at dancing at their three weddings, however, we must deal with three preliminary questions. The first, the historical question, asks how Israeli human rights activism originated. The second, the sociological question, tries to understand how Israel's identity as a "Jewish and democratic state" has constrained and benefited human rights NGOs. The third, the political question, asks how the public's perception of existential threat has affected its reception of the human rights message.

WHY ARE THERE ISRAELI HUMAN RIGHTS ACTIVISTS?

State-based human rights activism does not develop spontaneously in every country, not even in every Western-style democracy. To some extent, domestic human rights activism must travel a more difficult road than international activism. State-based NGOs have to establish themselves as a loyal opposition within the state while appealing for their legitimating authority to a group of institutions and treaties designed to be *beyond* the state, existing in the field of global governance. Each domestic human rights organization has to be established arduously, under discrete historical conditions particular to that state.[10] Nothing about this process is predetermined; everything about it is contingent.

When reconstructing the history of Israeli human rights activism, what jumps out immediately is that very little distinct human rights activity emerged in Israel until the late 1980s, that is, nearly a century after the first modern attempts at Jewish settlement in Palestine, and nearly half a century after the founding of the state. During the state's first twenty years, until 1967, an Israeli human rights movement did not coalesce, nor did it emerge for another twenty years after Israel occupied the West Bank and Gaza and annexed East Jerusalem and the Golan Heights. One might be tempted to ask the question of Israeli activists, why did it take you so long? But this is not the right question. Given the constant threats to Jews in the Yishuv (the prestate Jewish enclave in Palestine), and later to Israeli Jews, a better question is, how did Israeli human rights activism ever emerge?

One must admit, on inspection of Israel's history, that the conditions were rarely auspicious for the emergence of a domestic human rights activism. Zionist thinkers from Herzl forward were not notably universalist. Michael Stanislawski points out in *Zionism and the Fin de Siecle* that Herzl, Max Nordau, and other founders of Zionism were both nationalist and "cosmopolitan," inasmuch as they envisioned a Jewish state that would be established on a European model as a liberal democracy, guaranteeing equal rights for all. Yet Herzl's cosmopolitanism was firmly relegated to second priority; first priority was a state by, for, and of the Jewish people. For Herzl, the state was the natural entity for a people, and Jews' two thousand–year existence as an extraterritorial people was an aberration. In the Jewish state, Jews would return to normality. The state would serve as the guarantor of what the UN Charter later called the Jewish people's "right of self-determination" and would, through its own laws, justice system, government, and military, guarantee and secure Jews' rights. Hence, Jews in a Jewish state did not need to depend on international or cosmopolitan guarantees of human rights, which were themselves weakly institutionalized and implemented. For Herzl, "universal brotherhood is not even a beautiful dream."[11] For Nordau, cosmopolitan ideas were merely the mathematical axioms of the French Revolution "without reference to sentiment and emotion," where anti-Semitism continued to reign.[12] Of the three values of the French revolutionaries, equality was least to be trusted.

Leo Pinsker probably expressed the early Zionists' lack of interest in cosmopolitanism best in the epigraph to his influential tract, "Auto-Emancipation." He introduces the same passage by Hillel that serves as the conclusion of the previous chapter in this book ("If I am not for myself. . . ."). Yet he entirely omits the second question: "If I am only for myself, what am I?"[13] The omission represents an implicit argument that, in the wake of the Russian pogroms of 1881 that had inspired his tract, Zionism could not afford to spend too much energy worrying about individuals or groups other than Jews.

To be sure, from the 1920s on through 1967, there were always a few Zionist organizations concerned with reconciling with the Palestinian Arabs, mostly associated in the early years with Martin Buber and his circle of German-J ewish intellectuals, including Brit Shalom (Covenant of Peace), Kedma Mizraha (Forward to the East), Ha-shomer Ha-Tzair (The Youth Guard), and Ihud (Union).[14] All of these groups advocated a single, binational state comprised of Jews and Palestinian Arabs, with equal rights under the law for all. For these groups, the binational solution was not only the most practical means of securing peace, but the most democratic means of expressing the Zionist mission to the world. Yet these groups never gained more than a small handful of followers, comparable, on the other end of the Zionist political spectrum, to the following earned by right-wing terrorist groups like the Irgun and the Stern Gang.[15] As Amos Oz pointed out in a satirical portrait in *A Tale of Love and Darkness*, even David Ben-Gurion, the state's first prime minister, "published an essay in which he claimed that equality between human beings was impossible, although they could achieve a measure of fraternity."[16] That is, while Israel's founding leader always sought to placate Arabs, when pressed he prioritized national solidarity among Jews.

Between 1948 and 1967, Palestinian and Arab Israeli rights were not major subjects of public discourse, either in Israel or abroad. The major Arab areas, including East Jerusalem and the West Bank, were ruled by Jordan, and hence were outside the realm of Israeli responsibility. Quietly, the Israeli government sought to consolidate its gains during the 1948 war by preventing its Arab citizens—and certainly Palestinian refugees—from returning to villages from which they had fled in 1948. Israeli planners directed that moshavim and kibbutzim be built on the sites of many of those villages, and, as the novelist A. B. Yehoshua observed in his controversial short story, "Facing the Forests," the Jewish National Fund planted forests over others.[17] The government gave formerly Arab areas Jewish names, often inspired by biblical events, mostly without the non-Arab part of the international community raising an eyebrow. While the nascent Palestinian national movement considered the war of 1948 to be Al Nakba (the Catastrophe), the cause of the displacement of seven hundred thousand Palestinian refugees, Israel could generally rely on the recognition and support of the Jews' right to the land given by the international community, including the United Nations and the United States.[18] During these years most Israelis did not consider themselves—nor did much of the international community beyond the Arab world—to be violating Palestinian rights.

Because the state depended for its legitimacy on its recognition by the United Nations, and because the Holocaust heightened Jews' awareness of human rights violations, Israeli governments were eager to sign and ratify many of the early international human rights treaties. (For a complete list of treaties and the dates of Israel's signature and ratification, see appendix B.) Israeli ambassadors to the United Nations participated in drafting a number of these treaties, which they saw in both moral and pragmatic terms—morally, as means of expressing solidarity with the remaining Jews in the Diaspora whose rights the treaties protected, pragmatically, as a means of contributing to and becoming part of the international community.

Yet despite these formal gestures, no sustained Israeli human rights activism emerged in the decades between 1948 and 1967 to monitor the state's compliance with the treaties it had adopted. The primary reason was that the new Israeli Jewish public perceived itself to be under perpetual threat of extinction. The war of 1948–1949 did not end with peace, but with a series of cease-fire agreements. Israel was established without formal borders and the state of emergency proclaimed in 1948 has never been lifted. The series of crises—the Suez war, the formation of the Palestinian Liberation Organization, whose 1964 charter called for Israel's destruction, the moves of the anti-Israel alliance at the UN starting in the early 1960s to identify Israel as a racist state—made the Jewish population feel constantly threatened, in both the military and public relations arenas. This conviction of ever-present danger was heightened by pan-Arabist proclamations that Israelis must be driven into the sea, as well as by the recent memory of the Nazi murder of European Jewry. Under these conditions, Israeli Jews voiced little public dissent to government policies during Israel's formative years. The important project was to build and protect the Jewish state.

Political leaders, military officials, educators, and intellectuals all played a role in promoting and sustaining the mood of consensus. The Labor Party, in its various forms, had widespread support, co-opting or minimizing other voices and becoming Israel's sole ruling party until Likud's landmark victory in 1977.[19] Compulsory military service bred a sense of national solidarity, a common history, and a common respect for and trust in military leaders, who enjoyed great influence on public policy in urban and agricultural planning and infrastructure in addition to more traditional military pursuits. With some exceptions, the national education system and the popular culture both largely reinforced a tendency toward conformity with the national Zionist project.[20] In the arena of domestic pluralism, although conflicts existed from the beginning of the state (e.g., the religious/secular divide, ethnic tensions, the integration of Arab citizens, women's inequality), these had, for the most part, to be relegated to the background in times of perceived or actual national emergency—which meant always.[21] Threat-driven nationalism prevented a sustained public focus on internal diversity.

This history lends support to the theory of political scientists Gad Barzilai and Asher Arian, among others, that when public perception of threat is high, public dissent is low.[22] Only when public threat perception is low is it possible for significant levels of dissent to emerge. Given Israelis' perception of relatively permanent existential threat, one would not expect any kind of dissenting sector to emerge—much less a human rights network adopting international standards to question its own government's treatment of the state's enemies. Moreover, we can extrapolate from Barzilai and Arian to predict the conditions under which dissent is more likely to emerge. Public threat perception will generally be high at a conflict's outset, when the opponent is well organized and manifestly intent on causing sustained national and personal harm. Threat perception will generally be low when the government engages in wars of choice, when Israel's military force is directed against enemy civilians, when national existence does not seem to be at stake, and when war-fatigue sets in during a protracted conflict. We would therefore predict a greater likelihood that human rights activism would emerge at times when the nation seems to be more secure.

Yet this model implies that human rights organizations face a daunting and constitutive problem. For it is precisely during times when public threat perception is high that government officials are most likely to think they can engage in an increased rate of human rights abuses with impunity. The US response to 9/11 is a case in point: in the wake of the World Trade Center attacks, the US government weakened prisoner of war (POW) protections for enemy combatants; held detainees for extended periods without charge, trial, or counsel; tortured prisoners; rendered prisoners to countries that practice torture in interrogations; and engaged in widespread warrantless wiretapping. The government calculated that the American public was so fearful of terrorists that it would look the other way—which is, for the most part, what happened. At fearful moments citizens in wartime democracies are more inclined toward nationalism and less inclined to stand up for universal human rights. This assertion may seem obvious enough, but it poses a potentially debilitating challenge to domestic human rights activists; they can expect their message to be least effective when it is most needed. How they respond to this obstacle largely determines how successful they can be.

This model helps us account for why little human rights activism emerged in the period 1948–1967. Whether one measures the Israeli public's threat perception during these years using content analyses of journalistic opinion, polls, the rise of a civil society with allied activist movements (e.g., the peace movement), or attitudes toward the potential border with Palestine, one is struck by how high Israel's threat perception was during these years, and how low the incidence of dissent. Threat-driven nationalism prevented not only the formation of a sector advocating a pluralist agenda, but the formation of a sector advocating a cosmopolitan agenda. Two of the three wedding dances receded into the background, while the third, Zionism, dominated public discourse.

Even for two decades after the Six-Day War of 1967, when Israel was transformed from a fledgling state to a regional power and an occupying force, there was little public debate about how international human rights norms might apply in the territories, despite the state's formal commitments to international human rights treaties. Israel's initial disastrous loss during the first two weeks of the Yom Kippur War (1973) dampened the triumphalism Israelis felt after the complete victory of 1967 and once again increased the public's sense that Israel was fighting for its existence. Two domestic organizations did begin to monitor Israel's adherence to human rights norms in the 1970s, the liberal-centrist Association for Civil Rights in Israel (ACRI, est. 1972) and the communist Israel League for Human Rights (est. 1970). Yet, as we saw in chapter 4, these groups were in conflict with each other, and in the beginning neither was particularly well organized or funded.[23]

While Israelis were not very preoccupied during these years with the human rights questions raised by occupation, they were also not troubled by the internal question of how to ensure justice for the state's minorities. From the 1950s through the 1970s, the primary focus of the early state's attention was not on human rights but on how to absorb successive waves of Jewish immigrants (primarily from Iraq, Yemen, Syria, and Morocco) that would more than double the Jewish population. This was followed by the need to absorb Ethiopian and Soviet Jews in the 1980s and 1990s, many of whom could not be considered "Jewish" under any or all definitions.[24]

The model of absorption that Israeli sociologists, politicians, and urban planners adopted was assimilationist rather than pluralist: they encouraged the immigrants to aspire to imitate the Ashkenazic elites who had founded the country, as a means of creating an "Israeli" identity that would transcend the various Diaspora cultures brought into the country. They believed assimilationism was a crucial tool for securing national unity in the face of the state's struggle for existence. Once again, compulsory military service played a major part in the effort to socialize disparate Jewish ethnic groups as Israelis. Israeli immigration, education, and military policies discouraged the expression of diverse minority cultures. Moreover, the absorption planners often sent ethnic minority immigrants to live in development towns in Israel's "periphery" rather than to major cities in its "center." This policy was intended to help Israel build "facts on the ground"—settlements that would help underscore its claim to the territories captured in 1948 and 1967. The result, however, from the point of view of many of the immigrants, was their disenfranchisement and disillusionment with the Zionist dream of ingathering. Eventually, these immigrants, many of whom were religious Mizrahim, would form the core of a new political body that would challenge the predominantly secular Ashkenazim of the Labor Party for their preeminent status and make Israel's ethnic and religious diversity visible.

The latter part of the 1970s saw the government's increasing expropriation of land from Israeli Arabs and the growth of settlements in the West Bank on private Palestinian land requisitioned by the military. Nonetheless, the cracks in the façade of national consensus did not appear during this period.[25] A persistent, visible human rights presence in Israel only began to develop as a result of the war on Lebanon in 1982, which many Israelis perceived as an unnecessary war of choice. In the massacre of Palestinians at Sabra and Shatilla these Israelis found a cause célèbre. In its wake, new granting organizations, like the NIF, began to seed peace and human rights organizations. The New Historians, led by Benny Morris, Avi Shlaim, Tom Segev, and Ilan Pappé, began to articulate a post-Zionist critique of Israel's founding.[26] Popular singers like Chava Alberstein and Shalom Chanoch recorded protest songs.[27] The earliest of the protest organizations against the Lebanon war was the Four Mothers, founded by women whose sons had died in the conflict and who demanded that Israel pull its soldiers out of Lebanon. As the first major dissenting activists in Israel's history, the Four Mothers shocked the population but also won a large following. They used their maternal sacrifice as a powerful rhetorical tool for the cause of withdrawal. Because most Israelis consider motherhood sacrosanct, the Four Mothers' demands resonated with the public.[28]

While Lebanon shattered the national consensus, the first Palestinian intifada of 1987–1989 was the watershed event in the emergence of Israeli human rights activism.[29] Many Israelis perceived the government's struggle against the intifada as a conflict of choice, largely against unorganized Palestinian civilians, in which the threat to national existence was relatively low. Palestinians succeeded in calling attention to their everyday sufferings at the hands of Israeli occupiers, in reaction to which Israeli Jews formed as many as fifteen different human rights monitoring and advocacy groups. The 21st Year against the Occupation, an organization established to protest twenty years of Israeli presence in the West Bank and Gaza, spoke out against the consequences of Israeli human rights abuses for Israel's international moral and legal standing.[30] The most lasting and well organized of the primarily Jewish human rights groups organized in reaction to the intifada included:

- B'Tselem—Israeli Information Center for Human Rights in the Occupied Territories
- HaMoked—Center for the Defence of the Individual
- Physicians for Human Rights—Israel (PHR)
- Public Committee against Torture in Israel (PCATI)
- Rabbis for Human Rights (RHR)

In the late 1980s and early 1990s, these NGOs were sometimes joined by groups of reservists, former generals, peace organizations, and intellectuals. During the second intifada a "second wave" of organizations emerged. In 2001, a group of women formed Machsom Watch to monitor abuse of Palestinians at Israeli checkpoints, and a group of Jews and Arabs formed Ta'ayush (Arabic for "life in common") as an antiracist organization.[31] In 2004 and 2005 two groups of demobilized army personnel were established, Combatants for Peace and Breaking the Silence, the former combining Israeli soldiers and Palestinian combatants to work for peace. In 2005, Yesh Din ("there is judgment") formed to mobilize volunteers to work for human rights in the territories, and Gisha ("access" or "approach") was established to work with the military on behalf of Palestinians' freedom of movement. Not all of the second wave NGOs are exclusively dedicated to human rights, but they all contribute to the network.

With public threat perception relatively low in the late 1980s and during the Oslo period (1993–1999), these NGOs were able to seize the moment to influence public opinion on issues in the territories, including the military's use of torture, administrative detention, house demolitions, settlements, excessive force, unequal distribution of resources, and legal discrimination. Within the Green Line, activists focused on legal discrimination with regard to ethnic minority Jews and Israeli Arabs, rectification of unequal division of resources, gender and sexual equality, and educational equality.

The establishment of these organizations signaled a cultural as well as political shift in Israel. Dr. Ruchama Marton, who founded PHR—Israel in March 1988, has described the cultural shift and physical conditions many human rights activists experienced in those years:

> When I was young, no one could spell "human rights." We could talk about justice, freedom—we meant human rights. It's the same with feminism—the word "women's rights" was not there. You need good wording to do something. I had heard awful things going on in Gaza—the TV was spreading lies all the time—so I called friends in Gaza and they said, "Why don't you come?" So I took eleven people to Gaza—a psychologist and ten doctors. The next Shabbat I took another eleven people. We went to Ahli Arab hospital—and found dirty, smelly, old medical equipment, thirty to forty years behind Israel.
>
> In the beginning we didn't have a penny. The first four years we worked in a tiny one-bedroom apartment—no computer, no fax, no nothing. We were naïve and we believed that if we let people know what's really going on, people will be shocked and will react and everything will be okay. We didn't realize that the public actively doesn't want to know.[32]

Both the work conditions and the early optimism are typical of other NGOs at this period. ACRI, for example, although established in 1972, was in its early years entirely run by the board and did not even have a full-time lawyer on staff until Neta Ziv joined in 1984, as compared to the thirteen lawyers it had in 2006.[33] It would take a decade for these groups to become well established.

While the national context is crucial to understanding this history, the international context is no less so. It was not until the mid-1970s that an international human rights culture emerged that could provide the structure and support for domestic activism in individual countries. Michael Posner and Candy Whittome of the Lawyers Committee for Human Rights, an international NGO, have identified the development of domestic human rights activism as the "second phase" of the emergence of this culture, preceded by the creation and development of internationally focused NGOs.[34] One cannot understand many features of the Israeli NGOs without regarding them in a comparative framework, including their sources of funding, the strategies and tactics they adopt, and their motivations.

As an aggregate, these NGOs did not (and do not) have formal agreements to work together to achieve a common set of goals. In interviews with activists, funders, capacity-builders, and scholars, there was unanimity that there has never been a contractual structure to their alliances.

To be sure, many of the organizations have received funding from the same Israeli sources (NIF and the Abraham Fund). To some degree NIF has determined which of these groups could emerge and be sustained through its seed granting policies. According to Dorit Karlin, NIF's director of programs, strategic planning, grants, and partnerships, although NIF's grants have varied each year depending on what "bubbles up," the funder has typically allocated its grants as follows: 40 percent for social justice organizations (working on economic, social, and cultural rights), 40 percent for civil and political rights organizations, and 20 percent for groups working on religious pluralism issues.[35] The grants have ranged from $20,000 to $500,000.[36] By advertising new granting areas, such as its "Separation Fence Program," "Active Citizenship Education," and "Initiative to Promote the Rights of Arab Citizens of Israel," it has sought to influence the shape of the civil society.[37] The Abraham Fund has also established initiatives in order to provide a platform for those interested in a particular issue.[38]

The informality of their relationships has not prevented the groups from helping each other. Many of the NGOs have participated in trainings and forums organized by SHATIL, the NIF's capacity-building arm. Almost all of these NGOs have had lawyers on their boards or staffs who were trained in NIF's Israel-US Civil Liberties Law Program in association with American University in Washington, DC. In fact, the law fellows program has essentially created a human rights bar in Israel where none had existed, having established a community of over fifty lawyers who have built new organizations and developed human rights as a field of study and an area of litigation.[39] General-purpose civil and human rights organizations like ACRI, B'Tselem, and RHR have worked on a regular, if informal basis with more specialized groups on particular issues, like PCATI or the Israeli Coalition against House Demolitions (ICAHD).

At the same time, each group has had its own agenda and has received resources independently from unique grantors unshared by the others. B'Tselem, for example, after having been seeded by the NIF, soon began to receive the majority of its funding from sources outside Israel.[40] After its NIF seed grant ran out, RHR raised the majority of its budget from North American Jewry.[41] In some cases, human rights NGOs seeking outside funds have competed for the same dollars and euros. Initially, the NIF sought formal agreements with its American funders that it would be the only progressive Israeli organization they funded. From the NIF's perspective, this step was necessary to reduce competition among NGOs for the same sources and also to provide a coherent structure for givers who wished to fund progressive activity in Israel. The NIF's critics argued, however, that this represented the NIF's attempt to corner the market and prevent other potential funding intermediaries from becoming well established. When the NIF began to fund ACRI, its formal agreement included a provision that ACRI could not seek funds from American sources. Later the agreement was rescinded, but because the NIF began to fund (and still funds) ACRI at a uniquely high level of $500,000 per year, ACRI has generally continued to hold to the agreement, seeking outside resources from Europe rather than the United States, although it does receive funds from American foundations that are not in contact with the NIF.[42]

The funding strategies suggest what is true in programmatic areas as well: all these cooperative relationships have existed on an informal basis. The NGOs have formed ad hoc, time-limited strategic coalitions on particular issues, but have gone their own ways as necessary. According to Jessica Montell, within the context of the occupied territories B'Tselem "is a multi-issue organization and works in coalition with other organizations on particular issues. Human rights spans a broad spectrum of issues: working on domestic pluralism is quite different than advocating for Palestinian human rights. While we all take our starting point from basic principles of democracy and the rule of law, this is a basic affinity more than a formal coalition."[43]

As we saw with the various groups in the Soviet Jewry network in chapter 2, the informality of Israel's brand of domestic human rights activism can work to the NGOs' advantage, by allowing each one the flexibility, on a particular issue, to pursue its own tactics (e.g., individual casework, test case litigation, public campaigns, and so on). In the most successful cases, such independent efforts add up to more than the sum of their parts.

HUMAN RIGHTS IN A "JEWISH AND DEMOCRATIC STATE"

Israel's history of perpetual conflict is not the only factor that has helped to condition the emergence of its human rights movement; its political structure has also played a key role. The Basic Law: Human Dignity and Liberty (1992) officially classifies Israel as a "Jewish and democratic state" (Article 1), which has led to endless debates about whether the emphasis should be on preserving the dominance and prerogatives of a single ethnic/religious/national group or equal rights for all Israeli citizens. The debate itself implicitly assumes that democracy and human rights are both committed to political dignity for all, but this is not necessarily the case. As Jack Donnelly points out, "democracy allocates sovereign authority to the people. . . . Human rights, by contrast, aim to empower individuals, thus *limiting* the sovereign people and their government. . . . Only if a sovereign people wills respect for human rights, and thus constrains its own interests and actions, will democracy contribute to realizing human rights."[44]

Three different models of how the state balances (or should balance) its priorities have been proposed, each of which will be briefly detailed below.[45]

Israel as Liberal Democracy

For Aharon Barak, former president of the Israeli Supreme Court, Israel is a liberal democracy that seeks to guarantee universal citizenship rights and equality before the law. Barak points to Israel's periodic democratic elections, independent judiciary, free press, and separation of the political and military spheres.[46] Although discriminatory legislation and practices do exist, judicial review serves as a check on government abuses. For example, on March 9, 2000, the Supreme Court decided, in a precedent-setting case brought by Neta Ziv and Dan Yakir of ACRI, that Adel and Iman Ka'adan, who are Arab citizens of Israel, must be permitted to build a house in the all-Jewish town of Katzir, even though the land on which the neighborhood was built was state land that had been allocated through the Jewish Agency for Jews only.[47] The Supreme Court reasoned that, if Israel is a state for all its citizens, Arabs and Jews must have equal rights to purchase property. This example stands in for hundreds of cases in which judicial review has upheld the liberal-democratic foundations of the state. To be sure, judicial review has its sources in rabbinic practice in the *Bet Din*, or house of judgment, in the medieval autonomous community, but it also has its source in Ottoman and British law. It is an amalgam of various legal sources.

Barak does not believe that there is a necessary contradiction between the Jewish and democratic elements of the state. For him, "the state is not Jewish in the halakhic sense, but in the sense that Jews have the right of *aliyah* [immigration], and that their national culture is the culture of the state (expressed, for example, in the language and in the days of rest). Judaism's "foundational values" are the values of the state, but Barak interprets these values in a broad and abstract sense to coincide with the abstract values of democracy—"love of mankind, sanctity of life, social justice, . . . the protection of human dignity, the rule of law. . . ."[48]

Others, like Tel Aviv University philosopher Yael Tamir, disagree that Israel's democracy and its Jewishness can be made to coincide through a process of abstracting their foundational values. The ultimate source of authority for a democracy is the people, while for Judaism it is God. This is an irreconcilable difference. However, Tamir argues, while Judaism and democracy are doomed to be in a perpetual conflict, this conflict can be (and often is) ameliorated by concrete compromises between religious leaders and state officials.[49]

Still others, including the rabbis of all Israeli orthodoxy, criticize both of these positions from a "traditionalist" religious perspective that assumes that changes within the system of halakhah, or Jewish law, must be resisted as infringements of what is sacred and eternal. As Menachem Fisch, professor of history at Tel Aviv University, argues, this stance means that "there is no way in which even the most basic civil liberties can be accommodated."[50]

Israel as Ethnocracy

Some critics of the idea that Israel can be classified as a liberal democracy—including some Palestinians, some members of the international community, and some Israeli human rights activists—view Israel instead as an ethnocracy, a state devoted to preserving the dominance and prerogatives of the majority ethnic group and enshrining inequality and the tyranny of the majority in its laws and political structures.[51] The democratic features of the Israeli system are offset by its "rigid ethnic hierarchy, lack of inclusive territorial citizenship, and the power of religious institutions."[52] The favored "nation" is not restricted to a particular territory, because West Bank settlers and Jews in Diaspora are part of the nation, exerting influence on the political system from outside of Israel's boundaries and/or cease-fire lines. Israeli immigration, land, and settlement policies are all skewed toward Jewish and Zionist interests. In *Next Year in Jerusalem*, a memoir by one of the cofounders of B'Tselem, Daphna Golan-Agnon describes a "frightening similarity" between Israel's occupation and apartheid South Africa that "lies in the precise and consistent use of the legal system to normalize the abnormal state of discrimination. . . . Here, too, the state employs hundreds of attorneys and lawyers and consultants to explain how what is unjust is also legal."[53] In this model, Israel provides equal rights protections for its Jewish citizens, but administers a different set of laws and regulations to its non-Jewish citizens and the occupied people under its control.

Similarly, the radical sociologist Baruch Kimmerling prefers to describe Israel not merely as a state, but more broadly as a "control system," by which he means all of the geographic areas Israel governs: inside the Green Line, in the occupied territories, and in the annexed regions of East Jerusalem and the Golan Heights. Kimmerling asserts that each of these areas is governed using a different rights regime; and in some cases there are two different regimes within the same area.

For example, inside the Green Line, Jewish citizens have full rights, although there is a divide among rights provisions for Ashkenazic Jews (the minority, but strongly represented among Israel's elites) and other Jewish groups, especially Mizrahim and Ethiopians. Arab citizens of Israel (e.g., in Galilee, in East Jerusalem) are generally guaranteed full rights formally, with a number of exceptions. While the Law of Return (1950) guarantees Jews around the world who wish to immigrate to Israel automatic citizenship, Palestinians are denied their internationally recognized "right to return." Under the law, non-Jews immigrating to Israel must undergo a lengthy and grueling naturalization process.[54]

The Law of Return also treats different Jews differently. Its definition of "who is a Jew" has been controversial: Orthodox Members of Knesset have proposed to amend it so that non-Orthodox converts would not be considered Jews, essentially stripping Reform and Conservative rabbis in Diaspora of the power to perform conversions. These amendments were introduced after the Supreme Court accepted a series of petitions filled by ACRI and the Israel Religious Action Center (IRAC) and ordered the Ministry of Interior to register as a Jew anyone who was converted abroad in a Reform or Conservative conversion. The results are still pending.

Other distinctions within the "equality" guarantee in Israel involve political participation and economic and social rights. Under Article 7A of the Basic Law: The Knesset (1950), a political party may not participate in an election "if its objects or actions, expressly or by implication, include . . . negation of the existence of the State of Israel as the state of the Jewish people." Hence, a number of Arab political parties have been under threat of being disqualified. While Palestinian citizens are guaranteed equal economic and social rights, they are often systematically denied the ability to purchase property in "Jewish" areas, and their property is often expropriated by the state. If they sell property to the state, the state transfers its title to a private Diaspora organization, the Jewish Agency, which then leases the land only to Jews (e.g., in East Jerusalem) in perpetuity. Investments in urban planning, infrastructure, education, and medical care are enjoyed by Jewish citizens at highly disproportionate levels. While such discrimination mainly affects Arabs, Jewish ethnic minorities also experience disparities. Mizrahim and Ethiopians who immigrated to Israel were initially given no choice of where to live and have often been too poor to exercise their freedom of movement.

Israel as Ethnic Democracy

Sociologist Sammy Smooha has made an influential yet controversial case for a middle road, describing Israel as neither a liberal democracy nor an ethnocracy. He calls Israel an "ethnic democracy." Based on ten typical measures of Western democracies, Smooha performs a comparative analysis among Israel and several new Eastern European states, like Estonia and Slovakia, which give predominance to a single ethnic group. Like these states, Israel was built by a founding ethnic group for self-protection. Smooha identifies an emerging form of governance in which the state meets the minimum procedural standards of a democracy for all its citizens, is recognized as a democracy by other democracies, and guarantees basic rights equally for all. Yet in ethnic democracies, there is a dominant national or ethnic group, which commandeers the state for its own purposes and thereby assures its continuing dominance. Although this type of democracy formally guarantees all citizens the same rights in most cases, it discriminates in practice in the way it upholds these rights in favor of the dominant group. Smooha argues that, despite the tension between the ethnic and democratic components of such a state, this formation can be quite stable, and it provides for the gradual improvement of the ethnic minority's conditions.[55]

Smooha's notion of ethnic democracy presents a model of the state in which all citizens are equal, but, for the time being, some are more equal than others. This model has been criticized from both poles—for not giving sufficient weight to discriminatory laws and policies against Palestinians in Israel and the occupied territories, and for not giving sufficient weight to Israel's formal democratic guarantees and institutions—but it expresses quite well the tension that has been at the heart of the Zionist project.

The tension between whether Israel is a state for Jews (an *ethnos*) or for all its citizens (a *demos*) has shaped the development of the Israeli human rights network. On the one hand, elements of formal democracy have enabled the emergence of types of human rights activity familiar from other Western liberal democracies: legal challenges in the courts, media campaigns, and political advocacy with the Members of Knesset.

Israel's mechanism for judicial review is especially impressive. ACRI and other legal NGOs have made frequent use of a peculiar feature in Israeli's legal system called *bagatz*, which was a holdover from the British Mandate judicial system. In many cases, the Israeli Supreme Court sits as *bagatz* (a.k.a. the High Court of Justice), a court of first resort for any individual or group petitioner, including Palestinians in the occupied territories, who believes the state has violated his, her, or their human or civil rights. These cases do not need to be appealed from lower courts but are heard directly by an odd number of sitting justices (three, five, seven, . . . up to fifteen in high-profile cases). Since the 1980s, the High Court of Justice has been willing to hear petitions from individuals or groups who were not personally harmed by a state authority, opening the way for public interest lawyers associated with human rights NGOs to file petitions.[56] According to former Supreme Court justice Itzhak Zamir, the *bagatz* system ensures fairness of judicial review for Palestinians.[57] Of the approximately fourteen thousand cases the High Court hears each year, about twenty-three hundred are *bagatz* cases, approximately one thousand of which are brought by West Bank and Gaza Palestinians.[58] The judiciary actively checks governmental overreaching.

Despite these formal democratic elements, there are gaps in substantive democracy in many areas of equality and fairness. In the occupied territories Palestinians' right to self-determination has been denied through the settlement policy, which under the Drobles plan was designed to prevent a contiguous Palestinian territory from coming into existence.[59] The due process rights of detainees have been denied because of the perpetual state of emergency, which is also the rationale for detentions without charge or trial. Detainees have been systematically tortured by the General Security Service (GSS) in interrogations. Palestinians have experienced severe restrictions on their economic and social rights (e.g., curfews, work closures, checkpoints, poor access to medical care). Their homes have been demolished and olive groves destroyed as part of a systematic policy of collective punishment by the Israel Defense Forces (IDF). The Citizenship and Entry into Israel Law (Temporary Order, 2003) prohibits thousands of Palestinians living in the territories from joining their spouses in Israel. The law denies spouses from the territories who are married to Israeli citizens or permanent residents the opportunity to acquire Israeli citizenship or residency rights.[60] Meanwhile, Jewish settlers are daily protected by the IDF.

The gap between Israel's formal and substantive democratic practices has caused human rights activists to develop formal and informal mechanisms for aiding the Arab Israeli and Palestinian victims of legal, social, and economic discrimination. HaMoked has successfully used a caseworker approach to intervene with Israeli authorities refusing to provide social and economic services to Palestinians. B'Tselem and PHR have fielded large numbers of monitors in the territories to provide them with up-to-date data for their reports. From its founding in 1988, PHR doctors developed the practice of making unannounced site visits to Palestinian hospitals to measure the quality of and access to health care.[61] B'Tselem and PCATI have used public campaigns at various periods to sensitize the public to the concept of human rights in general or to particular issues. B'Tselem placed large-scale advertisements in daily newspapers (see examples on the following pages).

Grassroots initiatives have also been put to wide use. RHR and the ICAHD have led protests against house demolitions in East Jerusalem and the West Bank, many times lying down in front of bulldozers while their lawyers argued in the Supreme Court for dismissal of the demolition orders. During one of these events in April 2003, Rabbi Ascherman and two coworkers, Ori Omer and Shai Eliezer Tzvi, were arrested and charged with interfering with a police officer in the performance of his duties. The Magistrates Court in Jerusalem rejected their "passive resistance" and "defense of justice" defenses and found them guilty, which would have meant a sentence of three years in jail or a fine. At the last moment, the prosecution agreed that the court would cancel the conviction in return for community service, recognizing that the case was a test of legal principles.[62]

Along with the particular nature of Israeli democracy, the Jewish nature of the state has also conditioned a specific kind of human rights approach. The Supreme Court is bound to consider that, in its essence, the national culture is Jewish (e.g., the Jewish Sabbath is the official day of rest, the official calendar

We must protect ourselves. Israelis have the right to live in security. If we need a security fence to protect ourselves, we can build it without isolating villages, without separating children from their parents and patients from doctors, without dividing communities in half, and without enclosing people in crowded enclaves. We can build a security fence without taking land and inflaming hatred. After all, there are people on the other side too, and they too were created equal. (Courtesy of B'Tselem)

Killing civilians is not allowed. Not to prevent suicide attacks. Not in the struggle to end the occupation. Even in wars there are rules. (Courtesy of B'Tselem)

is largely comprised of Jewish holidays, national symbols like the flag and the menorah are drawn from Jewish history, kosher food is served in state institutions, etc.) Second, the courts' custom is to consider broad Talmudic principles regarding justice, peace, and war in interpreting laws. Third, there is no formal separation of religion and state in Israel. Maintaining the Ottoman millet system, each religion has its own religious courts, which are jurisdictionally empowered to employ Jewish law (halakhah*)*, Quranic law, or Christian law in determining Israelis' freedom to practice religion (or no religion) as they please, as well as to determine their freedom to marry, divorce, or remarry.

Don't put borders on love. The Citizenship Law tears apart husbands and wives, children and parents. (July 2004) (Courtesy of B'Tselem)

Fourth, many members of the public respond positively to human rights appeals grounded in the Prophets, Midrash, or other Jewish traditional sources, (although other, more secular, citizens sometimes reject these approaches, associating them with Orthodoxy).

For all these reasons, one might expect to find that appeals to Jewish law and practice would permeate both the court decisions and the petitions, briefs, media campaigns, and educational materials of the human rights network. In fact, to a large degree this is not the case. The Supreme Court, which has jurisdiction over most human rights issues (except freedom of religion) is separate from the religious courts. This separation enables the Supreme Court to minimize the impact of Jewish law within its domain.[63]

For their part, most human rights NGOs in Israel do not often invoke Jewish sources. If you hold a report by B'Tselem in your hand, you will see that its logo bears the cantillation marks used by the *chazzan* in the synagogue to chant Genesis 1:27 ("*b'tselem elohim bara oto*"—"in the image of God He created him"). This would suggest that B'Tselem sees its work as rooted in the Torah's conception of the fundamental dignity and equality of those made in the divine image. Yet, while B'Tselem has sometimes interspersed quotes from Jewish sources in its reports, for the most part it has appealed to the public in the neutral, legal, universalist language of international human rights.[64] Starting in 1998, B'Tselem tried to make its practice of hewing to such rhetoric (shared by ACRI and most other Israeli human rights NGOs) more accessible by publishing its *B'Tselem Quarterly for Human Rights in the Occupied Territories* in a large-scale magazine format in Hebrew and English.

Some activists and political theorists of social change movements, however, do not think this kind of approach is accessible enough, pointing to a need for "non-technical issue definition": activists should strive to use language the public can easily understand.[65] In the Israeli context, this means emphasizing those aspects of Jewish tradition and history amenable to a human rights orientation, particularly traditional universal concepts of human dignity, along with the history of Jewish persecution and Jewish social justice work.[66]

RHR and IRAC are the NGOs that have made the most systematic and visible attempts to ground their activism in Jewish values. These organizations can be seen as the Jewish equivalent of Latin American NGOs inspired by Catholic "liberation theology."[67] Rabbi Arik Ascherman, RHR's director, argues that it is necessary to merge the "Torah of international law" with the "Torah of Jewish tradition." "We can't be just fieldworkers or *luftmenschen* (visionaries)," he insists. "We really have to bridge those worlds." He recognizes that rabbis in the religious Zionist camp have tried to socialize Israelis to a different reading of Torah, which he characterizes as "a dangerous mixture of nationalism and particularism that they call Judaism—and most secular Jews *also* think this is the authentic Judaism." However, he wants to "introduce alongside this interpretation of Torah a different interpretation that is not less authentic, and is possibly more authentic."[68] In other words, he thinks it is important for human rights activists to take back the Torah from the religious nationalists.

To that end, in 1998, the fiftieth anniversary of Israel's independence, RHR began to work with Rabbi Yaariv Ben Aharon to develop Gemara—the type of commentary found in the Talmud—on the Israeli Declaration of Independence. By summer 2006, a draft of Tractate Independence had been produced and was being vetted for wider distribution.[69] Through programs like this and its human rights yeshiva, RHR has tried to augment its fieldwork and legal petitions with human rights education. Its Torah-based, grassroots human rights activism has focused on particular issues where for the rabbis in the NGO, the Torah seems to speak clearly—house demolitions in the occupied territories, including East Jerusalem, the destruction of Palestinian olive groves by the IDF, the expropriation of Bedouin land to grow a settlement outside of Jerusalem. If the grassroots activities are meant to stop individual abuses, the educational efforts are intended to effect a gradual change in the climate of Israeli opinion in a language most Israeli Jews understand.

RHR's Torah-based approach is certainly borne of its members' convictions, but it also has its uses as an outreach tactic, particularly for Jews outside of Israel. Many secularized Israelis, including human rights workers, resent Judaism as the preserve of right-wing Orthodox believers. However, many Jews in the United States and elsewhere, where Jewishness is less a national than a religious identity, resonate with references to the Torah. As Rabbi Ascherman remarked:

> No one in the US Jewish community wants to be seen as anti-Israel but at some level that Jewish *neshama* [soul] is still working. When you come in and start talking about apartheid, no one's going to listen. People come out of a talk that I give and they feel good. I often say, the real Zionism today is working for a better Israel—that's being pro-Israel. When people bring the universal human rights law language, it's abstract and distancing.[70]

Because RHR draws most of its funding from these audiences, it has had to calibrate its approach to their needs.

If RHR has sought to link its activism on behalf of Palestinian rights to a particular Jewish stance, IRAC, directed by Anat Hoffman, has done the same on behalf of Israeli pluralism issues. IRAC is the political advocacy arm of the Reform Movement in Israel. It was founded in 1987 to advocate for human rights and pluralism, particularly the freedoms of religion and conscience, issues with which the movement's international arm, the WUPJ, had been engaged since the 1960s.[71] IRAC's action on the "Who is a Jew?" controversy, the Law of Return, the state's privileging of the Orthodox establishment over other denominations, and the rights of new immigrants is grounded in a view of Judaism that is "open and renews itself in accordance with the spirit of the times, a Judaism that stands for both a Jewish and a democratic society, a Judaism that ensures equality of men and women, a Judaism that is Zionist and a Judaism that embraces universal, human values."[72] IRAC's mission statement neatly characterizes the tensions inherent in Jewish Israeli human rights work.

Israel's dual nature as a Jewish and democratic state has clearly influenced the direction in which the domestic human rights network has evolved. This result should not surprise us, because every human rights network in every state has to find a local language with which to make its universal appeal. Domestic activists manifest the "relative universality" of human rights—the need for the instrumental use of local traditions where those traditions express an overlapping consensus with internationally recognized human rights norms.[73]

THREAT PERCEPTION

The tension between Israel as *ethnos* or *demos* has been clearly exacerbated by the Israeli public's perception that the state has been subject to continuous existential peril. While Israel has certainly faced national security threats throughout its history, it is possible to make the case that, in some periods, Israel's existential threat has been relatively low. For example, during the Oslo period, 1993–1999, Israel had clearly become the regional superpower. It had developed a nuclear deterrent and its armed forces and intelligence services were widely conceived to be the best trained, most effective, and best armed in the region. Its enemies in the Arab world were in disarray and could not function collectively. It had peace treaties with Egypt and Jordan, and cold peace and/or friendly relations with many other Muslim and Arab countries, including Morocco, Turkey, Kuwait, and, under the table on certain issues, Saudi Arabia. Its northern border with Syria and Lebanon was relatively quiet. And its economy dwarfed that of its neighbors, in some cases by one hundred times.

Yet the public's perception of existential threat, while receding during the Oslo period, never disappeared. Ruchama Marton, founder of Physicians for Human Rights, put the issue this way (my translation):

> For Jews the most important question is, "How do we live?" For Israelis the most important question is *if* we can live. "How" is a moral question. "If" is a security question. Both are important, but not the same.[74]

When the Al-Aqsa intifada began after the failure of the Camp David summit in August 2000, the Israeli public's sense of being threatened increased exponentially, leading to broad public support for prime minister Ariel Sharon's unilateralist policies, including the destruction of the Palestinian Authority infrastructure in Ramallah, the increase in settlement activity, and the building of a seven hundred–kilometer separation barrier between Israel and the West Bank. Whether the second intifada actually constituted an existential threat has been disputed. Some Israelis believed that, although the series of suicide bombings Israelis suffered were tragic disasters for the individuals killed and their families, they did not pose a threat to the nation's very existence. But no one disputes that, with each suicide bombing, Israelis perceived that the risk to national security was grave. This public reaction is a common, predictable, and comprehensible response to terrorism. In fact, the heightening of the public's fear is, to a large extent, the central aim of those who target civilians.

Yet the continuously high level of public threat perception has conditioned what Israel's human rights organizations have been able to accomplish. Nongovernmental efforts generally cannot create a change of the tide, because such changes are dependent on prevailing security conditions. Dr. Tamar Hermann, a founding member of the B'Tselem Board of Directors and director of the Tami Steinmetz Center for Peace at Tel Aviv University, paints a vivid picture of how threat perception exacerbates the cultural divide that often separates human rights NGOs from their public:

> These organizations operate in a bubble—social, demographic, political. Their message meets the ear of the secular, middle class, urban, women, Ashkenazi—this is a distinct minority from the public at large. This group is less affected by threat. Their perception is not impaired by war. They are part of the socio-economic center, not the periphery—they're not blue collar, they live in big cities. They feel part of the global international human rights community more than the community here. This makes them the target of the other parts of the national collective—they sometimes aren't considered loyal to the nation. This limits their ability to change public opinion.[75]

Dr. Hermann does say that these considerations do not hamper the human rights work in more neutral venues, such as the Supreme Court, although the court may not always act neutrally. The court may be aware that its own reputation can be impaired among the broader public by its association with human rights. Moreover, the activists have sometimes been constrained to the extent that the judges are themselves Israeli citizens who may be ideologically hostile to the activists' aims.[76]

Human rights activists and funders dispute these critical assessments with a long list of accomplishments, and some assert that human rights workers can contribute to greater security. For example, Arik Ascherman remarked, in the midst of the Lebanon war of 2006,

> At some level we can't change policy—only the politicians can do that. We work at the micro level and they work at the macro level. But it was the human rights workers in the field who saw that all these human rights violations were building tensions that would erupt in the second intifada—because we were there. So the micro and macro levels each have a role to play and can have positive interchange.[77]

But regardless of whether high threat perception has partially or totally diminished the capacity of human rights activists to effect change, it has indisputably diminished the Israeli public's empathy for Palestinian suffering.[78]

Periods of high threat perception have also prevented human rights NGOs from doing their day-to-day fieldwork. A joint study by SHATIL, Amnesty International, the United Nations Relief and Works Agency for Palestine Refugees, and Israeli NGOs concluded that when a conflict is at its height, NGOs should not send human rights monitors into the field. Monitors should only be sent when both sides have an agreement and invite the monitors. Otherwise, as SHATIL's Rolly Rosen put it, "they get stuck in the checkpoints like everyone else."[79]

INNER DYNAMICS

Under the conditions of ethnic democracy and national insecurity, human rights activists have developed a variety of styles of public justification, issue specialization, and tactics. This stratification has resulted in an inner dynamic of both coordination and conflict among NGOs.

Some, like B'Tselem, focused on importing and applying international norms to the Israeli practices in the occupied territories. Others, like ACRI, confronted both threats to pluralism inside the Green Line and threats to human rights in the occupied territories, using the secular-liberal language of Israeli and international law.[80] Most women's rights organizations, with the exception of Bat Shalom (which worked with the Jerusalem Center for Women, a Palestinian NGO), made an early decision not to focus on issues in the occupied territories, in hopes of attracting right-wing Israeli women to work for women's issues.[81] RHR relegated both international and national-secular norms to a secondary status, developing a "Torah of human rights," based on traditional Jewish sources, to aid activists both inside and outside the Green Line. Finally, PHR has taken a more pragmatic line of using whichever law works in any given situation, and sometimes using one legal system against the other. "What is the source of value—Jewish law, international law, or Israeli law?" says PHR Israel's founder, Dr. Ruchama Marton.

> We are always using some laws against the others. You know, laws are not sacred; they are just laws. We remember that laws can be used against justice—as in Nuremberg. And sometimes you have to work against the laws.[82]

It should be noted that Dr. Marton's instrumentalism is not particularly unique, even where Jewish law is concerned. Every invocation of religious discourse in the public sphere is utilitarian, inasmuch as its purpose is to secure some resource, benefit, or change. This is as true for the religious nationalists as it is for the religious universalists—which is not in any way to impugn what may be the activists' sincerely held religious beliefs.

Some of the NGOs worked at the international level as well as the national level; others concentrated their resources at home. Even those that did work outside of Israel have not conceived of their activism as primarily directed toward the international human rights community. B'Tselem has maintained membership in the European-Mediterranean Human Rights Network through which it files a joint annual report to the European Union, and has worked with Amnesty International, Human Rights Watch, and other international NGOs. However, executive director Jessica Montell has wondered how B'Tselem benefits from formal membership in international networks. It regularly sends representatives to give reports to some of the UN bodies that monitor states' compliance with human rights treaties (the covenants, CERD, et al.), but on many more issues, Montell believes B'Tselem has been more effective working with the US administration in Washington.

ACRI, too, has cooperated with international NGOs like Amnesty International and Human Rights Watch by sharing information, particularly in a 1993 *bagatz* petition against the torture and detention of Lebanese in the al-Hyam Prison in Southern Lebanon. Like B'Tselem, it has sent representatives to give "shadow reports" (i.e., reports that fill in gaps in the country's own periodic reports to the UN's treaty bodies). Initially, it found that filing these reports required tremendous resources, and has become more selective in picking issues to focus on.[83] For its part, PHR has attended annual gatherings in The Netherlands of PHR affiliates worldwide.[84]

All these groups have considered international law to be a crucial tool in their struggle for social justice, but as domestic NGOs, they have not sought to become active contributors in the UN human rights system. Rather, their aim has been to direct the tools of international human rights and humanitarian law toward Israeli policies and practices. These NGOs adopt universalist tools, not to advance cosmopolitan democracy at the international level, but to advance Israeli democracy at home.

Tactically, the organizations developed a wide variety of tools and tended to specialize among themselves in their use, including legal petitions, advocacy, grassroots campaigns, education, and casework. PHR, for example, has engaged in advocacy to compel the IDF to ensure freedom of movement for patients and medical staff, fieldwork to measure standards of health care in hospitals and clinics in the territories, reporting of its findings, and direct provision of health care services for Palestinians. Its doctors engaged in public campaigns to expose Israel's practice of torture during interrogations and demanded the reduction of solitary confinement for detainees.[85]

On the cooperative side, B'Tselem and ACRI have had ongoing, open access to and discussions with HaMoked and PHR. According to Jessica Montell, these NGOs are "like sisters. . . . If we have a legal question, we call ACRI. If we are doing a report on a HaMoked issue, we say, why don't we do a joint report. Basically we specialize in research and publication, HaMoked in locating detainees and obtaining necessary permits, ACRI and HaMoked in legal petitions."[86] The larger organizations have also done a good deal of ad hoc work with single-issue organizations like PCATI, ICAHD, and Adalah—The Legal Center for Arab Minority Rights in Israel.[87]

Some kinds of coordination seem to have worked better than others. NGOs cannot always agree on strategy and tactics. They disagreed, for instance, on whether Israel's bombings of areas in which Hezbollah had used Lebanese civilians as human shields to protect weapons constituted a war crime. Joint advertisements rarely seem to have much impact or to be worth the energy in getting everyone to agree or the expense to produce them.[88]

Human rights NGOs have also sometimes come into conflict over the question of how closely to work with peace activists. While Peace Now advocates for particular policies and resolutions to the conflict, sometimes to the detriment of human rights positions, Israeli human rights organizations generally assert a nonpartisan stance, fearing that to take policy positions will compromise their support for neutral rights standards. In this stance, they often resemble their human rights counterparts in other countries.[89] Jessica Montell offered the following example:

> After 1992 some Israeli peace activists justified using torture in interrogations if it would prevent bus bombings, because these bombings were intended to derail the Oslo accords, but from a human rights perspective this consideration is irrelevant. Torture is prohibited in all circumstances. These peace activists would say, "we have to sacrifice human rights now in order to enable human rights in the future," but this reasoning contradicts one of the most basic human rights principles—the end doesn't justify the means. From a practical perspective, it's also deleterious to permit human rights violations because it courts international condemnation. . . . My job is not to ask if a particular policy is good for peace; my job is to make sure it respects human rights.[90]

For similar reasons, despite many Israelis' belief that the separation barrier helps peace negotiations by minimizing violent outbreaks, B'Tselem has criticized the barrier as a violation of numerous Palestinian human rights, including the rights to freedom of movement, economic security, access to health care, and national self-determination.

This stance sometimes puts B'Tselem at odds with peace activists, but also with other human rights NGOs, like the Israel Women's Network and RHR, who are less opposed to working with peace organizations on particular areas where they can agree. According to Arik Ascherman, "There are some issues in which our interest as human rights workers overlaps with peace camp interests. On other issues (final status, borders) we can't work together because we don't take a position on these issues and our rabbis come from a broad range of political perspectives."[91]

Tactical disagreements among network NGOs can sometimes, ironically, work to the advantage of their common goals. The more maverick groups are sometimes willing and able to take action on a given issue when the more mainstream groups will not take the risk of alienating the public, their donors, their staff, the government, or the court.[92] The action of the maverick group then creates a new "fact on the ground" that forces the hands of politicians. Then the splitting of the network into "radical" and "mainstream" factions enables the "mainstream" group's talk of a compromise solution to appear reasonable and face-saving to policymakers. The result can be partial movement in the direction of a given human right, where no movement might have occurred in the absence of the tactical split among the NGOs.[93] Because of this dynamic, the marginalization of the radical group does not indicate that it has failed to contribute to the total process of change-making—only that its contribution to change has been to stake out a pole in the continuum of possible action.

While stratification has its uses, it can also produce a certain amount of confusion about how member groups in the network should prioritize their goals. With so many sources of authority, issues, and tactics to choose from, where should they begin? This is less of a challenge for single-issue organizations and organizations with an articulated preference for a particular source of authority than it is for broad-spectrum NGOs like ACRI and B'Tselem. For ACRI, the only NGO in Israel dealing with the whole array of human rights and pluralism issues, prioritizing has been, according to Dan Yakir, ACRI's chief legal counsel, a "delicate balancing act" that can benefit or harm ACRI's effectiveness. "We hope those who oppose our work in the territories may be interested in other areas—like freedom of speech. We take into account the severity and scope of the violation, the means we have to deal with it, whether others specialize in it."[94] B'Tselem, although restricted to working in the territories, also has had to prioritize. A measure of its maturation as an NGO in recent years is that it has engaged in an in-house strategic planning process so that it can make more proactive choices.

EVALUATING THE ISRAELI HUMAN RIGHTS NETWORK

To what degree has the fluctuation in public threat perception affected the network's effectiveness? How successful has the network been at puncturing the public's indifference, denial, and/or apathy during periods of high threat perception? What victories has it won, and what major issues has it lost?

Overcoming Threat Perception

Over the years, activists in the Israeli network have developed numerous strategies to puncture the public's denial, apathy, lack of empathy, and indifference in the face of high threat perception. These range from carefully calibrating which issues are likely to resonate with the public, putting a human face on the issue, changing the venue of activities to arenas where they can be successful, and working for gradual long-term changes in the climate of public opinion.

Most of the time, particularly in a state as prone to crises as Israel, human rights organizations are in reactive mode, responding to the pressing needs of the moment. But, sometimes as a result of multiyear strategic planning processes, the more mature NGOs, funders, and capacity builders have been able to mount sophisticated efforts to determine the issues that should have priority on their agenda. In 2002, at the height of the second intifada, Norman Rosenberg, at that time the CEO of the NIF, determined that the NIF and its grantees were being marginalized by the media. He brought in Mark Melman, a campaign strategist for the Democratic Party in the United States. Melman engaged a polling company to administer a survey, the first of its kind, of the Israeli public's attitudes toward human rights. The survey concluded that in a time of crisis

> you can't move the public from 0 to 50, but you can move them from 50 to 60. You have to find out which issues Israelis already agree with a little and work on those issues, rather than wasting your resources and energy on other issues.[95]

For example, the survey found that Israeli Jews believed the West Bank checkpoints made them more secure (despite the determination by the UN Human Rights Committee that checkpoints are an unlawful form of collective punishment).[96] However, Israeli Jews wanted the IDF to alleviate Palestinian suffering at the checkpoints as much as possible. The public had been sensitized to this issue by several high-profile reports of pregnant Palestinian women who, because of the lines at the checkpoints, had been unable to reach the hospital in time and had given birth in their cars. On the basis of the survey's conclusion, the NIF encouraged its grantees to work toward increasing access to health care at the checkpoints.

A number of NGOs objected to this strategy, however. The activists in these organizations argued that ameliorating suffering at the checkpoints was too partial a solution; it ignored the fact that, from a human rights perspective, the checkpoints themselves are illegal. For these NGOs, the amelioration solution (i.e., moving policymakers from fifty to sixty based on public sensitivity to the issue) was too mainstream, and muddied the purity of the universal norm. Hence, these NGOs chose ideological purity at the cost of being publicly marginalized. Others, however, whom the purists considered too mainstream, chose to prioritize the amelioration issue, and were able to convince the IDF to increase access to health care for pregnant women, at least for a time.

Pictures and stories about individual Palestinian women giving birth in their cars are examples of another network tactic for overcoming public indifference: personalizing an issue by giving it a human face. Reports by most of the NGOs give space to individual testimonies about the impact of a given Israeli policy on their lives.[97] The hope is that, while the public can ignore abstract or collective data, a first-person narrative automatically inspires sympathetic identification in the reader. On the other hand, while personal testimony might persuade a member of the public, it is unlikely to have much impact in court or with a Knesset member, so it has limited usefulness.

Over the years, the NGOs have become more adept at picking the appropriate venue in which to raise an issue. At times of increased threat, it can be less effective to spend a great deal of money on a public campaign than to work quietly with Knesset members or to bring legal petitions. When threat perception is relatively low, however, advertisements and op-eds may be more successful. In recent years B'Tselem has mounted sophisticated media appeals making greater use of the web banners on ynet.com, the website of the daily newspaper, *Yediot Ahronot*. It has included video footage, photographs, PowerPoint presentations, and video testimonies in its reports and media releases.[98] It produced a music video, "Eyes Wide Open," which was offered on its website and received thirty-six thousand hits in the first year as well as radio play on Israel's VH1 television channel.[99]

While many of the tactics for overcoming denial and indifference are short-term, designed to address current problems, educational efforts take the long view. B'Tselem has offered a series of "study tours" of the West Bank for other NGOs, Israeli and international high school students and teachers, youth movement counselors, kibbutz members, and the general Israeli public.[100] Similarly, the Coalition of Women for Peace has offered "reality tours" in which it takes right-wing Israeli Russian women for tours of Nazareth, where they stay in Palestinian hotels, talk with Palestinians who speak Russian, and attend workshops and theatrical performances. The coalition also produces media campaigns to introduce the concept of "human security"—asking Israeli Jews whether the occupation has made them feel more secure.[101]

Whether any of these tactics correlates to a direct change in public opinion is unclear. Some political scientists have tried to establish influence by looking at changes in journalistic uses of human rights discourse.[102] Whether news articles are representative of public opinion, however, is questionable. If one looks only at mass circulation newspapers, one will find a very different story than if one looks at local newspapers. Most of the theoretical literature on public opinion has given up on direct correlations because it is difficult to assess an organization's direct influence on a specific issue. However, organizations may gradually help to create a different climate of opinion among policymakers that may influence future policies—at which point it would be impossible to establish the influence of the organizations' efforts empirically.

In the end, even after the deployment of all these tactics, there is probably a limit to what the Israeli human rights network can accomplish. Like all human rights activists under strained circumstances, the Israelis face certain structural, endemic challenges, which they can probably only overcome partially and for short periods of time. One can compare the network's effectiveness during the first intifada, when the enemy was neither well organized nor particularly threatening, to its difficulties during the Oslo period, and especially during the second intifada, when the enemy was well organized and intent on injuring Israeli civilians through a coordinated campaign of large-scale attacks and suicide bombs. In the Oslo years (1993–1999), the lowering of the threat perception, which theoretically ought to have increased the NGOs' effectiveness, brought with it its own set of problems. Oslo led many members of the public to think that human rights problems either had disappeared or were on the verge of doing so, while at the same time the continuing suicide bombings "foster a climate in Israel which demands the safety of Israeli citizens at any price."[103]

During the second intifada in 2000–2005, the threat perception was considerably higher than in the first intifada in 1987–1989—for good reason—and as expected the Israeli human rights network experienced stagnant growth and met increased public resistance. Here the public increasingly viewed many of the organizations in the network as part of the radical left in a polarized struggle against the religious-nationalist right, the latter of which it trusted more on security. The public was, for the most part, not persuaded by the NGOs' arguments against targeted assassinations, freedom of movement restrictions, and the growth of settlements. In its annual reports from 2000 to 2005, B'Tselem indicates that the public response to its work during the second intifada grew increasingly apathetic, if not hostile. In 2000, after two years, B'Tselem had to close its *Human Rights Quarterly* newsletter for lack of public interest. By 2002, the public "has become progressively more hostile and apathetic to any discussion of Palestinian rights" and the media pays "virtually no attention to the Palestinian reality in the mass circulation newspapers."[104] The public expresses "uncritical support for all military actions" and exhibits "the desire not to know," and the "grave human rights violations that once captured headlines have now become part of the routine to which Israelis are accustomed."[105] B'Tselem's experience was echoed by all of the other activists I interviewed.

Moreover, the second intifada by occupied Palestinians was accompanied by an increase in frustration and resentment by Arab citizens of Israel, who comprise about 18 percent of the population. This resentment was brought to a head in 2000 when Israeli police killed thirteen Israeli Arabs who were holding a protest at the start of the intifada on Galilee's main north-south highway. The subsequent government inquiry determined that the police were acting in self-defense, and no one was held responsible for the killings. These events signaled and caused a broader radicalization of Arab Israelis, what some scholars have referred to as the "Palestinization" of these citizens.[106] The predictable reaction among Israeli Jews was a hardening toward the country's largest ethnic minority, an attitude that Arabs were unentitled to the full set of human rights.[107]

Even during the second intifada, however, the human rights network did have a number of successes in temporarily stopping punitive house demolitions, decreasing the military's destruction of Palestinian olive trees, greatly reducing the IDF's use of Palestinians as human shields, and improving the conditions of detention.[108] The network was able to chalk up these successes in part because it had built up reserves of human, political, and economic capital during the Oslo period that it could now put to use. Just as important, however, was that the Israeli public itself had, to a degree, absorbed the language of human rights, and did not react to the threat to its national security by granting the government a blank check. The human rights discourse had so far penetrated public consciousness that even right-wing settlers began to claim their rights were being violated by the disengagement from Gaza.

Another potential obstacle to the network's effectiveness has been that by speaking out on behalf of Palestinians, human rights NGOs risked being perceived as the secular, left-wing antithesis of the religious right. The danger was that, by seeming to mark out the opposite pole in the political spectrum, the human rights NGOs might only succeed in polarizing the electorate. As a precaution against this, human rights NGOs like ACRI have underscored the nonpartisan nature of their efforts by defending members of the right from human rights violations. For example, when Noam Federman, a central activist in the extreme-right Kach movement, was held in administrative detention, ACRI took his case and defended his right to charge, trial, and counsel. Whether such activities have been perceived by most Israelis as authentically nonpartisan or as occasional media stunts is a harder question to answer.

Failures and Successes

If we use an outcome-based measure of success, we can see that the network's activities have produced mixed results. There have certainly been many disappointments, setbacks, and outright failures. The High Court of Justice has refused to recognize the validity of human rights NGO arguments in several cases. For example, the court has issued confused and evasive judgments regarding the construction of civilian settlements in the territories. According to Dan Yakir, chief legal counsel of ACRI,

> The Court ignores totally international law in this respect. In other areas the implementation and significance of [international] law has risen dramatically. But with this the Court evades declaring a clear position and thus continues support of the settlements. In the decision on the separation barrier, the Court said they have to balance the rights of settlers and Palestinians—as if they were both protected persons in an occupied territory accorded the same protection under international law.[109]

Similarly, when ACRI argued that the court should order the IDF to cease its practice of deporting alleged Hamas terrorists, the court ruled that suspects must be given a hearing prior to deportation but that deportation itself was legal, despite the Fourth Geneva Convention's prohibition of deportation.[110]

One of the largest issues on which the Israeli human rights network has been unable to prevail is family reunification for Arab Israelis with their Palestinian spouses. The state has argued that the law passed in 2003 denying Palestinian spouses of Israelis the right to seek Israeli citizenship is necessary because such unions are often a means of smuggling suicide bombers and weapons into the country. Human rights organizations have questioned the evidence for these claims and have filed seven petitions before the High Court asking it to rule the law invalid, but it has refused to do so.[111] Given that the effort to free Soviet Jews often turned on family unification, a Jewish and democratic state's denial of unification represents an ironic turn of events.

Apart from its failure to win support on specific issues, some critics within the network suggest that since 2000 it has failed to articulate a broad, accessible vision to the public. According to Daphna Golan-Agnon, in its early days, B'Tselem tried every year not only to respond to the issues of the day, but also, at least in one report, to "give a comprehensive picture of the territories." Now, however,

> the main problem with Israeli human rights is we don't have a vision. We respond to the government's actions—reactively not proactively. SHATIL and NIF give a place to meet and sit and develop strategies—but this is not vision in the big sense—how this place is going to look in twenty years. . . . Human rights here is not radical at all—we take a very limited view of what can be done, and our discourse is unfriendly to people.[112]

Furthermore, she says, the network has not done as well as it could to make clear to the public how various human rights issues (e.g., house demolitions, checkpoints) are interrelated as collective punishments. Nor has it made a powerful enough case that what happens in the territories "contaminates the democracy here." It is difficult to assess how widely this critique is held.

Other issues they have cultivated have resulted in more ambiguous fruit, neither fully ripe nor rotten. The most important example of this type of result is the security barrier. Jessica Montell calls the human rights approach to the barrier "a work in progress," but asserts that when it was first constructed, no one in Israel was talking about it as a human rights issue. B'Tselem was "the vanguard" in asserting the relevance of rights law. Although the Israeli High Court of Justice did not go as far as the International Court of Justice, which ruled the entire barrier unlawful, it did reroute significant portions of the barrier in an attempt to alleviate the most severe humanitarian hardships it created.[113]

For all the failures and ambiguous outcomes, however, there have also been many outright successes, even during the most difficult times. In general, Israeli human rights activists are not prone to despair. In the midst of the Lebanon war of 2006, many of the activists I spoke with told me that they were tremendously saddened. With family, friends, and colleagues in Haifa and other northern cities where Hezbollah bombs were falling, the activists were visibly and understandably shaken by the toll of the war on Israelis. They were also enormously depressed by the humanitarian suffering the war had wrought on Lebanese civilians, whether because of Hezbollah's use of human shields or the humanitarian crisis precipitated by Israel's bombing (legitimate from a military standpoint) of the airport, roads, and bridges.

Yet when I asked Rabbi Ascherman of RHR whether he ever became despondent, he replied that although the first weeks of the war had been "humbling," he did not despair, because "the religious personality is basically optimistic." Although most activists in the network describe themselves as secular Jews, Ascherman's response nonetheless struck me as applicable to human rights activists in general. Given Irwin Cotler's description of human rights as the modern "civic religion," Ascherman's insight helps explain why activists are drawn to the scene of the darkest actions of which human beings are capable, and why they keep going back in the midst of continual setbacks and disappointments.

Israeli activists' persistence has paid off in a number of triumphs. The first, not to be underestimated, is that the level of public awareness of human rights issues is high compared to what it was in the early 1980s. The Israeli public celebrates an annual day for human rights and the high school curriculum includes it as a subject. Moreover, activists have created a sustainable human rights sector, comprising organizations and knowledgeable individuals who can carry the work forward.[114]

Many of the network's victories have occurred in the Supreme Court. The court's ruling on September 6, 1999, that torture in any form is illegal represents the network's high water mark to date.[115] B'Tselem was the first organization to document the interrogation methods of the GSS and to label them torture. In 1984, the Landau Commission Report confirmed the torture charges and ruled that the GSS could not cause major physical injury to detainees during interrogations, but could continue to apply "moderate physical pressure." During the Oslo years, NGOs engaged in a variety of activities at every level attempting to persuade the court and the public that such pressure still constituted torture, and that torture of any kind should be forbidden. PCATI, ACRI, and HaMoked prepared the legal arguments. Led by Hannah Friedman and Leah Tsemel, PCATI demonstrated the significance of this issue to the public by mounting a compelling single-issue public advocacy campaign with policymakers, in the media, and through public symposia, films, and exhibitions.[116] In its reports it demonstrated that the GSS was "outsourcing" torture of Palestinian detainees to Palestinian collaborators.[117] It monitored the implementation of the High Court of Justice ruling prohibiting the use of torture by visiting detainees in detention centers and collecting testimonies and affidavits.[118] It gave written submissions to the UN Committee against Torture on what it termed Israel's "blatant violations" of the prohibition.[119] And in the wake of the victory, it continued to monitor and report on violations of the ruling.[120]

For its part, PHR issued a report describing the traumatic physical and mental effects of the GSS torture on its victims.[121] It repeatedly petitioned the High Court of Justice to stop the torture of individual detainees. It held a two-day international conference against torture in Tel Aviv for experts from Europe and the United States to help spread the word internationally. The conference helped raise public awareness about the issue in Israel and abroad.

B'Tselem also contributed greatly to the effort. Between 1984 and 1999, it published a total of nine reports on the subject and made two appearances before the UN Committee against Torture. In 1999, B'Tselem was actively engaged in advocacy surrounding the High Court petitions, particularly in generating widespread media coverage and international attention.[122] It lobbied justices around the world to contact President Barak to provide comparative information.[123] Following the High Court decision, B'Tselem produced a position paper and lobbied local and international bodies regarding possible legislation legalizing torture.

The result of all this activity was a victory so total that it stunned both public officials and the activists themselves. In the 1999 ruling, the court ruled that the GSS did not have the authority to employ even "moderate physical pressure." The court also held that the "necessity defense," found in the Israeli Penal Law, could not serve in advance as a justification for GSS investigators to employ such interrogation practices, although it could be used as a defense ex post facto—either in the choice made by the attorney general in deciding whether to prosecute, or according to the discretion of the court if criminal charges were brought against them. Acknowledging that "ever since it was established, the State of Israel has been engaged in an unceasing struggle for its security—indeed, its very existence," the court admitted that "we are aware that this decision does not make it easier to deal with that reality." However, it concluded:

> This is the destiny of a democracy—it does not see all means as acceptable, and the ways of its enemies are not always open before it. A democracy must sometimes fight with one hand tied behind its back. Even so, a democracy has the upper hand. The rule of law and the liberty of an individual constitute important components in its understanding of security. At the end of the day, they strengthen its spirit and this strength allows it to overcome its difficulties. . . .
>
> Deciding these petitions weighed heavily on this Court. True, from the legal perspective, the road before us is smooth. We are, however, part of Israeli society. Its problems are known to us and we live its history. We are not isolated in an ivory tower. We live the life of this country. We are aware of the harsh reality of terrorism in which we are, at times, immersed. The possibility that this decision will hamper the ability to properly deal with terrorists and terrorism disturbs us. We are, however, judges. We must decide according to the law. This is the standard that we set for ourselves. When we sit to judge, we ourselves are judged. Therefore, in deciding the law, we must act according to our purest conscience.

The network has also been able to make some shorter-term inroads with the military. A notable success was in abolishing many house demolitions, and this success also represented a joint effort of many NGOs. In November 2004, B'Tselem issued a report condemning house demolitions as forms of collective punishment and land expropriation. It documented the emotional and mental harm demolitions cause families and communities. It described the demolitions as violations of the right to housing and due process, and asserted that each one constitutes a war crime.[124] In February 2005, in response to the report, the military convened a committee that concluded that there was no evidence that demolitions are effective as a deterrent to terrorism while there was evidence that the practice both increases the hostility of the Palestinian population and harms Israel's international reputation.

Perhaps the greatest acknowledgment of the effectiveness of the human rights network came from prime minister Yitzhak Rabin. Rabin was no fan of human rights NGOs, which he considered to be interfering with peace negotiations by highlighting Israeli abuses. He often remarked that the Palestinian Authority would be fortunate to build its state "*bli bagatz u'bli b'tselem*" [without a High Court of Justice and without B'Tselem]. In other words, the Palestinian Authority is able to act without fear of a court of first resort or a strong human rights network monitoring its practices. In a backhanded way, there could hardly be a better demonstration of the degree to which the network has sometimes been able to worry and check Israeli leaders.

CONCLUSION

While Jewish human rights activism in the international arena declined during the half-century after World War II, in Israel the reverse has been true. During the same period, Israel's human rights sector increased from almost nothing to a network of well-established organizations characterized by stratification of authorities, issues, and tactics, and by the use of time-limited strategic alliances. While the anti-Israel alliance has often succeeded in quashing Jewish dissent at the international level, in Israel the fragmentation of the national consensus that had coalesced during the state-building period has enabled Israeli dissidents to find their voice.

Yet activists in the Israeli network have faced daunting constraints, operating in the context of an ethnic democracy in which the public perceives itself to be confronting a perpetual existential threat. The network has had to endure constant attacks from its critics, who have sometimes claimed that human rights activism was treasonous, or at least that it was the naïve preserve of bleeding hearts, successful only in eroding the state's legitimacy in the eyes of the world. The activists have responded that their appeals have actually strengthened Israel's democracy by helping to establish and maintain the rule of law for all its citizens. Activists have felt compelled to respond to their critics with continuous efforts to establish their credibility and effectiveness. They have had to invent an intricate Israeli dance while being buffeted by the ethnocentrism of some forms of Zionism, the lack of official Israeli commitment to pluralism, and the anti-Zionism at the heart of so much international politics.

Given these constraints, disappointments have been inevitable, and progress sometimes excruciatingly slow. Yet Israeli human rights activists remain convinced of the justice of their efforts. They have persisted through limitations and setbacks. They have often succeeded in influencing their society by exploiting all the avenues available to them: Israeli, Jewish, human.

6

Epilogue: The Road from Durban

My aim in this book has been to offer more light than heat on a range of issues often rife with controversy, issues on which public debate frequently lacks either intellectual depth or moral nuance. As a preliminary overview of the inner dynamics of Jews' three major political commitments, this study makes no claim to comprehensiveness. Readers will be able to add many details from their own experience, and I hope that historians, political scientists, sociologists, and legal scholars will continue filling in the picture sketched out here. For example, an expert in the history of apartheid might explore Jews' anti-apartheid activism in the broader context of international human rights. Others might do the same for persecuted Jewish communities in Ethiopia, Iraq, Syria, Lebanon, and Iran, among others. These are not just Jewish stories; they are human rights stories.

Just as Jacob received the name Israel by wrestling all night with an angel, Jews have often established their political identities through their long wrestling match with human rights. Here, a few general comments may be hazarded about the result and significance of that struggle.

As a globally dispersed set of political communities—working sometimes together, sometimes apart, and sometimes at cross-purposes—Jews have made signal contributions to the development of the international human rights system. They have played every possible role: victims, advocates, violators, and judges. For modern Jews, securing human rights has not always been a predominant goal, but it has nonetheless played a constant part in Jewish political decision-making, both in the world at large and in the state of Israel. During and after the French Revolution, Jews did not merely embrace Enlightenment universalism; they were in many instances the occasion for its expression, and they largely made the universal their particular contribution to world politics. Whether in their capacities as state officials, members of NGOs, or as empowered individuals, Jews have stood for—and stood up for—human rights.

Jews could succeed in advocating for universal rights protections because their suffering conferred moral standing on their cause, because they could plumb a rich religious and philosophical tradition to find support for a cosmopolitan and pluralist worldview, and because they nurtured generations of experienced organizers. Jews did not always seek, find, or emphasize the universalism in their tradition. Most found themselves living in the contact zone among various, sometimes competing, ideals.

When we look at the arc of development of Jewish human rights activism since 1945, we find that Diaspora Jewish NGOs' activity on human rights has declined while Israeli Jewish human rights activity has increased. After a period of initial enthusiasm for universal norms, Diaspora Jews' dedication cooled from 1967 through the end of the twentieth century, although it never disappeared. Jews remained active where, as in the Soviet case, there was a need to protect a vulnerable part of the Diaspora, or where, as in the case of the formal prohibition and punishment of genocide, Jews' own history cried out for action.

The decline of international Jewish human rights activism must be understood primarily as a reaction against the world community's misuse of treaties, bodies, conferences, and courts to delegitimize Israel. These misguided, often atrocious, efforts have led many Diaspora Jews to view international forums with ambivalence at best, and often with outrage. The Zionism=Racism charge, in its many forms, has taken enormous resources to combat and has caused many vicarious Zionists to harden their positions. Moreover, Jews' internal transformation from radicals to liberals and/or neoconservatives has also exercised a dampening effect on their human rights enthusiasm. The ironic consequence has been that Diaspora Jews are now often more hawkish on Israel, less predisposed toward debating or supporting Palestinian rights, than their Israeli counterparts. As the world has taken up against Israel, Diaspora Jews have decreased their trust in the world. To the extent that domestic organizations in the United States—churches, ethnic minorities, civil rights groups—have identified their own causes with the Third World or pro-Palestinian movements, their relationships with American Jews have become strained, even with regard to domestic civil rights issues.

Yet while Jewish activism on human rights has declined, the opposite trend has been observable in Israel. While the first century of modern Jewish settlement in Palestine and Israel saw very little Jewish human rights activity, toward the end of the twentieth century increasing levels of activism and discourse appeared. Israeli activists worked both inside and outside the Green

Line, both with regard to Jewish and non-Jewish minorities. Ironically, this development was the consequence of Israel's growing military, economic, and political strength. During the first intifada and the Oslo years, the Israeli public experienced a decreased level of existential threat perception and a recalibration of their priorities. Some Israeli Jews no longer believed it was necessary to abide by a strict national consensus; there was room for dissent. During these years, the militarized culture in place since before the founding of the state began to be challenged by a bourgeoning civil society that included protest against the government's human rights practices. Unfortunately, the demoralizing effects of the collapse of the Camp David peace talks in 2000, the organized violence against Israeli civilians mounted by Palestinians during the second intifada, Ariel Sharon's provocative measures to destroy the Palestinian infrastructure, Hezbollah's bombing campaign of 2006, and Iran's nuclear threat to "wipe Israel off the map" have combined once again to increase Israelis' insecurity and decrease their sympathies for human rights.

Which vision will prevail depends on the future of the conflict, but also on whether the UN is willing to stop endorsing its member states' anti-Zionism and anti-Semitism. The immediate signs in this regard are mixed. Although outwardly the World Conference against Racism in Durban seemed a reprise of all the worst tendencies of the international human rights system, beneath the surface it marked the beginnings of a transformation in the UN's relationship with Israel and Jews—how profound remains yet to be seen.

Signs of change were evident even before the conference, making its ugliness all the more disconcerting for Jews. In the late 1990s, the AJC's Felice Gaer successfully prodded the Organization for Security and Cooperation in Europe to establish an ombudsman to monitor anti-Semitism in Eastern Europe and work with governments there to resolve conflicts. Taking note of these efforts, the UN General Assembly passed its first-ever condemnation of anti-Semitism on December 9, 1998, on the fiftieth anniversary of the adoption of the Genocide Convention.[1] While Israel had long been the only UN member state to be denied a place in a regional group, in May 2000 it was finally admitted to the Western European and Others Group.

The disturbances at Durban produced a backlash from inside the United Nations itself. Secretary-General Kofi Annan stated, albeit not until after the conference, that UN human rights procedures had to change so that the world body would not continue to be torn apart by outbreaks of propaganda against Israel. Annan came to see UN-sponsored anti-Zionism as bad for relations with the United States, harmful to Jews and Israel, and perhaps most pointedly, a hindrance to the UN in doing its work. These views were shaped by political events, especially the September 11, 2001, Al Qaeda attacks on the

United States. After the attacks, the Bush administration criticized the HCHR for allowing the charter and treaty bodies to be overrun by inhumane and anti-Zionist forces, exemplified when Sudan held the chair of the Commission on Human Rights at the very moment its government was superintending genocide in Darfur. The Bush administration's criticisms, combined with its unilateralism, caused consternation among UN officials. Secretary-General Annan argued that if the UN did not want to become irrelevant it would have to undertake a program of widespread reforms to ensure greater fairness in its human rights bodies.

A priority among these reforms, for Annan, was effecting a rapprochement between the United Nations organization and the international Jewish community. Under his leadership, the UN took a series of small steps that, at least for a time, subtly changed the atmosphere for Israel and Jews. Annan praised Gaer's election to the Committee against Torture as a sign that the "healing of wounds" between the UN and the Jewish community was taking place.[2] He encouraged the Blaustein Institute to build on an extensive memorandum it had produced in preparation for the Durban conference, "Antisemitism: An Assault on Human Rights," by organizing the first conference on anti-Semitism at the UN's headquarters in New York on June 21, 2004.[3] Recognizing the work of the conference, on December 16, 2005, the General Assembly reaffirmed its condemnation of anti-Semitism.[4] For the next several months these efforts seem to have changed the atmosphere of anti-Zionism at the UN. When Iranian president Mahmoud Ahmadinejad threatened to destroy Israel, he was roundly condemned.

Still another change may have been registered by the dissolution of the discredited Commission on Human Rights in 2006, and its replacement by a Human Rights Council. Secretary-General Annan worked to ensure that the new council would broaden its focus beyond the Middle East.[5] However, it is unclear whether the changes will enable the council to produce a fairer track record toward Israel than its predecessor. The council ended its first session with a resolution criticizing Israel for its military operations in Gaza during the summer of 2006, without citing the Hamas-sponsored kidnapping of Corporal Gilad Shalit or the rocket attacks on Israeli cities that had provoked Israel's response.[6] To many Jews, this resolution seemed like sour old wine in a new bottle. There is still much to be done before Israel can take its seat at the UN as just another member state.

Yet even if the world community's relations with Israel remain fraught, the historical record suggests that Jews are not likely to abandon the struggle for human rights altogether. While acknowledging the flaws in the current system, some Jews will nonetheless keep working to improve its fairness and efficacy. They will do so because they believe it is better to struggle for human rights than to revert to the old system of unquestionable state sovereignty. They will do so because they carry deep historical memories and have witnessed recent instances of Jewish suffering. They will do so in answer to their tradition's call for universal justice. They will do so because they hope to strengthen Israel's democracy. They will do so because genocide should not happen—to anyone—ever again. They will keep dancing at three weddings.

Appendix A: Genocides and Other Mass Killings

Table A.1. Genocides and Other Mass Killings

Country	*Years*	*Perpetrators*	*Victims*	*Estimated Number of Deaths*
Namibia	1904–1905	German Colonialists in Southwest Africa	Hereros	65,000
Turkey	1915	Ottomans	Armenians	1.3–1.8 million
Ukraine	1919	Cossack groups aided by the Petlurian government	Jews	35,000–100,000
USSR	1929–1933	Stalin-led Communist government	Collectivized peasants (Kulaks)	5–15 million
Germany	1939–1945	Nazis	Jews, Roma and Sinti (Gypsies), the Disabled	6 million, 20,000, 200,000
Indonesia	1965–1966	Anti-Communist army units	Communists	500,000
Nigeria	1967–1970	Nigerian government	Igbo in Biafra	2 million
Bangladesh	1971–1972	Pakistani government	Hindus	100,000
Uganda	1972–1979	Idi Amin government	Asians, tribal groups	200,000– 500,000
Paraguay	1974	Paraguayan government	Aché Indians	Entire tribe (approx. 1,000)
Cambodia	1975–1979	Khmer Rouge	Monks, Cham, Buddhist, and Vietnamese minorities, Eastern Khmer	1.7 million

East Timor	1975–1979, 1999	Indonesian army	Timorese	60,000–80,000, 2,000
Guatemala	1966–1986	Government and counterinsurgency forces	Mayan Indians	200,000
Iraq	1988	Iraqi government	Kurds	50,000–100,000
Yugoslavia	1992–1995	Serbs, Croats	Bosnian Muslims, Croats, Serbs	300,000
Burundi	1972, 1993	Tutsis	Hutus	100,000, 200,000–300,000
Rwanda	1994	Hutus	Tutsis	800,000
Democratic Republic of the Congo (formerly Zaire)	1998–2005	Government forces, rebels, and their backers in 7 neighboring countries	Civilian Tutsis, Hutus, Lari caught in the civil war	3.3 million
Kosovo	1999	Serbian paramilitary organizations	Ethnic Albanians	10,000– 15,000
Darfur, Sudan	2002–	Janjaweed militias associated with the Sudanese government	Members of the Fur Tribe	200,000 (continuing)

Sources: Totten, Parsons, and Charny, eds., *Century of Genocide* (2004); Totten, ed., *Genocide at the Millenium* (2005); Kuper, *Genocide: Its Political Use in the Twentieth Century* (1981).

Appendix B: Israel's Adoption of Major Human Rights Treaties

Table B.1. Israel's Adoption of Major Human Rights Treaties

Treaty	*UN Adoption*	*Entry into Force*	*Israeli Signature*	*Israeli Ratification or Accession*
Convention on the Prevention and Punishment of the Crime of Genocide	9 Dec. 1948	12 Jan. 1951	17 Aug. 1949	9 March 1950
Convention Relating to the Status of Refugees	28 July 1951	22 April 1954	1 Aug. 1951	1 Oct. 1954
Convention Relating to the Status of Stateless Persons	28 Sept. 1954	6 June 1960	1 Oct. 1954	23 Dec. 1958
Convention on the Reduction of Statelessness	30 Aug. 1961	13 Dec. 1975	30 Aug. 1961	None to date
International Convention on the Elimination of All Forms of Racial Discrimination (CERD)	7 March 1966	4 Jan. 1969	7 March 1966	3 Jan. 1979
International Covenant on Economic, Social, and Cultural Rights (CESCR)	16 Dec. 1966	3 Jan. 1976	19 Dec. 1966	3 Oct. 1991
International Covenant on Civil and Political Rights (CCPR)	16 Dec. 1966	23 March 1976	19 Dec. 1966	3 Oct. 1991
Convention on the Elimination of All Forms of Discrimination against Women (CEDAW)	18 Dec. 1979	3 Sept. 1981	17 July 1980	3 Oct. 1991
Convention against Torture and Other Cruel, Inhuman or Degrading Treatment or Punishment (CAT)	10 Dec. 1984	26 June 1987	22 Oct. 1986	3 Oct. 1991
Convention on the Rights of the Child (CRC)	20 Nov. 1989	2 Sept. 1990	3 July 1990	3 Oct. 1991

Sources: Multilateral Treaty Framework: An Invitation to Universal Participation, Treaty Event: 13-15 September, 2006, United Nations Headquarters (New York: United Nations, 2006); Office of the United Nations High Commissioner for Human Rights, http://www.ohchr.org/english/countries/ratification/11.htm.

Appendix C: Glossary of Abbreviations

The world of the international human rights system is an alphabet soup of organizations. For aid in identifying an organization, treaty, or conference abbreviated in this book, please consult the following list:

ACRI	Association for Civil Rights in Israel
AJC	American Jewish Committee
AJCongress	American Jewish Congress
AJWS	American Jewish World Service
AI	Amnesty International
BBI	B'nai B'rith International
Blaustein	Jacob Blaustein Institute for the Advancement of Human Rights
CAT	Convention against Torture
CBJO	Coordinating Board of Jewish Organizations
CCJO	Consultative Council of Jewish Organizations
CEDAW	Convention on the Elimination of Discrimination against Women
CERD	Convention on the Elimination of All Forms of Racial Discrimination
CHR	Commission on Human Rights
CP Covenant	International Covenant on Civil and Political Rights
CRC	Convention on the Rights of the Child
CSCE	Conference on Security and Cooperation in Europe
ECOSOC	Economic and Social Council
ESC Covenant	International Covenant on Economic, Social, and Cultural Rights

FSU	Former Soviet Union
HCHR	High Commissioner for Human Rights
HWG	Moscow Helsinki Watch Group
HRW	Human Rights Watch
ICAHD	Israeli Coalition against House Demolitions
ICC	International Criminal Court
ICJ	International Court of Justice
ICJW	International Council of Jewish Women
ICTR	International Criminal Tribunal for Rwanda
ICTY	International Criminal Tribunal for the Former Yugoslavia
ILC	International Law Commission
NCSJ	National Conference of Soviet Jewry
NIF	New Israel Fund
OSCE	Organization for Security and Cooperation in Europe
PCATI	Public Committee against Torture in Israel
PHR	Physicians for Human Rights
RHR	Rabbis for Human Rights
UCSJ	Union of Councils for Soviet Jews
UDHR	Universal Declaration of Human Rights
UNGA	United Nations General Assembly
UNSC	United Nations Security Council
USCIRF	United States Commission on International Religious Freedom
WCAR	World Conference against Racism, Racial Discrimination, Xenophobia and Related Intolerance
WJC	World Jewish Congress
WJRO	World Jewish Restitution Organization
WUPJ	World Union for Progressive Judaism

Notes

INTRODUCTION

1. Felice D. Gaer, "Reality Check: Human Rights NGOs Confront Governments at the UN," in *NGOs, the UN, and Global Governance*, ed. Thomas G. Weiss and Leon Gordenker (Boulder, Colo.: Lynne Rienner, 1996), 51–66; William Korey, *NGOs and the Universal Declaration of Human Rights: "A Curious Grapevine"* (New York: St. Martin's Press, 1988), 31–33.

2. Raphael Lemkin, *Axis Rule in Occupied Europe* (Washington, D.C.: Carnegie Endowment for International Peace, 1944); William Korey, *NGOs*, 4.

3. William Korey, *NGOs*, 45; biographical sketch of Cassin in Sidney Liskofsky and Karel Vasak, eds., *The Right to Leave and Return: Papers and Recommendations of the International Colloquium Held in Uppsala, Sweden, 19–20 June 1972* (New York: AJC, 1976); John Humphrey, *Human Rights and the United Nations: A Great Adventure* (Dobbs Ferry, N.Y.: Transnational Publishers, 1984).

4. Aviezer Ravitzky of the Department of Jewish Thought at Hebrew University has called such values "meta-halakhic principles," that is, the guiding principles driving the majority of decisions in relevant Jewish law. See *Messianism, Zionism, and Jewish Religious Radicalism* (Chicago: University of Chicago Press, 1996), introduction. See Peter J. Haas, *Human Rights and the World's Major Religions, Volume 1: The Jewish Tradition* (Westport, Conn.: Praeger Publishers, 2005), 118.

5. For an early expression of the compatibility of Zionism and American values, see Louis D. Brandeis, "Zionism Is Consistent with American Patriotism" (June 1915), in *The Jew in the Modern World: A Documentary History*, 2nd ed., ed. Paul Mendes-Flohr and Jehuda Reinharz (New York: Oxford University Press, 1995), 496.

6. Benedict Anderson, *Imagined Communities: Reflections on the Origin and Spread of Nationalism*, revised ed. (New York: Verso, 2006). Also see E. J. Hobsbawm, *Nations and Nationalism since 1780* (New York: Cambridge University Press, 1990); Jeffrey Alexander, *The Civil Sphere* (New Haven, Conn.: Yale University Press, 2007).

7. Horace M. Kallen, "Democracy versus the Melting-Pot," in *Jewish American Literature: A Norton Anthology*, ed. Jules Chametzky et al. (New York: W. W. Norton, 2001), 207–216; David Biale, "The Melting Pot and Beyond," in *Insider/Outsider: American Jews and Multiculturalism*, ed. David Biale, Michael Galchinsky, and Susannah Heschel (Berkeley: University of California Press, 1998), 17–33; David Theo Goldberg, ed., *Multiculturalism: A Critical Reader* (Oxford: Basil Blackwell, 1994); Will Kymlicka, *Multicultural Citizenship: A Liberal Theory of Minority Rights* (New York: Oxford University Press, 1996).

8. Lawrence Fuchs, *The Political Behavior of American Jews* (Glencoe, Ill.: Free Press, 1956). For American Jews' civil rights commitments, see Jerome A. Chanes, "Who Does What? Jewish Advocacy and Jewish Interest," in *Jews in American Politics: Essays*, ed. L. Sandy Maisel and Ira N. Forman (Lanham, Md.: Rowman and Littlefield, 2004), who declares that in these decades "civil rights *were* the Jewish agenda" (101).

9. The UN Commission on Human Rights (CHR)—a body comprised of the delegates of UN member states and thus overtly political—has dealt harshly with Israel from just after the Six-Day War through ritual annual condemnations. One month after the start of the second intifada in September 2000, CHR held only its fifth "special session" to condemn Israel for "grave and massive violations of the human rights of the Palestinian people." (Geneva, October 17–19, 2000) UN Doc. E/CN.4/RES/S-5/1. Also see UN Economic and Social Council, "Report of the Commission on Human Rights on its fifth Special Session" (Geneva, November 9, 2000) UN Doc. E/2000/112. As a sample of the condemnations, from 2001 through 2003, CHR adopted the following resolutions condemning Israel (far more than for any other country): from the 57th session, "Situation in Occupied Palestine" (Geneva, April 6, 2001) UN Doc. E/CN.4/RES/2001/2; "Human Rights in the Occupied Syrian Golan" (Geneva, April 18, 2001) UN Doc. E/CN.4/RES/2001/6; "Question of the Violation of Human Rights in the Occupied Arab Territories, including Palestine" (Geneva, April 18, 2001) UN Doc. E/CN.4/RES/2001/7; "Israeli Settlements in the Occupied Arab Territories" (Geneva, April 18, 2001) UN Doc. E/CN.4/RES/2001/8. In its 58th session, CHR adopted these resolutions: "Situation of Human Rights in the Occupied Palestinian Territory" (Geneva, April 5, 2002) UN Doc E/CN.4/RES/2002/1; "Situation in Occupied Palestine" (Geneva, April 12, 2002) UN Doc. E/CN.4/RES/2002/3; "Human Rights in the Occupied Syrian Golan" (Geneva, April 12, 2002) UN Doc. E/CN.4/RES/2002/6; "Israeli Settlements in the Occupied Arab Territories" (Geneva, April 12, 2002) UN Doc. E/CN.4/RES/2002/7; "Question of the Violation of Human Rights in the Occupied Arab Territories, including Palestine" (Geneva, April 15, 2002) UN Doc. E/CN.4/RES/2002/8; "Human Rights Situation of Lebanese Detainees in Israel" (Geneva, April 19, 2002) UN Doc. E/CN.4/RES/2002/10; "The Situation of Human Rights in the Occupied Palestinian Territory" (Geneva, April 26, 2002) UN Doc. E/CN.4/RES/2002/90. In its 59th session, CHR adopted the following resolutions: "Situation in Occupied Palestine" (Geneva, April 14, 2003) UN Doc. E/CN.4/RES/2003/3; "Human Rights in the Occupied Syrian Golan" (Geneva, April 15, 2003) UN Doc. E/CN.4/RES/2003/5; "Question of the Violation of Human Rights in the Occupied Arab Territories, including Palestine" (Geneva, April 15, 2003) UN

Doc. E/CN.4/RES/2003/6; "Israeli Settlements in the Occupied Arab Territories" (Geneva, April 15, 2003) UN Doc. E/CN.4/RES/2003/7; "Human Rights Situation of the Lebanese Detainees in Israel" (Geneva, April 16, 2003) UN Doc. E/CN.4/RES/2003/8. Since 1993, Israel has been the subject of annual reports by John Dugard, the special rapporteur of the Commission on Human Rights on "the situation of human rights in the Palestinian territories occupied since 1967." Israel has been investigated by CHR's thematic mechanisms, including working groups or special rapporteurs on torture, arbitrary detention, and extrajudicial and summary executions. On the website of the Office of the High Commissioner for Human Rights, Palestinian human rights are the only specific situation mentioned in CHR's "Main Themes." See www.ohchr.org/english/bodies/chr/intro.htm.

10. Asian preparatory meeting, World Conference against Racism, Racial Discrimination, Xenophobia and Related Intolerance, "Declaration and Plan of Action," Tehran, Islamic Republic of Iran, February 19–21, 2001, available at www.unhchr.ch/html/racism/02-recomtehr.html. See chapter 1 and the conclusion for the full story.

11. On the so-called New Anti-Semitism, see Henry F. Carey and John Carey, "Hostility in United Nations Bodies to Judaism, the Jewish People and Jews as Such," *Israel Yearbook of Human Rights* 17 (Dordrecht: Martinus Nijhoff, 1987), 29–40.

12. See Landau Commission Report, 1987, paragraphs 2.25–2.46; Human Rights Committee, concluding comments, 63rd Session, CCPR/C/79/Add93 (Geneva, 1998); Committee on Economic, Social, and Cultural Rights, concluding comments, 19th Session, E/C.12/1Add.27 (Geneva, 1998); Human Rights Watch/Middle East *Torture and Ill-Treatment: Israel's Interrogation of Palestinians from the Occupied Territories* (New York: Human Rights Watch, 1994); N. Gordon and R. Marton, eds., *Torture: Human Rights, Medical Ethics, and the Case of Israel* (Atlantic Highlands, N.J.: Zed Books, 1995); B'Tselem, "Torture during Interrogations: Testimony of Palestinian Detainees and Israeli Interrogators," information sheet, November 1994; International Court of Justice, "Legal Consequences of the Construction of a Wall in the Occupied Palestinian Territory," advisory opinion, general list no. 131 (The Hague, July 9, 2004) paragraphs 74ff., 117–22, 134; Reporters without Borders, ed., *Israel/Palestine: The Black Book* (Sterling, Va.: Pluto Press, 2003); David Kretzmer, *The Occupation of Justice: The Supreme Court of Israel and the Occupied Territories* (Albany: State University of New York Press, 2002), 21–25, 34–40, 43–56.

13. Anna Greenberg and Kenneth D. Wald, "Still Liberal after All These Years? The Contemporary Political Behavior of American Jewry," in *Jews in American Politics*, ed. Sandy Maisel and Ira N. Forman (Lanham, Md.: Rowman and Littlefield, 2004), 184.

14. Natan Lerner, *The U.N. Convention on the Elimination of All Forms of Racial Discrimination* (Rockville, Md.: Sijthoff and Noordhoff, 1980), 2–73; Hersch Lauterpacht, *The International Bill of the Rights of Man* (New York: Cambridge University Press, 1944); Louis Henkin, ed., *The International Bill of Rights: The Covenant on Civil and Political Rights* (New York: Columbia University Press, 1981), and ed., *World Politics and the Jewish Condition: Essays Prepared for a Task Force on the World of the 1970s of the American Jewish Committee* (New York: Quadrangle Books, 1972); Yoram Dinstein, "The International Law of Belligerent Occupation and Human Rights," *Israel Yearbook on Human Rights* 8 (1978): 104–143.

15. See Natan Sharansky, *Fear No Evil*, trans. Stefani Hoffman (New York: Random House, 1988); Korey, *NGOs*; Moses Moskowitz, *The Politics and Dynamics of Human Rights* (Dobbs Ferry, N.Y.: Oceana Publications, 1968); Nehemiah Robinson, *The Universal Declaration of Human Rights* (London: WJC, 1958) and *The Genocide Convention: A Commentary* (London: WJC, 1960); and Felice Gaer, "And Never the Twain Shall Meet? The Struggle to Establish Women's Rights as International Human Rights," in *The International Human Rights of Women: Instruments of Change*, ed. Carol Elizabeth Lockwood, Daniel Barstow Magraw, Margaret Faith Spring, S. I. Strong (Washington, D.C.: ABA Section of International Law and Practice, 1998), 1–89.

16. A recent exception to this rule is in Nelly Las, *Jewish Women in a Changing World: A History of the International Council of Jewish Women (ICJW), 1899–1995*, trans. Stephanie Nakache (Jerusalem: A. Harman Institute of Contemporary Jewry, 1996).

17. Eckart Otto, "Human Rights: The Influence of the Hebrew Bible," *Journal of Northwest Semitic Languages* 25, no. 1 (1999): 1–20. Thanks to Shalom Goldman for this reference.

18. Irwin Cotler, "Jewish NGOs and Religious Human Rights: A Case Study," in *Human Rights in Judaism: Cultural, Religious, and Political Perspectives*, ed. Michael J. Broyde and John Witte, Jr. (Northvale, N.J.: Jason Aronson, 1998), 167.

19. Cotler, "Jewish NGOs," 168.

20. Milton Konvitz, ed., *Judaism and Human Rights* (New York: W. W. Norton, 1972), 13.

21. Haas, *Human Rights.*

22. Haas, *Human Rights,* 6, 49, 199.

23. Lenn E. Goodman, *Judaism, Human Rights, and Human Values* (Oxford: Oxford University Press, 1998), xiv.

24. René Cassin, "From the Ten Commandments to the Rights of Man," at www.udhr50.org/history/tencomms.htm.

25. Haim Cohn, *Human Rights in the Bible and Talmud* (Tel Aviv: MOD Books, 1989), and a digest of an earlier work commissioned by the WJC, *Human Rights in Jewish Law* (London: Institute of Jewish Affairs, 1984). On the reciprocal relation of rights and duties, see also David Novak, *Covenantal Rights* (Princeton, N.J.: Princeton University Press, 2000), 31; and Haas, *Human Rights*, 49.

26. Cohn, *Human Rights in the Bible and Talmud*, 27.

27. Cohn, *Human Rights in the Bible and Talmud*, 52.

28. Konvitz, *Judaism and Human Rights*, 11. Haas avoids this pitfall altogether by historicizing the development of human rights concepts at each particular period in the development of Judaism.

29. Goodman, *Judaism*, 49.

30. On the Noachide laws, see Gen. 6:7–10; On the stranger, see, e.g., Exod. 12:49, 22:21, 23:9; Lev. 19:10, 19:33–34, 24:22; Num. 15:15–16; Deut. 10:19, Jer. 7:6; Zech. 7:10, Mal. 3:5; Pss. 94:6, 146:9; on the pursuit of justice, see Amos 5:24.

31. On Jubilee, see Lev. 25. On the institutions of justice and charity, see Richard G. Hirsch, "There Shall Be No Poor," in Konvitz, *Judaism and Human Rights*, 234–246.

32. 2 Sam. 12:1–14.

33. Deut. 12:1. For a brief and tense consideration of the Bible's treatment of "pagans and gentiles," see Emanuel Rackman, "Judaism and Equality," in *Judaism and Human Rights*, ed. Milton Konvitz (New York: W. W. Norton and B'nai B'rith Commission on Adult Jewish Education, 1972), 52–54.

34. See Samson Raphael Hirsch, "Do Not Destroy!" in Konvitz, *Judaism and Human Rights*, 259–264. Similarly, the Israeli NGO, Rabbis for Human Rights, has mounted a campaign to save Palestinian olive trees from destruction by the Israel Defense Forces.

35. Num. 21:21–25, 33–35; Deut. 2:32–25; Josh. 10:28–40; 11:11–12, 21.

36. Num. 31:7–18. Of the slaughters of Midianite prisoners in Numbers, the Torah commentator W. Gunter Plaut asks, "How can the idea of slaughtering so many prisoners be reconciled with the humanitarian ideals and the deep sense of compassion that are the very heart of the Torah?" in W. Gunter Plaut, ed., *The Torah: A Modern Commentary* (New York: Union of Hebrew Congregations, 1981), 1230.

37. Haas, *Human Rights*, 6.

38. Michael Broyde, "The Bounds of Wartime Military Conduct in Jewish Law: An Expansive Conception," Herbert Berman Memorial Lecture, Center for Jewish Studies, Queens College, CUNY, November 3, 2004, 8–9.

39. Baruch Spinoza, *Theological Political Treatise*, chap. 18, qtd. in Michael Walzer, Menachem Lorberbaum, and Noam J. Zohar, *The Jewish Political Tradition*, v. 1 (New Haven, Conn.: Yale University Press, 2000), 216.

40. Walzer, Lorberbaum, and Zohar, *Jewish Political Tradition*, xxvii.

41. Jack Donnelly, *Universal Human Rights in Theory and Practice*, 2nd ed., (Ithaca, N.Y.: Cornell University Press, 2003).

42. Caryn Aviv and David Schneer, *New Jews: The End of the Jewish Diaspora* (New York: New York University Press, 2005). Other work on the theory of the Jews' Diaspora includes Robin Cohen, *Global Diasporas: An Introduction* (Seattle: University of Washington Press, 1997); Michael Galchinsky, "Scattered Seeds: A Dialogue of Diasporas," in Biale, Galchinsky, and Heschel, *Insider/Outsider*, 185–211; Arnold Eisen, *Galut: Modern Jewish Reflection on Homelessness and Homecoming* (Bloomington: Indiana University Press, 1986); Jonathan Boyarin and Daniel Boyarin, *Powers of Diaspora: Two Essays on the Relevance of Jewish Culture* (St. Paul: University of Minnesota Press, 2002).

43. Steven J. Gold, *The Israeli Diaspora* (Seattle: University of Washington Press, 2002).

44. Lynn Hunt, *Inventing Human Rights: A History* (New York: W. W. Norton, 2007).

45. For the protection of religious minorities in the Treaty of Westphalia, see Hersch Lauterpacht, *International Law* (Cambridge: Cambridge University Press, 1978), and Brian Orend, *Human Rights: Concept and Context* (Calgary: Broadview Press, 2002). For the Jewish concern pervading Locke's Letter concerning Toleration, see Marc Shell, "Marranos (Pigs), or from Coexistence to Toleration," *Critical Inquiry* 17, no. 2 (Winter 1991): 306–335.

46. See Lynn Hunt, *Inventing Human Rights*, 146–160, 179–180; Arthur Hertzberg, *The French Enlightenment and the Jews: The Origins of Modern Anti-Semitism* (New

York: Columbia University Press, 1968), and George L. Mosse, *Toward the Final Solution: A History of European Racism* (New York: Harper Colophon Books, 1978).

47. See, for example, Carole Fink, *Defending the Rights of Others: The Great Powers, the Jews, and International Minority Protection, 1878–1938* (New York: Cambridge University Press, 2004), 3–38; Mitchell Knisbacher, "The Jews of Iraq and the International Protection of the Rights of Minorities (1856–1976)," in *Essays on Human Rights: Contemporary Issues and Jewish Perspectives*, ed. David Sidorsky, with Sidney Liskofsky and Jerome J. Shestack (Philadelphia: JPSA, 1979), 157–178; Michael Galchinsky, *The Origin of the Modern Jewish Woman Writer* (Detroit, Mich.: Wayne State University Press, 1996); David Sorkin, *The Transformation of German Jewry, 1780–1840* (Oxford: Oxford University Press, 1987); Hertzberg, *French Enlightenment*; Cotler, "Jewish NGOs," 179.

48. See Hunt, *Inventing Human Rights*, 185–196, 209–214.

49. For an extensive and detailed history of Zionism's relation to human rights, see Haas, *Human Rights*, 125–145.

50. On the minorities treaties, see Carole Fink, *Defending the Rights of Others*; Francesco Capotorti, special rapporteur on the question of minorities for the UN Subcommission on Prevention of Discrimination and Protection of Minorities, whose report, written in June 1977, was published as *Study on the Rights of Persons Belonging to Ethnic, Religious, and Linguistic Minorities* (New York: United Nations, 1991); and Thomas Buergenthal, *International Law in a Nutshell*, 2nd ed. (St. Paul, Minn.: West Publishing, 1995), 10–13.

51. Ben Halpern, "Jewish Nationalism: Self-Determination as a Human Right," in Sidorsky et al., *Essays on Human Rights*, 317.

52. Some legal scholars have suggested that the UN Charter made such intervention unlawful, since the charter sanctions only those hostilities undertaken for the purpose of a state's self-defense or under the direction of the UN Security Council (Articles 51 and 42, respectively). On the other hand, the continuing behavior of states (e.g., Tanzania's intervention in Uganda or the NATO intervention in Kosovo) might suggest that there is still room for this kind of activity under the law of nations. For recent justifications of humanitarian intervention, see Richard B. Lillich, *A United States Policy of Humanitarian Intervention and Intercession*, qtd. in ed. David Weissbrodt, Joan Fitzpatrick, and Frank Newman. *International Human Rights: Law, Policy, and Process*, 3rd ed. (Cincinnati, Ohio: Anderson Publishing, 2001), 346–348.

53. Immanuel Kant, "Toward Perpetual Peace: A Philosophical Project," in *Practical Philosophy*, Cambridge Edition of the Works of Immanuel Kant, trans. and ed., Mary J. Gregor (New York: Cambridge University Press, 1996), 326.

54. Fred Halliday, "Global Governance: Prospects and Problems" in *The Global Transformations Reader: An Introduction to the Globalization Debate*, ed. David Held and Anthony McGrew (Malden, Mass.: Polity Press, 2000), 431–441; David Held and Anthony McGrew, Introduction, *Global Transformations Reader*, 11–13.

55. David Held, "Regulating Globalization?" in Held and McGrew, *Global Transformations Reader*, 425–429; and Anthony McGrew, "Democracy Beyond Borders?" in Held and McGrew, *Global Transformations Reader*, 413.

56. See Gerald M. Pomper and Miles A. Pomper, "Movers, Shakers, and Leaders," in Maisel and Forman, *Jews in American Politics,* 93.

57. For neo-conservative Jews' embrace of anti-Communism and rejection of liberal rights discourse where Israel was concerned, see Michael Taub, *Torn at the Roots: The Crisis of Jewish Liberalism in Post-War America* (New York: Columbia University Press, 2002), 19–44, 280–308.

58. On the rejection of human rights discourse by Chabad, see Aviezer Ravitzky, *Messianism, Zionism, and Jewish Religious Radicalism* (Chicago: University of Chicago Press, 1996), 183.

59. The primary examples are UN Watch, founded by Morris Abram, and Committee for UN Reform Education, founded by Harris Schoenberg. See Schoenberg, "Enhancing and Advancing Human Rights: An Essay on Improving UN Human Rights Instruments, Mechanisms, and Procedures Prepared as a Contribution to the UN Decade for Human Rights Education, 1995–2004, in Commemoration of the 50th Anniversary of the Universal Declaration of Human Rights," Center for UN Reform Education, 1999; *The World Conference against Racism: The Adoption and Repeal of the Z=R Resolution and the Implications for UN Reform* (Wayne, N.J.: Center for UN Reform Education, 2001); *War No More! A Concrete Action Plan to Revitalize the United Nations Security Council* (New York: Center for Public Policy, 1995).

60. David Harris, *In the Trenches: Selected Speeches and Writings of an American Jewish Activist, 1979–1999* (New York: Ktav Publishing House, 2000), 271; Felice Gaer, "Antisemitic Incidents Are Not Hooliganism—They Are Human Rights Abuse: The United Nations Should Address Them as Such," remarks to "Confronting anti-Semitism: Education for Tolerance and Understanding," UN Headquarters, New York, June 21, 2004; Anthony Julius, Robert S. Rifkind, Jeffrey Weill, Felice D. Gaer, "Antisemitism: An Assault on Human Rights," memorandum submitted to the UN World Conference Against Racism, Racial Discrimination, Xenophobia, and Related Intolerance, Durban, South Africa, Jacob Blaustein Institute, August 2001.

CHAPTER 1. BUILDING HUMAN RIGHTS

1. Benjamin Ferencz, "Opening Statement of the Prosecution," *Trial of the Major War Criminals*, vol. 1 (Nuremberg, Germany: Tribunal Secretariat, 1947), 32.

2. Irwin Cotler, ed., *Nuremberg Forty Years Later: The Struggle against Injustice in Our Time*, International Human Rights Conference, November 1987, Papers and Proceedings, and Retrospective, 1993 (Montreal: McGill-Queen's University Press, 1995), 104.

3. David Held, "Regulating Globalization?" in *The Global Transformations Reader: An Introduction to the Globalization Debate*, ed. David Held and Anthony McGrew (Malden, Mass.: Polity Press, 2000), 425–429; Anthony McGrew, "Democracy Beyond Borders?" in Held and McGrew, *Global Transformations Reader*, 405–419.

4. William Korey, *NGOs and the Universal Declaration of Human Rights: "A Curious Grapevine"* (New York: St. Martin's Press, 1998), 35–38. This fear was codified as Article 2(7) of the UN Charter, which states that "nothing contained in the

present Charter shall authorize the United Nations to intervene in matters which are essentially within the domestic jurisdiction of any state."

5. *American Jewish Year Book* 2 (1900–1901) (Philadelphia: Jewish Publication Society of America, 1901), 46.

6. See *American Jewish Year Book* 45 (1942–1943); Jacob Blaustein, "Human Rights—A Challenge to the United Nations and to Our Generation," Dag Hammarskjold Memorial Lecture, Columbia University, December 4, 1963.

7. Lily Montagu, "Religion and the United Nations," West Central Congregation, London, October 25, 1958, Lily Montagu Papers, MS282/4/5, AJA.

8. Conference of Jewish Communities of the British Commonwealth, "Report on the Work of the Foreign Affairs Committee of the Board of Deputies of British Jews and of the Coordinating Board of Jewish Organizations," July 1950, 4, CBJO Collection, MS76/1/6, AJA.

9. NGO consultants to the Delegation of the United States of America at Dumbarton Oaks to Edward R. Stettinius, Jr., chair of the US Delegation to the UN Conference on International Organization, memorandum, May 2, 1945; Felice D. Gaer, "Reality Check: Human Rights NGOs Confront Governments at the UN," in *NGOs, the UN, and Global Governance*, ed. Thomas G. Weiss and Leon Gordenker (Boulder, Colo.: Lynne Rienner, 1996), 51–66; Korey, *NGOs*; Irwin Cotler, "Jewish NGOs and Religious Human Rights: A Case Study," in *Human Rights in Judaism: Cultural, Religious, and Political Perspectives*, ed. Michael J. Broyde and John Witte, Jr. (Northvale, N.J.: Jason Aronson, 1998).

10. See Raphael Lemkin, *Axis Rule in Occupied Europe* (Washington, D.C.: Carnegie Endowment for International Peace, 1944); UN Doc. E/CN.4/Sub.2/L.565, May 23, 1972; Cotler, "Jewish NGOs," 184–185; Korey, *NGOs*; Leslie C. Green, "Jewish Issues on the Human-Rights Agenda in the First Half of the Twentieth Century," in *Essays on Human Rights: Contemporary Issues and Jewish Perspectives*, ed. David Sidorsky, with Sidney Liskofsky and Jerome J. Shestack (Philadelphia: JPSA, 1979), 297–308; William Korey, *NGOs*, 205–207; CCJO, Reports, 1947–1952, BL; and CCJO, Memoranda, Statements, Releases, etc., 1947–1953, BL.

11. ECOSOC Res. 75(V), August 5, 1947.

12. Thomas Buergenthal, *International Human Rights in a Nutshell*, 2nd ed. (St. Paul, Minn.: West Publishing, 1995), 87.

13. Jerome Shestack, Raymond Nasher, and Sidney Liskofsky, "Human Rights and International Organizations: Objectives, Methodology and Program of AJC's Committee on International Organizations," April 17, 1972, 1, FAD-IO [Foreign Affairs Department—International Organizations], BL.

14. Liskofsky, memo on "Draft Conventions on the Elimination and Reduction of Future Statelessness," February 12, 1959, in Human Rights Conventions Refugees, 51-66, RAD-TO, BL.

15. See, for example, the following reports of the Commission on Human Rights on the drafting of the International Covenant on Civil and Political Rights, 1947: 6th Session, Supplement 1; 7th Session, Supplement 2; 9th Session; Supplement 10; 13th Session, Supplement 9; 14th Session, Supplement 4; 16th Session, Supplement 8; and 18th Session, Supplement 7. Also see Consultative Council of Jewish Organizations,

Reports, 1947–1952 and Memoranda, Statements, Releases, etc., 1947–1953, BL. On the contributions of the WJC and the ICJW to the Convention on the Rights of the Child, see Michael Longford, "NGOs and the Rights of the Child," in *The Conscience of the World: The Influence of Non-Governmental Organizations in the UN System*, ed. Peter Willetts (Washington, D.C.: Brookings Institution, 1996), 214–240 and E/CN.4/1982/WG.1/WP.1. On the Declaration on the Elimination of All Forms of Intolerance or Discrimination Based on Religion or Belief (adopted 1981), see Liskofsky, "The Santa Clara University and UNESCO (Bangkok) Conferences on Religious Intolerance, December, 1979 (Draft)," in FAD-IO, 1979, "Religious Freedom, International Protection of." On the WJC's contributions to the UDHR and the Civil and Political Rights Covenant, see A. L. Easterman and F. R. Bienenfeld, memorandum, "To All Members of the European Executive," WJC European Secretariat, December 16, 1948, WJC Collection, MS361/B84/7, AJA; WJC, "Many WJC Proposals Adopted by Committees of UN Human Rights Commission in Session at Geneva," December 15, 1947, WJC Collection, MS361/B137/6, AJA; Provisional Summary Record of the Two Hundred and Thirty-first Meeting, ECOSOC, 7th Session, May 8, 1951, WJC Collection, MS361/B137/6, AJA; WJC, "Memorandum on the Draft First International Covenant on Human Rights Submitted by the World Jewish Congress to the Third Committee of the U.N. General Assembly," October 20, 1950, WJC Collection, MS361/B141/33, AJA; WJC, "Observations Concerning the Draft First International Covenant on Human Rights, Submitted to the Eleventh Session of the Economic and Social Council of the United Nations," n.d., WJC Collection, MS361/141/33, AJA; "Memorandum Submitted to the Thirteenth Session of the Commission on Human Rights," February 12, 1957, WJC Collection, MS361/B116/9, AJA. On the treaty on statelessness, see WJC, United Nations General Assembly, International Law Commission, reports, 1948–1957, WJC Collection, MS361/B106/5, AJA. The Coordinating Board of Jewish Organizations' contributions were also extensive. See CBJO Collection: CBJO submission, E/CN/NGO/26, April 23, 1951, AJA; G. Warburg, "Final Report on UN Conference of Plenipotentiaries on the Status of Refugees and Stateless Persons," Geneva, August 1951, MS76/1/1, AJA; G. Warburg to A. Brotman, letter, July 21, 1951, MS76/1/1, AJA. On slavery, status of women, freedom of information, UDHR, the covenants, the subcommission, and genocide, see Bernard Bernstein, "Report of Activities of the Coordinating Board of Jewish Organizations," January 1, 1949 to June 20, 1950, CBJO Collection, MS 76/1/1, AJA; CBJO memorandum, "Protection of Human Rights Pending Adoption of the Covenant," May 16, 1949, CBJO Collection, MS76/1/1, AJA.

16. The first such effort may have been the creation of an AJC Film Division (under CCJO auspices) to assist UNESCO in the production of films dealing with "intergroup education." See Robert Disraeli to Moses Moskowitz, memorandum, September 25, 1951, fourth regular meeting of the Governing Board, Paris, November 4, 1951, appendix E, CCJO Reports, 1947, BL. Also see CCJO, "Report on Methods and Techniques Used to Combat Discrimination and Prejudice," January 18, 1955, in Memoranda, Statements, Releases, etc., 1955, BL; B'nai B'rith International, text of interview between Frank Goldman, president of B'nai Brith, and Clark M. Eichelberger,

director of the American Association for the United Nations on "The UN Is My Beat," National Broadcasting Company, April 15, 1950, CBJO Collection, MS76/2/1, AJA.

17. CBJO, "Report of Activities," 41. An example of coordination is "Consultation of London Representatives of Non-governmental Organizations Having Consultative Status at the Economic and Social Council," July 27, 1950, CBJO Collection, MS76/1/6, AJA, which lists the participant NGOs as CBJO, CCJO, WJC, and Agudas Israel.

18. CBJO, "Note Supplementary to the Report on the Work of the Foreign Affairs Committee," n.d., 1, CBJO Collection, MS76/16, AJA.

19. See, for example, Jules Braunschvig, vice president of Alliance Israélite Universelle; Joseph Proskauer, president of AJC; Leonard Stein, president of the Anglo-Jewish Association; Moses Moskowitz, secretary of CCJO; and Norman Bentwich, professor of international relations, Hebrew University, "Proposals for the Consideration of the Commission on Human Rights Relative to the Suggestions of the Drafting Committee for Articles of an International Declaration on Human Rights and the Draft Articles on Human Rights and Fundamental Freedoms to Be Considered for Inclusion in a Convention," November 21, 1947, BL.

20. CBJO, "Coordination of Jewish Organizations with Consultative Status in the United Nations," n.d., CBJO Collection, MS76/1/6, AJA; Phil Baum to Dr. Joachim Prinz, letter, February 12, 1969, Joachim Prinz Papers, MS673/2/1, AJA.

21. CBJO, "Coordination," 43.

22. CBJO, "Coordination."

23. Qtd. in Korey, *NGOs*, 384.

24. Liskofsky, "Draft Proposal for International Covenant on Civil and Political Rights: A Commentary," CCPR, 1977, Box 19, FAD-IO, BL; Schedule of Actual and Projected Expenses for Approved Projects, 1979–1981, Jacob Blaustein Institute, Administrative Council, FAD-IO 1980, BL; Louis Henkin, ed., *The International Bill of Rights: The Covenant on Civil and Political Rights* (New York: Columbia University Press, 1981).

25. One can get an idea of the extent of the Ad Hoc Committee's commitment from the names of its files during its first twelve years of work: Human Rights Conventions, Senate Foreign Relations Sub-Committee Hearings, FAD-I0, 1957–1967, BL; Human Rights and Genocide Treaties, Ad Hoc Committee, FAD-I0, 1960–1970, BL; Human Rights Conventions, Genocide, Slavery, Women, Forced Labor, FAD-IO, 1963–1966, BL; Human Rights Conventions, Country Ratifications and Senate Support for US Ratification, FAD-IO, 1963–1967, BL; Human Rights Conventions—Slavery, Women, Senate Foreign Relations Committee, FAD-I0, 1967, BL; Efforts on Genocide Ratification in US, 1968–1972, FAD-IO, 1968–1972, BL; Genocide Convention—Correspondence with Sen. Claiborne Pell, FAD-IO, 1969, BL.

26. Letter to the chair of the Commission on Human Rights (unsigned), March 2, 1954, WUPJ Collection, MS16/D32/5, AJA.

27. CBJO submission on asylum, February 26, 1960 in UN secretary-general, "Declaration of the Right of Asylum: Comments of Non-Governmental Organizations," UN Doc. E/CN.4/794/Add.2; A. L. Easterman and F. R. Bienenfeld, memorandum, "To All Members of the European Executive," WJC European Secretariat,

December 16, 1948, WJC Collection, MS361/B84/7, AJA; WJC, "Many WJC Proposals Adopted by Committees of UN Human Rights Commission in Session at Geneva," December 15, 1947, WJC Collection, MS361/B137/6, AJA; Provisional Summary Record of the Two Hundred and Thirty-first Meeting, ECOSOC, 7th Session, May 8, 1951, WJC Collection, MS361/B137/6, AJA; WJC, United Nations General Assembly, International Law Commission, reports, 1948–1957, WJC Collection, MS361/B106/5, AJA; WJC, "Memorandum on the Draft First International Covenant on Human Rights Submitted by the World Jewish Congress to the Third Committee of the U.N. General Assembly," October 20, 1950, WJC Collection, MS361/B141/33, AJA; WJC, "Observations Concerning the Draft First International Covenant on Human Rights, Submitted to the Eleventh Session of the Economic and Social Council of the United Nations" n.d., WJC Collection, MS361/141/33, AJA; "Memorandum Submitted to the Thirteenth Session of the Commission on Human rights," February 12, 1957, WJC Collection, MS361/B116/9, AJA.

28. See, for example, Agudas Israel World Organization, oral submission to the Commission on Human Rights, UN Doc. E/CN.4/Sub.1/SR.102.

29. WUPJ, statement from the World Union for Progressive Judaism to the Governments of the United Nations, 1945, WUPJ Collection, MS16/D32/5, AJA.

30. Bruno Woyda, "Notes on a Convention on Human Rights," 1952, 2, WUPJ Collection, MS16/D32/5, AJA; WUPJ, "Study of Discrimination in the Matter of Religious Rights and Practices," July 1957, Conference Room Paper No. 19, September 10, 1958, WUPJ Collection, MS16/D32/7, AJA.

31. See the following documents from Box 20, FAD-IO, BL: "Preparation of a World Wide Legal Instrument to Protect Religious Freedom" (Santa Clara Law School), 79; Nives Fox to Sidney Liskofsky, letter, October 11, 1977; Dinah Shelton to Liskofsky, letter, May 10, 1978; Liskofsky to Shelton, letter, October 8, 1979; Shelton to Liskofsky, letter, October 17, 1979; Liskofsky to Shelton, letter, October 19, 1979. Also see ICJW, program, 10th Triennial Convention, April 25–May 1, 1975, Melbourne, Australia, 110, BL.

32. Michael Galchinsky, "Gaer, Felice D.," *Encyclopedia Judaica*, v. 7, 2nd ed. (Detroit, Mich.: Thomson Gale, 2006), 333.

33. Moses Moskowitz, *The Politics and Dynamics of Human Rights* (Dobbs Ferry, N.Y.: Oceana Publications, 1968), 170; also see Francesco Capotorti, *Study on the Rights of Persons Belonging to Ethnic, Religious, and Linguistic Minorities* (New York: United Nations, 1991), written June 1977.

34. Liskofsky to Morris Abram, letter, October 29, 1964, Human Rights Conventions, Racial Discrimination, Correspondence, FAD-IO, 1964–1967, BL.

35. WJC, "Additional Memorandum Submitted to the U.N. Economic and Social Council by the World Jewish Congress on the Situation of the Jewish Population in Certain Moslem and Arab Countries," February 25, 1948, WJC Collection, MS361/B137/4, AJA; WJC, "Memorandum concerning the Situation of Jews in Moslem Lands," WJC Collection, MS361/B143/2, AJA; A. L. Easterman, WJC political secretary, to Charles Malik, president of ECOSOC, letter, August 20, 1948, WJC Collection, MS361/137/4, AJA; Robert S. Marcus, WJC political director, to Trygve Lie, UN secretary-general, letter, November 8, 1949, WJC Collection,

MS361/137/4, AJA; "Jews in Arab Countries," resolutions adopted by the Second Plenary Assembly of the WJC, June 27–July 6, 1948, WJC Collection, MS361/C74/8, AJA; WJC, *The Treatment of Jews in Egypt and Iraq* (New York: Institute for Jewish Affairs, 1948), MS/361/C74/8, AJA; Bernard Bernstein, "Report of Activities of the Coordinating Board of Jewish Organizations," January 1, 1949 to June 20, 1950, 40, Annex 14, CBJO Collection, MS76/1/6, AJA; "American Jewish Committee Asks U.S. Government on Iraq's Treatment of Jews," *JTA Newsletter*, May 9, 1951, CBJO Collection, MS76/2/4, AJA; CBJO, "Background," n.d., CBJO Collection, MS76/2/4, AJA.

36. CBJO, "Background."

37. I. Schwartzbart to A. B. David, letter, August 3, 1948, WJC Collection, MS361/H191/5, AJA; WJC Collection MS361/H71/12, 13, AJA; Max Melamet, memorandum, "re: The Jewish Situation in Chile," September 28, 1970, WJC Collection, MS361/H86/8, AJA; Max Melamet, memorandum, "Report on Chile," April 5, 1971, WJC Collection, MS361/H86/8, AJA; minutes from the Collectividad Israelita de Chile on Arab propaganda, WJC Collection, MS361/H84/3, AJA; WJC Collection, MS361/H84/3, AJA; Peter E. Tarlow, head rabbi Círculo Israelita synagogue, Report, June 1981, WUPJ Collection, MS16/G1/8, AJA; David Harris, "Indochinese Refugees—'We Are All Boat People,'" *Forward*, April 22, 1988, in Harris, *In the Trenches: Selected Speeches and Writings of an American Jewish Activist, 1979–1999* (New York: Ktav Publishing House, 2000), 436; Richard Maas to AJC members, December 27, 1979, www.ajcarchives.org/AJC_DATA/Files/735.PDF; Rabbi Marc H. Tanenbaum, partial transcript of testimony before the House of Representatives Subcommittee on Asian and Pacific Affairs of the Foreign Affairs Committee, December 18, 1979, ajcarchives.org/ajcarchive/DigitalArchive.aspx.

38. CBJO, "July Meeting—Human Rights Agenda," July 1950, n.p., CBJO Collection, MS76/1/6, AJA.

39. Felice D. Gaer, "And Never the Twain Shall Meet? The Struggle to Establish Women's Rights as International Human Rights," in *The International Human Rights of Women: Instruments of Change*, ed. Carol Elizabeth Lockwood, Daniel Barstow Magraw, Margaret Faith Spring, and S. I. Strong (Washington, D.C.: ABA Section of International Law and Practice, 1998), 1–89.

40. Michael Longford, "NGOs and the Rights of the Child," in "*The Conscience of the World": The Influence of Non-Governmental Organizations in the UN System*, ed. Peter Willetts (Washington, D.C.: Brookings Institution, 1996), 214–240; UN Doc. E/CN.4/1982/WG.1/WP.1; WUPJ, response to United Nations Department of Public Information, "Questionnaire for Non-Governmental Organizations," August 1979, WUPJ Collection, MS12/G5/24, AJA; Norma Levitt to constituents of the WUPJ, letter, May 16, 1977, WUPJ Collection, MS16/G5/24, AJA; Norma Levitt, "Rainbow of Understanding: The Asian Mission to China and Indonesia of the United States Committee for UNICEF," New York, 1980, WUPJ Collection, MS16/G7/18, AJA.

41. Nelly Las, *Jewish Women in a Changing World: A History of the International Council of Jewish Women (ICJW), 1899–1995*, trans. Stephanie Nakache (Jerusalem: A. Harman Institute of Contemporary Jewry, 1996).

42. Maurice L. Perlzweig to the WJC executive, memorandum, September 11, 1950 and F. R. Bienenfeld to Robert S. Marcus, letter, July 25, 1950, WJC Collection, MS361/B141/29 and MS361/B141/27, AJA; Perlzweig, oral submission to the ECOSOC Committee on Non-Governmental Organizations, February 9, 1950, E/C.2 /SR.69/Add.1; Bienenfeld, oral submission to the Commission on Human Rights, May 16, 1951, E/CN.4/SR.245; Perlzweig, oral submission to the Commission on Human Rights, April 14, 1952, E/CN.4/SR.253; WUPJ, "Notes on a Convention," 3; Bruno Woyda, WUPJ, form letter, May 15, 1953, WUPJ Collection, MS16/D32/5, AJA; Woyda, "A Challenge to Implement Our Ideas," in *The Work of the World Union for Progressive Judaism in Connection with the United Nations* (London: WUPJ, 1953), 8–9; Bernard Bernstein, "Report of Activities," Annex 2 and 3.

43. WJC, "Memorandum on the Draft First International Covenant on Human Rights submitted by the World Jewish Congress to the Third Committee of the U.N. General Assembly," October 20, 1950, 8, WJC Collection, MS361/B141/33, AJA.

44. See Moses Moskowitz, "Confidential Memorandum," November 3, 1950. The resolution to consider a UN attorney general was supported by France, India, Guatemala, Australia, Sweden, Denmark, Ethopia, and Chile. The United States agreed to it as a special protocol, but not as part of the covenant. The Uruguay proposal influenced by Moskowitz is UN Doc. A/C.3/L/741 November 1950.

45. Moses Moskowitz, *Human Rights and World Order* (Dobbs Ferry, N.Y.: Oceana Publications, 1958), forward by René Cassin, esp. 142–144.

46. Sidney Liskofsky, "Notes on Draft Covenants on Human Rights: Final Phases of General Assembly Review," October 10, 1962.

47. Human rights seminar, FAD-I, 1962–1964: preparation, programs, and speeches from "Seminar on the International Protection of Human Rights," May 27, 1963.

48. Felice Gaer, "NGOs and the U.N. High Commissioner for Human Rights," (Atlanta: Carter Center, 1997), 81–96; Gaer, "Reality Check"; Andrew Clapham, "Creating the High Commissioner for Human Rights: The Outside Story," *European Journal of International Law* 5 (1994): 556–568.

49. Gaer, "NGOs and the U.N. High Commissioner."

50. Gaer, "NGOs and the U.N. High Commissioner," 15.

51. On Humphrey's contribution, see Korey, *NGOs*, 58.

52. For a detailed analysis of the debates in the intervening years, see Shestack, Nasher, and Liskofsky, "Human Rights and International Organizations," 28; Adlai Stevenson, ambassador to the US Mission to the UN, to Blaustein, letter, February 4, 1964; Ralph J. Bunche to Blaustein, letter, January 28, 1964; Andrew Clapham, "Creating the High Commissioner," 569–571.

53. UN Doc. E/CN.4/NGO/136, March 18, 1966; UN Doc. E/CN.4/NGO/140, May 5, 1966.

54. The public procedure is called the "1235 procedure," based on ECOSOC Res. 1235 (XLII) of June 6, 1967; the secret procedure is called the "1503 procedure," based on ECOSOC Res. 1503 (XLVIII) of May 27, 1970.

55. Interview with Felice Gaer, American Jewish Committee Building, New York, July 9, 2002.

56. Gaer, "NGOs and the U.N. High Commissioner," 81.

57. Schoenberg, "Enhancing and Advancing Human Rights"; interview with Felice D. Gaer, Spring 2002; Korey, *NGOs* 299.

58. Korey, *NGOs*, 81–82.

59. Interview with Dr. Harris Schoenberg, UN Plaza Hotel, New York, July 10, 2002.

60. Gaer, "NGOs and the U.N. High Commissioner," 85.

61. Gaer, "NGOs and the U.N. High Commissioner, 85–93.

62. Human Rights Conventions, Racial Discrimination, Correspondence, FAD-IO, 64–67, BL.

63. Natan Lerner, *The U.N. Convention on the Elimination of all Forms of Racial Discrimination* (Rockville, Md.: Sijthofff and Noordhoff, 1980), 214.

64. Marcus R. Einfeld, "Africa and the Jews," December 1973, WJC Collection, MS361/B30/1, AJA.

65. Norma U. Levitt to Dr. Arthur Sackler, letter, April 29, 1975, WUPJ Collection, MS16/G3/12, AJA.

66. Norma U. Levitt, "Forum '85: A Festival and a Mixed Adventure," July 1985, WUPJ Collection, MS16/G7/18, AJA, 3; Felice D. Gaer, "And Never the Twain Shall Meet?"; Galchinsky, "Gaer, Felice D.," *Encyclopedia Judaica*, 333.

67. Las, *Jewish Women*, 103.

68. Qtd. in Las, *Jewish Women*, 104.

69. Las, *Jewish Women*, 107.

70. Levitt, "Forum '85," 4.

71. Permanent Mission of Israel to the United Nations, "Israel and the UN—An Uneasy Relationship," www.israel-un.org/Israelun/isrun/isrun2.htm.

72. For the history of the charge and its repeal, see Harris O. Schoenberg, *The World Conference against Racism: The Adoption and Repeal of the Z=R Resolution and the Implication for UN Reform*, Monograph 18 (Wayne, N.J.: Center for UN Reform Education, 2001).

73. For a Palestinian response, see Shawqui Issa, "Palestinian and Arab Response to Mary Robinson, Durban, South Africa, 5 September 2001," at www.hrea.org/lists/wcar/markup/msg00039.html.l

74. Amnesty International, *Broken Lives—A Year of Intifada: Israel/Occupied Territories/Palestinian Authority* (London: AI Publications, 2001). For the relevant law on collective punishment, see UDHR Art. 13, CCPR Art. 12, and Geneva Convention IV Art. 33.

75. Arab Lawyers Union, "That is the fact. . . . Racism of Zionism and 'Israel'," pamphlet distributed at the World Congress against Racism (WCAR), August 2001, WCAR file, BL.

76. Statement of the Jewish Caucus on the NGO Process and Concluding Document, Durban, South Africa, September 1, 2001, World Conference against Racism, WCAR file, BL.

77. Statement of Reservation by the Canadian Delegation to the World Conference against Racism, Racial Discrimination, Xenophobia and Related Intolerance (WCAR), Durban, South Africa, September 8, 2001, WCAR file, BL.

78. See Lerner, *The U.N. Convention*, 214.

79. ICJW, summary of the tenth Triennial Convention, April 25–May 1, 1975, Melbourne, Australia, BL; ICJW, summary of the fourteenth Triennial Convention, May 1987, BL. Also see Nelly Las, *Jewish Women,* 103–108.

80. ICJW, summary of the tenth Triennial Convention, 1975; ICJW, summary of the fourteenth Triennial Convention, 1987. Also see Las, *Jewish Women,* 103–108.

CHAPTER 2. FREEING SOVIET JEWS—AND AFTER

1. These questions are being asked today by policymakers, think tanks, and political scientists. See Michael Walzer et al., ed., *The Jewish Political Tradition*, vol. 1 (New Haven, Conn.: Yale University Press, 2000); "The Jewish People 2004: Between Thriving and Decline," the first annual assessment by the Jewish People Policy Planning Institute (JPPPI), founded in 2002 by the Jewish Agency, based in Jerusalem, and chaired by former Clinton Middle East negotiator Dennis Ross; and Scott Lasensky, "A System of Its Own? Mapping Jewish Foreign Policy and World Politics," paper given at the Association of Israel Studies Annual Meeting, May 2005.

2. For year-by-year emigration numbers, see Fred A. Lazin, *The Struggle for Soviet Jewry in American Politics: Israel versus the American Jewish Establishment* (Lanham, Md.: Lexington Books, 2005), "Table 3. Soviet Jewish Emigration, 1954–1994," 309. For emigration to Israel, see Sergio DellaPergola, "Demography in Israel at the Dawn of the Twenty-first Century," in *Jews in Israel: Contemporary Social and Cultural Patterns*, ed. Uzi Rebhun and Chaim I. Waxman (Hanover, N.H.: University Press of New England, 2004), 24.

3. Stephen J. Roth, "The Right to Jewish Culture in the Soviet Union," in *Jewish Culture and Identity in the Soviet Union*, ed. Yaacov Ro'i and Avi Becker (New York: New York University Press, 1991), 355–377.

4. Louis Henkin, *World Politics and the Jewish Condition: Essays Prepared for a Task Force on the World of the 1970s of the American Jewish Committee* (New York: Quadrangle Books, 1972), 33–34.

5. For the use of these loopholes, see International Council of the World Conference on Soviet Jewry in cooperation with the Jewish communities concerned, *The Position of Soviet Jewry 1983–1986: Report on the Implementation of the Helsinki Final Act since the Madrid Follow-Up Conference* (London: Institute of Jewish Affairs, 1986), 19, 23, 27.

6. For concurring assessments, see Sidney Liskofsky, "Human Rights in the Twenty-third United Nations General Assembly," *Bulletin of the International League for the Rights of Man* (Fall 1968), 2; Natan Lerner, *The U.N. Convention on the Elimination of All Forms of Racial Discrimination* (Rockville, Md.: Sijthofff and Noordhoff, 1980), 2–73; Jonathan Frankel, "The Soviet Regime and Anti-Zionism: An Analysis," in Ro'i and Becker, *Jewish Culture and Identity*, 310–354.

7. For a description of the attack on the credentials of Jewish NGOs with consultative status, see William Korey, *NGOs and the Universal Declaration of Human*

Rights: "A Curious Grapevine" (New York: St. Martin's Press, 1988), 78–94; and Sidney Liskofsky, "International Protection of Human Rights," in Henkin, *World Politics and the Jewish Condition*, chap. 8.

8. Petrus Buwalda, *They Did Not Dwell Alone: Jewish Emigration from the Soviet Union, 1967–1990* (Baltimore, Md.: Johns Hopkins University Press, 1997), 64; Vera Yedidya, "The Struggle for the Study of Hebrew," in Ro'i and Becker, *Jewish Culture and Identity,* 154.

9. On the UN specialized agencies, see Yoram Dinstein, "Soviet Jewry and International Human Rights," in *Essays on Human Rights: Contemporary Issues and Jewish Perspectives*, ed. David Sidorsky, with Sidney Liskofsky and Jerome Shestack (Philadelphia: Jewish Publication Society of America, 1979), 126–143.

10. On Soviet nationalities policy, see Dinstein, "Soviet Jewry," 131–132; Benjamin Pinkus, "Soviet Government Policy toward the Extraterritorial National Minorities: Comparison between the Jews and the Germans," in Ro'i and Becker, *Jewish Culture and Identity*, 290–309. On education taxes, see Michael Meerson-Aksenov, "The Influence of the Jewish Exodus on the Democratization of Soviet Society," in Sidorsky, *Essays on Human Rights*, 148.

11. Joshua Rubenstein, *Soviet Dissidents: Their Struggle for Human Rights*, revised ed. (Boston: Beacon Press, 1985), 316.

12. Pinkus, "Soviet Government Policy," 290–309.

13. Zvi Gitelman, "The Evolution of Jewish Culture and Identity in the Soviet Union," in Ro'i and Becker, *Jewish Culture and Identity,* 10–14.

14. Buwalda, *They Did Not Dwell Alone,* 135.

15. International Council of the World Conference on Soviet Jewry, *The Position of Soviet Jewry*, 62–63.

16. Rubenstein, *Soviet Dissidents*, 89–90.

17. Rubenstein, *Soviet Dissidents*, 183.

18. In some cases, as with Trofim Kichko's crude tract, *Judaism without Embellishment*, published by the Ukrainian Academy of Sciences in 1964, propagandists went too far even for Soviet officials. In the spirit of the reaction against the excesses of Stalinism, Khrushchev ordered Kichko's book removed from the stores. See Richard N. Gardner, *In Pursuit of World Order* (New York: Praeger, 1964), 257–259.

19. Rubenstein, *Soviet Dissidents*, 19.

20. Sharansky, *Fear No Evil*, 65.

21. Sharansky, *Fear No Evil*, xxiii.

22. Sharansky, *Fear No Evil*, 24.

23. "Babi Yar" was still a touchy subject under Brezhnev. See Colin Shindler, *Exit Visa: Détente, Human Rights, and the Jewish Emigration Movement in the USSR* (London: Bachman and Turner, 1978), 46–53.

24. Rubenstein, *Soviet Dissidents*, 31.

25. Qtd. in Rubenstein, *Soviet Dissidents*, 165, 181; Valery Chalidze, *The Soviet Human Rights Movement: A Memoir* (New York: AJC, 1984); and "Human Rights Movement USSR FAD-I, 1972," BL.

26. Paul Goldberg, *The Final Act: The Dramatic, Revealing Story of the Moscow Helsinki Watch Group* (New York: William Morrow and Company, 1988), 110–113.

27. Aleksandr Voronel, "The Subject and Object in a Study of the National Character," in *Jewishness Rediscovered: Jewish Identity in the Soviet Union*, ed. Aleksandr Voronel and Viktor Yakhot, pref. Irving Louis Horowitz, ed. Harris O. Schoenberg (Washington, D.C.: US Anti-Defamation League of B'nai B'rith, 1974), 15–32.

28. Voronel, "Subject and Object," 29.

29. Shindler, *Exit Visa*, 184.

30. Rubenstein, *Soviet Dissidents*, 234.

31. Rubenstein, *Soviet Dissidents*, 183; Shindler, *Exit Visa*, 68, 240–241.

32. Shindler, *Exit Visa,* 6.

33. Shindler, *Exit Visa* 3.

34. On the important place of the hijacker trial in the creation of the emigration movement, see Shindler, *Exit Visa*, 8

35. Qtd. in Goldberg, *Final Act*, 37.

36. Qtd. in Goldberg, *Final Act*, 245.

37. Yedidya, "Struggle," 136–167.

38. Yaacov Ro'i, "Nehama Lifshitz: Symbol of the Jewish National Awakening," in Ro'i and Becker, *Jewish Culture and Identity*, 168–190.

39. Ro'i, *Jewish Culture and Identity*, 128. See also Sharansky, *Fear No Evil*, preface; Michael Galchinsky, interview of Lev Goradetsky, September 12, 2005; Rubenstein, *Soviet Dissidents*, chap. 5; Union of Councils for Soviet Jews, *UCSJ Quarterly Report* (Winter 1986); Stephani Hoffman, "Jewish Samizdat and the Rise of Jewish National Consciousness," in Ro'i and Becker, *Jewish Culture and Identity*; Yossi Goldstein, "The Jewish National Movement in the Soviet Union: A Profile," in Ro'i and Becker, *Jewish Culture and Identity*, 27–41; Yaacov Ro'i, "The Role of the Synagogue and Religion in the Jewish National Consciousness," in Ro'i and Becker, *Jewish Culture and Identity*, 112–135; Yedidya, "Struggle," 136–167.

40. Hoffman, "Jewish Samizdat," 88–111.

41. Rubenstein, *Soviet Dissidents*, 162.

42. Hoffman, "Jewish Samizdat," 255–261.

43. See Hoffman, "Jewish Samizdat."

44. Lazin, *Struggle for Soviet Jewry*, 139.

45. Eliahu Essas, "The Moscow Symposium: Ten Years Later," in Ro'i and Becker, *Jewish Culture and Identity*, 262–265; and Hoffman, "Jewish Samizdat," 109–111.

46. Subcommittee on International Organizations of the Committee on International Relations, House of Representatives, *Anti-Semitism and Reprisals against Jewish Emigration in the Soviet Union*, 94th Cong., 2nd sess. (Washington, D.C.: GPO, 1976). Also see the reflections of David Harris, executive director of the American Jewish Committee, in David Harris, *In the Trenches: Selected Speeches and Writings of an American Jewish Activist, 1979–1999* (New York: Ktav Publishing House, 2000), 17.

47. Cf. House of Representatives, Committee on Foreign affairs, *Religious Persecution in the Soviet Union, Part I—Soviet Jewry: Hearing before the Subcommittees on Europe and the Middle East and on Human Rights and International Organizations*, 99th Cong., 2nd sess., Sept. 11, 1985 (Washington, D.C.: GPO, 1985) and *Religious Persecution in the Soviet Union, Part II*, July 30, 1986 (Washington, D.C.: GPO, 1986).

Part I, which is by far the longer, deals exclusively with Soviet Jewry, with statements by the National Conference on Soviet Jewry (NCSJ), Union of Councils for Soviet Jews (UCSJ), the Coalition to Free Soviet Jews, the International Council of the World Conference on Soviet Jewry (WCJ), and a number of other Jewish and non-Jewish organizations. Part II deals with Ukrainian and Lithuanian Catholics, Evangelical Baptists, Evangelical Lutherans, Seventh-Day Adventists, Reform Pentecostals, Jehovah's Witnesses, Muslims, Russian Orthodox, and Hare Krishnas.

48. United States Commission on Security and Cooperation in Europe, *Implementation of the Helsinki Accords: Hearing before the Commission on Security and Cooperation in Europe*, 101st Cong., 2nd sess., East-West Trade and the Helsinki Process June 13, 1990 CSCE 101-2-18 (Washington, D.C.: GPO, 1990), 5–6.

49. Buwalda, *They Did Not Dwell Alone*, 57.

50. See US Mission press release, "Remarks Delivered by U.S. Representative Mrs. Rita E. Hauser During Discussion of Question of Jews in Soviet Union," March 10, 1969.

51. Richard Maas to Arthur J. Goldberg, letter, April 4, 1978.

52. Shindler, *Exit Visa*, 240–241; United States Congress, Commission on Security and Cooperation in Europe, "Activities Report: 98th Congress" (Washington, D.C.: n.d. [circa 1984]).

53. US Congress, CSCE, "Activities Report," 24, 26.

54. Buwalda, *They Did Not Dwell Alone*, 89–112.

55. For Nixon's resistance to tying Jewish emigration to Most Favored Nation status, see Shindler, *Exit Visa*, 41, 60.

56. See, for example, US Commission on International Religious Freedom, *Annual Report of the United States Commission on International Religious Freedom* (Washington, D.C.: May 2002).

57. Testimony by Preeta D. Bansal, chair, United States Commission on International Religious Freedom, Hearing on the Annual Report on International Religious Freedom 2004 and the Designation of Countries of Particular Concern Before the House International Relations Committee of the United States House of Representatives, October 6, 2004.

58. Bansal, testimony before USCIRF; USCIRF press release, "Anti-Semitism: USCIRF Vice Chair Gaer on U.S. Delegation to Berlin OSCE Meeting," April 23, 2004; USCIRF press release, "Anti-Semitism: Commissioner Gaer Addresses OSCE rights meeting," October 15, 2003; USCIRF press release, "Commission Asks Clinton to Raise Religious-Freedom Issues in Meeting with Russian President," October 26, 2003; USCIRF press release, "Russia: Religious Communities, Extremist Movements, and the State," January 31, 2005.

59. Elie Wiesel, *The Jews of Silence* (Philadelphia: Jewish Publication Society, 1967); Liskofsky, "International Protection of Human Rights," 301.

60. Buwalda, *They Did Not Dwell Alone*, 35–36.

61. Extrapolated from Lazin, *Struggle for Soviet Jewry*, "Table 4. Exit, Aliyah, and Dropouts of Soviet/FSU Jews, 1968–1992," 310.

62. Lazin, *Struggle for Soviet Jewry*, chaps. 3–4.

63. Buwalda, *They Did Not Dwell Alone*, 72–88.

64. For negotiations on behalf of political prisoners, see WJC website, http://www.wjc.org.il/wjc/Changes.html. For the goal of using symposia to stimulate "moral concern," see Sidney Liskofsky to Bert Gold, January 29, 1971, "Proposal for a Conference of Experts on the 'Right to Leave,'" BL. For the NGOs' use of UN and regional bodies, see, for example, Natan Lerner, "The World Jewish Congress and Human Rights" (Geneva: WJC, 1978), 16–17; "Council of Europe, 72–79," Box 19, FAD-IO [Foreign Affairs Department–International Organizations], BL; Jerome Shestack to Bert Gold, February 5, 1971, BL. For tying-in with other NGOs, see, for example, Liskofsky to Gold, February 10, 1971, BL.

65. International Council of the World Conference on Soviet Jewry, *Position of Soviet Jewry.*

66. International Council of the World Conference on Soviet Jewry, *Position of Soviet Jewry*.

67. CBJO, *Memorandum on Discrimination in the Matter of the Right of Everyone to Leave Any Country Including His Own and to Return to His Country* (New York: CBJO, 1960).

68. See *American Jewish Yearbook, 1961* (Philadelphia: AJC and JPSA, 1962), 369.

69. Qtd. in Korey, *NGOs*, 66.

70. José D. Ingles, *Study of Discrimination in Respect of the Right of Everyone to Leave Any Country, Including His Own, and to Return to His Country* (New York: United Nations, 1963).

71. The story is well told in Korey, *NGOs*, 48–94.

72. Irwin Cotler, "Jewish NGOs and Religious Human Rights: A Case Study," in *Human Rights in Judaism: Cultural, Religious, and Political Perspectives*, ed. Michael J. Broyde and John Witte, Jr. (Northvale, N.J.: Jason Aronson, 1998), 225.

73. Buwalda, *They Did Not Dwell Alone*, 38.

74. Union of Councils for Soviet Jews, *UCSJ Quarterly Report* (Winter 1986); Goldberg, *Final Acts*, 198, 202. For an extensive account of UCSJ's activities, see Stuart Altshuler, *From Exodus to Freedom: The History of the Soviet Jewry Movement* (Lanham, Md.: Rowman and Littlefield, 2005).

75. Subcommittee on International Organizations of the Committee on International Relations, House of Representatives, *Anti-Semitism and Reprisals against Jewish Emigration in the Soviet Union*, 94th Cong., 2nd sess. (Washington, D.C.: GPO, 1976), 19.

76. Korey, *NGOs*, 192–202.

77. See Lazin, *Struggle for Soviet Jewry*, "Table 10. HIAS Assisted Refugees Resettled in the United States, 1980–2002," 316.

78. Sharansky, *Fear No Evil*, 25; Shindler, *Exit Visa*.

79. Goldberg, *Final Acts*, 253.

80. Much of the lone ranger activity was coordinated with officials from Russian synagogues. See Ro'i, "Role of the Synagogue," 129–135.

81. References in this section are to the following sources. "Meeting of Jewish Organizations Concerning Persecution of Jews Behind the Iron Curtain," January 8, 1953, CBJO Collection, MS76/2/3, AJA; "The Prague Trials Memorandum by the

Ambassador of Israel," n.d., CBJO Collection, MS72/2/3, AJA; American Zionist Council, press release, "U.S. Zionist Groups Issue Joint Condemnation of Soviet Policy," January 14, 1953, CBJO Collection, MS76/2/5, AJA; "Jewry Called to World Parley to Fight Soviet Anti-Semitism," *Herald Tribune*, February 17, 1953, CBJO Collection MS76/2/5, AJA; American Zionist Council, press release, "Gigantic Protest Rally against Soviet Anti-Semitism Calls upon Russia to Release Jews and Pledges Cooperation of World's Jews in Effecting Transfer to Israel," February 17, 1953, CBJO Collection, MS76/2/5, AJA; Sidney Liskofsky to Bert Gold, letter, February 3, 1971, BL; Liskofsky to Gold, letter, January 18, 1971, BL; Liskofsky to Gold, letter, January 29, 1971, BL; Sidney Liskofsky and Karl Vasak, eds., *The Right to Leave and Return: Papers and Recommendations of the International Colloquium Held in Uppsala, Sweden, 19–20 June 1972* (New York: AJC, 1976); Hurst Hannum, *The Right to Leave and Return in International Law and Practice* (Boston: Martinus Nijhoff Publishers, 1987). For other examples of conferences and symposia, see AJC archive box labeled "Human Rights Seminar, FADI, 1962–1964," BL; Sidney Liskofsky, "Report on Israel-Related and Other Issues." BL. Also see US Mission to the United Nations, press release USUN-102 (70), August 3, 1970; letter from Rita E. Hauser, US representative to the UN Commission on Human Rights on July 30, 1970, in reply to a letter from Congressman Richard L. Ottinger, July 28, 1970; US Mission, Geneva, press release, March 10, 1969, "Remarks Delivered by U.S. Representative Mrs. Rita E. Hauser During Discussion Question of Jews in Soviet Union"; Yuri Orlov to Sen. Fascell of the US Commission on Security and Cooperation in Europe, letter, January 7, 1977, qtd. in Goldberg, *Final Act*, 187; Goldberg, *Final Act*, 188–191.

82. Liskofsky to Gold, letter, February 3, 1971, Bert Gold Memos—70–71, FAD-IO, BL. Jewish members of the Ad Hoc Committee included CBJO (William Korey and Harris Schoenberg), WJC (Max Melamet and Roberta Cohen), Agudas Israel (Isaac Lewin), ICJW (Nettie Levy), WIZO (Evelyn Somer), and CCJO (Moses Moskowitz).

83. Goldberg, *Final Act*, 197–198.

84. Avi Becker, "Superpower Relations and Jewish Identity in the Soviet Union," in Ro'i and Becker, *Jewish Culture and Identity*, 445–462.

85. For a detailed account of the "freedom of choice" debate, see Lazin, *Struggle for Soviet Jewry,* chaps. 3–4.

86. Goldberg, *Final Acts*, 271–274.

87. Becker, "Superpower Relations," 447.

88. Natan Lerner, "Religious Human Rights Under the United Nations," in *Religious Human Rights in Global Perspective: Legal Perspectives*, ed. Johan D. van der Vyver and John Witte, Jr. (Cambridge, Mass.: Kluwer Law International, 1996), 79–134; Helsinki Watch Committee, *Glasnost in Jeopardy: Human Rights in the USSR* (New York: Human Rights Watch, 1991); Lawyers Committee on Human Rights, *Human Rights and Legal Reform in the Russian Federation* (New York: Lawyers Committee for Human Rights, 1993); Stephen J. Roth, "The Right to Jewish Culture in the Soviet Union," in Ro'i and Becker, *Jewish Culture and Identity*, 355–377. CSCE documents, including the 1975 Final Act of the Helsinki Conference on Security and Cooperation

in Europe (Principle VII), the Concluding Documents of the Vienna Meeting (1989) and Copenhagen Meeting (1990), and the Paris Charter for a New Europe (1990) are in Council of Europe, *Human Rights in International Law: Basic Texts* (Strasbourg, 1991).

89. Lawyers Committee on Human Rights, *Human Rights and Legal Reform*, 8.

90. For the declaration, see UNGA res. 36/55 (1981). Principles 16 and 17 of the Final Document of the Helsinki follow-up conference in Vienna of 1989 provide a greater number of religious rights than the parallel UN Declaration on the Elimination of All Forms of Intolerance and Discrimination Based on Religion or Belief of November 25, 1981. For the Vienna Concluding Document, see OSCE Human Dimension Commitments vol. 2 (Warsaw: OSCE Office for Democratic Institutions and Human Rights, 2005), 49–50. Also see Document of the Copenhagen Meeting of the Conference on the Human Dimension of the CSCE, 1990 in *Basic Documents on Human Rights*, 3rd ed., ed. Ian Brownlie (Oxford: Oxford University Press, 1992), 454–473, especially sections 9.4, 9.5, and 32–40.

91. Lawyers Committee on Human Rights, *Human Rights and Legal Reform*, 78.

92. For a comparison of the environments in post-Soviet Russia and Ukraine, see Yohanan Petrovsky-Shtern, "The Revival of Academic Studies of Judaica in Independent Ukraine," in *Jewish Life after the USSR*, ed. Zvi Gitelman, with Musya Glants and Marshall I. Goldman (Bloomington: Indiana University Press, 2003), 152–172.

93. Mark Tolts, "Demography of the Jews in the Former Soviet Union," in Gitelman, Glants, and Goldman, *Jewish Life after the USSR*, 173–206, claims that official governmental anti-Semitism in Russia was "replaced" by grassroots anti-Semitic activities.

94. United States Commission on Security and Cooperation in Europe, *Implementation of the Helsinki Accords*, 6.

95. For a similar shift in emphasis to some of the 168 ethnic groups in Russia other than Jews in the 1990–1991 period, see Helsinki Watch Committee, *Glasnost in Jeopardy: Human Rights in the USSR* (New York: Human Rights Watch, 1991), 3.

96. See WJC, *Restitution of Jewish Property in Central and Eastern Europe* (Jerusalem: Institute of World Jewish Congress, 1994).

97. WJC, *Restitution of Jewish Property*, 2.

98. Laurence Weinbaum, "Righting an Historic Wrong: Restitution of Jewish Property in Central and East Europe," (Jerusalem: WJC, 1995); Cotler, "Jewish NGOs," 242–244; WJC website,http://www.wjc.org.il/wjc/Changes/html.

99. Weinbaum, "Righting an Historic Wrong," 38.

100. Ro'i and Becker, *Jewish Culture and Identity*.

101. Ro'i and Becker, *Jewish Culture and Identity*, 459.

102. National Conference on Soviet Jewry, "National Meeting on Revitalization of Jewish Life in the Soviet Union," October 3, 1989, WUPJ Collection, MS16/G15/37, AJA.

103. "Exodus: Reform Synagogues of Great Britain Soviet Jewry Campaign, Report of Trip to USSR," November 6–13, 1989 and Rabbi Robert F. Shafritz, "A Panorama of Soviet Jewish Life: With Special Emphasis on the Central Asian Cities of Dushanbe, Samarkand and Tashkent, a Report on a Fact-finding Mission to the USSR," April 11, 1989, WUPJ Collection, MS16/G15/37, AJA; also see, in general,

WUPJ Collection, MS16/G14/12-13, AJA; Andrea D. Freedman to Rabbi Richard Hirsch, letter, October 26, 1992, WUPJ Collection, MS16/I4/45, AJA; Rabbi Joel Oseran to Rabbi Cliff Kulwin, memorandum, August 9, 1992, WUPJ Collection, MS16/I4/45, AJA; WUPJ, "Project Proposals for Implementation in the Former Soviet Union," WUPJ Collection, MS16/I4/45, AJA; "Project Budget," and "Project Summary," 1992, WUPJ Collection, MS16/I4/45, AJA; WUPJ, "Summary of Activities in the Former Soviet Union," October 1994, WUPJ Collection, MS16/I8/19, AJA; "WUPJ Operations in Former Soviet Union, January 1, 1994–December 31, 1994," WUPJ Collection, MS16/I6/38, AJA; Bar/Bat Mitvah Matching Program, WUPJ Collection, MS16/I6/37, AJA; Caryn Aviv and David Schneer, *New Jews: The End of the Jewish Diaspora* (New York: New York University Press, 2005), 37.

104. Zvi Gitelman, "Evolution of Jewish Culture and Identity," 21.

105. Sarai Brachman Shoup, "From Leadership to Community: Laying the Foundation for Jewish Community in Russia," in Gitelman, *Jewish Life after the USSR*, 127–140.

106. Aviv and Schneer, *New Jews*, 48; Judith Baskin, "Journal of Professional Proceedings, Jewish Studies Delegation to Russia, September 9–18, 2005" [unpublished].

107. Albert D. Chernin, "Letter from Russia," 1992, WUPJ Collection, MS16/I4/45, AJA.

108. Sarai Brachman Shoup, "From Leadership to Community," 129–130; and Petrovsky-Shtern, "Revival of Academic Studies." Also see Baskin, "Journal of Professional Proceedings."

109. See Baskin, "Journal of Professional Proceedings."

110. Jack Donnelly, *Universal Human Rights in Theory and Practice*, 2nd ed. (Ithaca, N.Y.: Cornell University Press, 2003), 219.

111. Robert J. Brym, "Russian Anti-Semitism, 1996–2000," in Gitelman, *Jewish Life after the USSR*, 99–113; Helsinki Watch Committee, *Glasnost in Jeopardy*, 57–61.

112. Tolts, "Demography of the Jews," 197–198.

113. Zvi Gitelman, "Thinking about Being Jewish in Russia and Ukraine," in Gitelman, *Jewish Life after the USSR*, 59.

114. Union of Councils for Jews in the Former Soviet Union, "Public Campaign to Combat Racism, Xenophobia, Antisemitism and Ethnic Discrimination in the Multi-National Russian Federation," www.fsumonitor.com/EC/aboutproject.shtml.

CHAPTER 3. JEWISH RESPONSES TO NON-JEWISH GENOCIDES

1. Qtd. in William Korey, *NGOs and the Universal Declaration of Human Rights: "A Curious Grapevine"* (New York: St. Martin's Press, 1998), 523.

2. Hyman Bookbinder, *Off the Wall: Memoirs of a Political Junkie* (Washington, D.C.: Seven Locks Press, 1991), 132.

3. American Jewish World Service, "Disaster Response," www.ajws.org/disaster.cfm.

4. Helen Fein, *Accounting for Genocide* (New York: Free Press, 1979); Leo Kuper, *Genocide: Its Political Use in the Twentieth Century* (New Haven, Conn.: Yale University Press, 1981); and Israel W. Charny, ed., *Toward the Understanding and Prevention of Genocide: Proceedings of the International Conference on the Holocaust and Genocide* (Boulder, Colo.: Westview Press, 1984).

5. Samuel Totten, "Non-governmental Organizations Working on the Issue of Genocide," in *The Widening Circle of Genocide: A Critical Bibliographic Review*, ed. Israel W. Charny, 325–357 (New Brunswick, N.J.: Transaction Publishers, 1994); and "The Role of Nongovernmental Organizations in Addressing the Prevention, Intervention, and Punishment of Genocide in the 1980s, 1990s, and Early 2000s," in *Genocide at the Millenium*, ed. Samuel Totten, 75–11 (New Brunswick, N.J.: Transaction Publishers, 2005).

6. On early warning systems, see Jennifer Leaning, "Identifying Precursors," in *Will Genocide Ever End*? ed. Carol Rittner, John K. Roth, and James M. Smith (St. Paul Minn.: Paragon House, 2002); Henry R. Huttenbach, "Anticipating Genocide"; and Barbara Harff, "Early Warning and Genocide Prevention" in *Will Genocide Ever End?* ed. Carol Rittner, John K. Roth, and James M. Smith (St. Paul, Minn.: Paragon House, 2002), 117–122, 123–126, 127–130; Leo Kuper, "Reflections on the Prevention of Genocide," in *Genocide Watch*, ed. Helen F. Fein (New Haven, Conn.: Yale University Press, 1992), 135–161.

7. On the constraints facing those who wish to prevent and intervene in genocide, see David Nyheim, "What Can Be Done?" in *Will Genocide Ever End?* 113–116.

8. Samantha Power, *"A Problem from Hell": America and the Age of Genocide* (New York: Basic Books, 2002), 34.

9. Jewish Black Book Committee, WJC, *The Black Book: The Nazi Crime against the Jewish People* (New York: Nexus Press, 1946); Arieh Tartakower to W. Keller, letter, July 20, 1944, WJC Collection, MS361/H71/14, AJA; Dr. Jacob Robinson, Abraham Duker, Oscar Karbach, Malva Schaeffer, and Gerhard Jacoby, "Part IV. Catastrophe, *The Black Book—The Nazi Crime against the Jewish People*, observations, draft, Institute for Jewish Affairs, 1946," [unpublished], 40, WJC Collection, MS361/C82/8, AJA.

10. Qtd. in Paul Mojzes, "Ethnic Cleansing," *Will Genocide Ever End?* 56.

11. Helen Fein, "States of Genocide and Other States," *Will Genocide Ever End?* 47.

12. James E. Mace, "Soviet Man-Made Famine in Ukraine," in *Century of Genocide*, 2nd ed., ed. Samuel Totten, William S. Parsons, and Israel W. Charny (New York: Routledge, 2004), 93–124.

13. Human Rights Watch, *Kosovo: Rape as a "Weapon of Ethnic Cleansing"* (New York: Human Rights Watch, 2000); Carol Rittner, "Using Rape as a Weapon of Genocide," *Will Genocide Ever End?* 91–97.

14. See Raphael Lemkin Papers MS60, boxes 6 and 7, *passim*, AJA; Steven Leonard Jacobs, "Genesis of the Concept of Genocide According to Its Author from the Original Sources," *Human Rights Review* 3, no. 2 (January–March 2002): 98–103; special rapporteur Nicodème Ruhashyankiko, "Study of the Question of the Prevention and Punishment of the Crime of Genocide," report to the UN Subcommission on

Prevention of Discrimination and Protection of Minorities, 25th Session, UN doc. E/CN.4/Sub.2/L.565, May 23, 1972, remarks that "some of the premises of this concept [i.e., genocide] were postulated by Professor Raphael Lemkin in a special report to the Fifth International Conference for the Unification of Penal Law," Madrid, October 14–20, 1933.

15. Korey, *NGOs*, 205; also Kuper, *Genocide*, 22.

16. See Raphael Lemkin, "I Draft: Hitler Case," 1-2, n.d., Raphael Lemkin Papers, MS60/7/13, AJA.

17. William Korey, *An Epitaph for Raphael Lemkin* (New York: AJC, June 2001); Korey, *NGOs*, 207; Samantha Power, *A Problem from Hell,* 32–60.

18. John W. Davis to Raphael Lemkin, letter, May 8, 1947, Raphael Lemkin Papers, MS60/D1/4, AJA.

19. United States Committee for a United Nations Genocide Convention, "Genocide," June 1948, Raphael Lemkin Papers, MS60/6/13, AJA.

20. "Memorandum Submitted to the U.N. Economic and Social Council by the World Jewish Congress," July 30, 1947, WJC Collection, MS361/B84/6, AJA, and February 6 and again June 9, 1948, WJC Collection, MS361/B84/7, AJA; United Nations Document E/C.2/52, August 8, 1947; UN Economic and Social Council, February 6, 1948, E/C.2/78; Oscar Karbach to A. Leon Kubowitzki, memorandum, re: Convention for the Prevention and Punishment of Genocide, June, 1947, WJC Collection, MS361/B84/6, AJA; Nehemiah Robinson, *The United Nations and the World Jewish Congress* (London: Institute of Jewish Affairs, 1956), 20–25; Irwin Cotler, "Jewish NGOs and Religious Human Rights: A Case Study," in *Human Rights in Judaism: Cultural, Religious, and Political Perspectives*, ed. Michael J. Broyde and John Witte, Jr. (Northvale, N.J.: Jason Aronson, 1998), 185.

21. UN ECOSOC, "Genocide: Communication from the Government of Pakistan," E/660, February 12, 1948.

22. Verbatim Report of Statement by Dr. Robert S. Marcus, Acting Political Director of the WJC, before the United Nations Ad Hoc Committee on Genocide, Lake Success, April 6, 1948, 1–2, WJC Collection, MS361/B84/7, AJA.

23. Verbatim Report of Statement, 3.

24. See Louis E. Shecter, "Does the U.S. Stand Opposed to Mass Murder?" n.d., Louis E. Shecter Papers (1921–1985), MS169/2/4, AJA; and "American Jewish Congress [Genocide Convention], 1953–1985," Louis E. Shecter Papers (1921–1985), MS169/1/2, AJA.

25. Memorandum for Rabbi Robert R. Marcus, August 12, 1947, WJC Collection, MS361/B84/6, AJA; Saul Hayes, memorandum for national executive, No. 211 confidential, August 14, 1947, WJC Collection, MS361/B84/6, AJA; for Stephen S. Wise's letters to WJC affiliates in Australia, Luxembourg, France, India, Argentina, Czechoslovakia, Brazil, Canada, Guatemala, El Salvador, Poland, Yugoslavia, Mexico, The Netherlands, Belgium, Chile, and South Africa, see August 28, 1947, WJC Collection, MS361/B84/6, AJA; for Robert S. Marcus's letters to affiliates in Peru, Venezuela, Denmark, Sweden, China, France, and Canada the following year, all dated January 26, 1948, see WJC Collection, MS361/B133/13, AJA.

26. CCJO, release, July 29, 1947, in Memoranda, Statements, Releases, Etc., 1947–1953, BL.

27. CCJO, Report no. 4, "Reports" [minutebook], 1947, BL; "CCJO Proposals regarding the Draft Convention on the Crime of Genocide," sent to secretary-general of the UN, Trygve Lie, July 24, 1947, in Memoranda, Statements, Releases, Etc., 1947–1953, BL.

28. CCJO, Report no. 1, in "Reports," 1947, BL; CCJO, "Proposals for the Consideration of the Economic and Social Council Regarding the Draft Convention on the Crime of Genocide," July 1947, WJC Collection, MS361/B84/6, AJA; UN document E/C.2/49, July 30, 1947.

29. Convention on the Prevention and Punishment of the Crime of Genocide, December 9, 1948, *United Nations Treaty Series* 78, 277.

30. Raphael Lemkin, *Axis Rule in Occupied Europe* (Washington, D.C.: Carnegie Endowment for International Peace, 1944), preface.

31. Memorandum [untitled], July 23, 1947, WJC Collection, MS361/B84/6, AJA.

32. See in particular the contributions by Helen Fein, Leo Kuper, David Hawk, and Lyman H. Legters in the conference proceedings *Toward the Understanding and Prevention of Genocide*, ed. Israel W. Charny, 3–66.

33. For examples, see several essays in George J. Andreopoulos, ed., *Genocide*, Pennsylvania Studies in Human Rights (Philadelphia: University of Pennsylvania Press, 1994), especially essays by Leo Kuper, 31–46; Israel W. Charny, 64–94; and Helen Fein, 95–108.

34. WJC, "Memorandum Concerning the Formulation of the Nuremberg Principles," submitted to the 2nd session of the UN International Law Commission, June 2, 1950, WJC Collection, MS361/B106/6, AJA.

35. Gerhardt M. Riegner to Robert S. Marcus, letter, June 15, 1950, WJC Collection, MS361/B106/7, AJA.

36. See Jacob Blaustein Institute for the Advancement of Human Rights, *Twenty-five Years on the Cutting Edge of Human Rights: JBI's 25th Anniversary Review* (New York: AJC, 1997), 8; US secretary of state Madeleine K. Albright to Felice D. Gaer, letter, December 2, 1999.

37. On Lemkin's massive efforts to track ratification prospects, country by country, and influence the US legislative process, see the Raphael Lemkin Papers, MS/60, especially box 1, AJA.

38. Resolutions Adopted at the Meeting of the Plenary Session of the Executive of the WJC, Geneva, September 10–14, 1951, WJC Collection, MS361/B137/11, AJA.

39. Nehemiah Robinson, *The Genocide Convention: A Commentary* (New York: Institute of Jewish Affairs, 1960); and *The Genocide Convention: Its Origins and Interpretation* (New York: Institute of Jewish Affairs, 1949).

40. Bernard Bernstein, Report of Activities of the Coordinating Board of Jewish Organizations, January 1, 1949 to June 20, 1950, 30, Annex 14, CBJO Collection, MS76/1/6, AJA.

41. Power, *"A Problem from Hell,"* 68; Nehemiah Robinson, "The Attitude of the American Bar Association toward the Genocide Convention," unpublished manuscript, WJC Collection, MS361/C130/2, AJA.

42. AJCongress and Union of American Hebrew Congregations, "United States Ratification of the United Nations Genocide Convention: A Background Analysis," n.d., 13–14, Louis E. Shecter Papers, MS169/1/2, AJA.

43. See S Res. 81, 83rd Cong. (August 7, 1954); Louis E. Shecter, "Talk," January 28, 1954, Louis E. Shecter Papers, MS169/1/2, AJA.

44. Korey, *NGOs*, 203–228.

45. Power, *"A Problem from Hell,"* 72; International Covenant on Civil and Political Rights (1966), in *Basic Documents on Human Rights*, ed. Ian Brownlie, 3rd ed. (New York: Oxford University Press, 1992), Art. 6, parts 2–3, 127–128.

46 See, for example, "Bar Association Attacks on Genocide Pact Disputed at Senate Hearings," press release, AJCongress, January 23, 1950, WJC Collection, MS361/B132/6, AJA; Statement of the American Jewish Congress Urging Ratification of the Genocide Convention before the Senate Foreign Relations Committee, Sub-Committee on Genocide, January 23, 1950, WJC Collection, MS361/B106/8, AJA.

47. Ad Hoc Committee on the Human Rights and Genocide Treaties, Member Organizations, in "Human Rights Conventions—Slavery, Women—Senate Foreign Relations Committee," FAD-IO 1967, BL; William Korey, "Popular New Initiative for Human Rights Treaties," reprint from the Conference Group of US National Organizations *News Bulletin* 7, no. 2 (1965): 8–10, in "Human Rights and Genocide Treaties, Ad Hoc Committee," FAD-IO, 1960-1970, BL; and Statement of Hon. Arthur J. Goldberg on Behalf of the Ad Hoc Committee on the Human Rights and Genocide Treaties Before the Senate Foreign Relations Subcommittee on the Genocide Convention, March 10, 1971 in "Genocide Convention," FAD-IO, BL.

48. See AJC archive boxes, including Efforts on Genocide Ratification in US, 1968–1972, FAD-IO, 1968–1972, BL; Genocide Convention: Correspondence with Sen. Claiborne Pell, 1969, FAD-IO, BL; Human Rights Conventions, Senate Foreign Relations Sub-Committee Hearings, FAD-IO, 1957-1967, BL; Human Rights Conventions, Genocide, Slavery, Women, Forced Labor, FAD-IO, 1963-1966, BL; Human Rights and Genocide Treaties, Ad Hoc Committee, FAD-IO, 1965-1966, in Human Rights Conventions—Slavery, Women, Senate Foreign Relations Committee, 1967, FAD-IO, BL. For the efforts of WJC/AJCongress, see Statement of American Jewish Congress Urging Ratification of the Genocide Convention before the Senate Foreign Relations Committee Sub-Committee on Genocide, January 23, 1950, WJC Collection, MS361/B84/9, AJA; and the massive documentation of the committee's (largely ineffectual) work in WJC Collection, MS361/B84/12, AJA; MS361/B85, AJA; and MS361/B133/7, AJA.

49. James N. Rosenberg to Nehemiah Robinson, letter, May 18, 1949, WJC Collection, MS361/B84/8, AJA.

50. Korey, *NGOs*, 223.

51. Jerome Shestack, Raymond Nasher, and Sidney Liskofsky, "Human Rights and International Organizations: Objectives, Methodology and Program of AJC's Committee on International Organizations," April 17, 1972, 29, BL.

52. Human Rights Conventions—Slavery, Women, Senate Foreign Relations Committee, 1967, FAD-IO, BL.

53. Hyman Bookbinder, *Off the Wall*, 132.

54. President's Commission on the Holocaust Report, September 27, 1979, qtd. in "First Draft of Proposal for a Committee on Conscience," September 22, 1994, 1, US Holocaust Memorial Museum Collection, MS712/12/10, AJA.

55. Proceedings of the Ad Hoc Exploratory Group on the Committee on Conscience, December 6, 1993, US Holocaust Memorial Museum Collection, MS712/10/4, AJA.

56. Marian Craig, US Holocaust Memorial Museum Council secretary, to Exploratory Task Group on the Committee of Conscience, memorandum, December 6, 1993, US Holocaust Memorial Museum Collection, MS712/10/4, AJA; "First Draft of Proposal for a Committee on Conscience."

57. "Former President Reagan Dies at 93," *Los Angeles Times,* June 6, 2004.

58. Power, *"A Problem from Hell,"* 160–163.

59. Herbert Hirsch, *Anti-Genocide: Building an American Movement to Prevent Genocide* (Westport, Conn.: Praeger, 2002), 41.

60. David Harris, *In the Trenches: Selected Speeches and Writings of an American Jewish Activist, 1979–1999* (New York: Ktav Publishing House, 2000), 437.

61. Ad Hoc Exploratory Group on the Committee on Conscience Meeting, May 24–25, 1994, US Holocaust Memorial Museum Collection, MS712/11/10, AJA.

62. Israel W. Charny and Chanan Rapaport, "A Genocide Early Warning System (a Pilot Project): Establishing a Data Bank for Events of Genocide and other Major Violations of Human Rights," Henrietta Szold Institute, National Institute for Research in the Behavioral Sciences, Jerusalem, Israel, n.d., US Holocaust Memorial Museum Collection, MS712/11/2, AJA.

63. Power, *"A Problem from Hell,"* 288–293, 358–363, 369.

64. Bill Clinton, *My Life* (New York: Alfred A. Knopf, 2004), 512.

65. Clinton, *My Life*, 593.

66. Hirsch, *Anti-Genocide*, 40–43.

67. Power, *"A Problem from Hell,"* 373–374.

68. Israel W. Charny, "Leo Kuper: A Great Pioneer," in *Pioneers of Genocide Studies*, ed. Samuel Totten and Steven L. Jacobs (New Brunswick, N.J.: Transaction Publishers, 2002); Kumar Rupesinghe (general secretary of International Alert), "International Alert and the Prevention of Genocide" in *Encyclopedia of Genocide*, ed. Israel W. Charny (Santa Barbara, Calif.: ABC-Clio, 1999).

69. Hirsch, *Anti-Genocide*, 173.

70. I. Schwartzbart to A. B. David, letter, August 3, 1948, WJC Collection, MS361/H191/5, AJA; also cf. WJC attempts to contact the officers of Musmeah Yeshua Synagogue, Rangoon, Burma (a community of ten to fifteen families) and the Jewish communities in Jakarta, Indonesia, and Usumbura, Burundi, WJC Collection, MS361/H71/12, 13, AJA.

71. Max Melamet, memorandum, "re: The Jewish Situation in Chile," September 28, 1970, WJC Collection, MS361/H86/8, AJA; Max Melamet, memorandum, "Report on Chile," April 5, 1971, WJC Collection, MS361/H86/8, AJA; also, clippings from 1969 on anti-Semitic discrimination from Chilean newspapers, and minutes from the Collectividad Israelita de Chile on Arab propaganda, MS361/H84/3, AJA.

72. Gary Rubin to Irving Levine, memorandum, "Meeting of the National Coalition for Refugee Resettlement," Washington, DC, June 18, 1979, ajcarchives.org/ajcarchive/DigitalArchive.aspx.

73. David Harris, "Indochinese Refugees—'We Are All Boat People,'" *Forward*, April 22, 1988, in Harris, *In the Trenches*, 436; Richard Maas to AJC members, December 27, 1979, www.ajcarchives.org/AJC_DATA/Files/735.PDF.

74. Rabbi Marc H. Tanenbaum, partial transcript of testimony before the House of Representatives Subcommittee on Asian and Pacific Affairs of the Foreign Affairs Committee, December 18, 1979, ajcarchives.org/ajcarchive/DigitalArchive.aspx.

75. Qtd. in Jerry Fowler, "Out of the Darkness: Responding to Genocide in the Twenty-first Century," in Totten, Parsons, and Charny, *Century of Genocide*, 456; also see Clinton, *My Life*, 512.

76. Human Rights Watch, *Yugoslavia: Human Rights Abuses in Kosovo, 1990–1992* (New York: Human Rights Watch, 1992).

77. Among them were Yehuda Bauer of the Hebrew University, Robert Melson, president of the International Association of Genocide Scholars, and directors of university Holocaust and genocide programs like Stephen Feinstein of the University of Minnesota, Steven Jacobs of the University of Alabama, and Colin Tatz at the University of New South Wales. www.genocidewatch.org/DirectorsAdvisors.htm.

78. Qtd. in Power, *"A Problem from Hell,"* 278.

79. Power, *"A Problem from Hell,"* 278.80. Dana Priest, "Coalition Calls for Action in Bosnia," *Washington Post*, August 1, 1995, A14; Korey, *NGOs*, 327; Jacob Blaustein Institute, *JBI Newsletter*, December 1995, 6.

81. "On Bosnian War Criminals: An Open Letter," *New York Review of Books* 43, no. 13 (August 8, 1996), signed by 112 organizations and individuals.

82. Michael Berenbaum, "The Pin-Stripe Approach to Genocide," January 19, 1994, US Holocaust Memorial Museum Collection, MS712/11/6, AJA.

83. See "The 'Jews of Africa,'" *Economist*, August 19, 2004; Power, *"A Problem from Hell,"* 357.

84. Robert Walker, "Rwanda Remembers the Holocaust," *BBC News*, January 27, 2005, news.bbc.co.uk/1/hi/world/africa/4211621.stm.

85. David Harris, "Letter from a Diplomatic Marathoner," October 13, 2003, www.ajc.org/site/apps/nl/content3.asp?c=ijITI2PHKoG&b=845459&ct=1089261.

86. Eric Reeves, "Cheap Talk: Europe's Indifference to Darfur," *The New Republic Online*, October 27, 2006, www.tnr.com/docprint.mhtml?i=w061023$s=reeves102706.

87. Nicholas D. Kristof, "If Not Now, When?" op-ed, *New York Times*, October 29, 2006, 13.

88. David Harris and Ruth Messinger, "Bitter Jewish Experience Means Community Can't Be Silent on Darfur," *Jewish Telegraphic Agency*, July 18, 2005; Allison S. Cohen, "Crisis in Darfur: Determining Genocide," JBI Human Rights Discussion Paper, November 2004; Allison S. Cohen, "We Must Halt the Genocide in Darfur, Sudan, Now," JBI Human Rights Discussion Paper, June 2005.

89. Ruth Messinger, email, November 8, 2006.

90. The groups were American Jewish Committee, Conference of Presidents of Major American Jewish Organizations, Hillel: The Foundation for Jewish Campus

Life, Jewish Healthcare International, Jewish Labor Committee, Jewish Reconstructionist Federation, Jewish World Watch, MAZON: A Jewish Response to Hunger, National Council of Jewish Women, National Jewish Democratic Council, Progressive Jewish Alliance, Congress of Secular Jewish Organizations, Jewish Family and Life, Union of Orthodox Jewish Congregations of America, United Jewish Communities, Canadian Federation of Jewish Students, Canadian Jewish Congress.

91. Ruth Messinger, email, November 8, 2006.

92. Rachel Silverman, "On Rwanda Visit, Students Learn of the Consequences of Genocide," United Jewish Communities website, April 25, 2006, www.ujc.org/content_display.html?ArticleID=182205.

93. Jennifer Hoar, "Jews for Justice in Darfur," CBS News, May 1, 2006, www.cbsnews.com/stories/2006/05/01/world/main1567410.shtml; Neela Banerjee, "Muslims' Plight in Sudan Resonates with Jew in U.S.," *New York Times*, April 30, 2006, 19.

94. Jewish World Watch, "Jewish World Watch . . . a Call to Conscience," www.jewishworldwatch.org/about/.

95. Nicholas D. Kristof, "Walking the Talk," op-ed, *New York Times*, October 9, 2005, 13.

96. Phone interview with Lily Baxter, October 23, 2006. Lily Baxter, Margo Dix-Gold, and Lois Frank were responsible for bringing the exhibit "The Littlest Voices" for the UN's International Day of Commemoration for the Holocaust, January 27, 2005. The drawings presented to the public were replicas of the originals, and were exhibited free of charge in the "Discovery Area" of the museum, generally reserved for material of interest to children.

97. Ruth Messinger, letter to the editor, *New York Times*, June 2, 2006.

98. Ruth Messinger, Saturday morning *d'var torah*, Ahavath Achim Synagogue, Atlanta, Ga., October 7, 2006.

99. Mission statement of UN Watch, Geneva, 1995, qtd. in Cotler, "Jewish NGOs," 251.

100. Jewish World Watch, "Call to Conscience."

101. United Nations Convention on the Prevention and Punishment of the Crime of Genocide, Art. VI, in Adam Roberts and Richard Guelff, eds., *Documents on the Laws of War*, 3rd ed. (New York: Oxford, 2001), 181–82.

102. Benjamin Ferencz website, www.benferencz.org/bio.html.

103. José Ayala Lasso, former United States high commissioner for human rights, qtd. in "Rome Statute of the International Criminal Court," www.un.org/law/icc/general/overview.htm.

104. WJC, "Memorandum Concerning the Formulation of the Nuremberg Principles and the Question of International Criminal Jurisdiction, Submitted by the World Jewish Congress to the General Assembly of the United Nations," October 18, 1950, WJC Collection, MS361/B141/31, AJA and August 1, 1951, WJC Collection, MS361/B106/5, AJA; WJC, "Memorandum Concerning the Draft Statute for an International Criminal Court Adopted by the Committee on International Criminal Jurisdiction, Submitted by the World Jewish Congress," November 13, 1952, WJC Collection, MS361/B106/5, AJA.

105. Gerhard Jacoby, "United Nations General Assembly, 3rd Committee, 'The Draft Code against the Peace and Security of Mankind and the Draft Statute for an International Criminal Court,' 1957," November 6, 1957, WJC Collection, MS361/B102/13, AJA; "United Nations General Assembly, 6th Committee, 'The Draft Code against the Peace and Security of Mankind and the Draft Statute for an International Criminal Court,' 1957," WJC Collection, MS361/102/21, AJA.

106. Robinson, *Genocide: A Commentary*, 48.

107. See WJC, "Memorandum Concerning the Draft Statute for an International Criminal Court."

108. *Democratic Republic of the Congo v. Belgium*, February 14, 2002, Separate Opinion of Judge Guillaume, president, International Court of Justice.

109. Henry A. Kissinger, "The Pitfalls of 'Universal Jurisdiction,'" *Foreign Affairs* (July–August, 2001): 86–96; for a response, see Kenneth Roth, "The Case for Universal Jurisdiction," *Foreign Affairs* (September–October, 2001): 150–154.

110. "Former Yugoslavia," S/RES/771, August 13, 1992, para. 5.

111. The report was later published as Aryeh Neier, *War Crimes: Brutality, Genocide, Terror, and the Struggle for Justice* (New York: Random House, 1998).

112. Korey, *NGOs*, 323–334.

113. Rome Statute of the International Criminal Court, Article 8(2)(b)(viii) (Rome, 1998). For an extensive analysis of the language in this paragraph, see Michael Galchinsky, "The Jewish Settlements in the West Bank: International Law and Israeli Jurisprudence," *Israel Studies* 9, no. 3 (Fall 2004): 115–136.

114. For example, Goldstone spoke to B'nai B'rith in Chicago on October 3, 1996. See "Is Genocide Here to Stay?" *The Jewish Monthly* (December 1996–January 1997): 27.

CHAPTER 4. AMERICAN JEWS AND VIOLATIONS IN ZION: A CASE STUDY

1. For example, "Herzog to Diaspora Jews: Keep Israel Criticism to Ourselves," *The Jewish Week*, July 15, 1983.

2. For references in the opening paragraph, see "Politicization in the UN: 76–77," BL. The Special Committee to Investigate Israeli Practices Affecting the Human Rights of the Palestinian People and Other Arabs of the Occupied Territories was established by the General Assembly in Resolution 2443 (XXIII) of December 19, 1968. For specific details of the charges of many of these bodies, see Y. Manor, *To Right a Wrong: The Revocation of the UN General Assembly Resolution 3379 Defaming Zionism*, 2nd ed. (New York: Shengold Publishers, 1977); Harris Schoenberg, *A Mandate for Terror: The United Nations and the PLO* (New York: Shapolsky Publishers, 1989); *The World Conference against Racism: The Adoption and Repeal of the Z=R resolution and the Implications for UN Reform* (Wayne, N.J.: Center for UN Reform Education, 2001).

3. Irwin Cotler, "Jewish NGOs and Religious Human Rights: A Case Study," in *Human Rights in Judaism: Cultural, Religious, and Political Perspectives*, ed. Michael J.

Broyde and John Witte, Jr. (Northvale, N.J.: Jason Aronson, 1998), 245–246; World Union for Progressive Judaism, "Zionism: One of the Earliest Examples of a National Liberation Movement," 1989, UN Doc. E/CN.4/2004/NGO/89.

4. Henry F. Carey and John Carey, "Hostility in United Nations Bodies to Judaism, the Jewish People and Jews as Such," *Israel Yearbook of Human Rights* 17 (Dordrecht: Martinus Nijhoff, 1987): 29–40.

5. Reporters without Borders, ed., *Israel/Palestine: The Black Book* (Sterling, Va.: Pluto Press in association with Reporters without Borders, 2003).

6. David Kretzmer, *The Occupation of Justice: The Supreme Court of Israel and the Occupied Territories* (Albany: State University of New York Press, 2002), 21–25, 34–40, 43–56.

7. See "United Nations: Expulsion, Question of Israel's, 75," BL.

8. Sidney Liskofsky, "General Assembly Action on Proposal to Condemn Anti-Semitism in Convention on the Elimination of All Forms of Racial Discrimination," November 11, 1965, Human Rights Conventions, Racial Discrimination, Correspondence, FAD-IO [Foreign Affairs Department–International Organizations], 64–67, BL; William Korey, "The United Nations Convention on the Elimination of All Forms of Racial Discrimination, Summary of Analysis Presented to the NCRAC [National Community Relations Advisory Council] Executive Committee," January 23, 1966, Human Rights Conventions, Racial Discrimination, FAD-IO, 64–67, BL; Natan Lerner, *The U.N. Convention on the Elimination of All Forms of Racial Discrimination* (Rockville, Md.: Sijthoff, and Noordhoff, 1980), 2–73.

9. *American Jewish Year Book* (Philadelphia: Jewish Publication Society of America, 1908), 238.

10. *American Jewish Year Book* (Philadelphia: Jewish Publication Society of America, 1929), 383–386.

11. See "Efforts on Genocide Ratification in US, 1968–1972," from AJC archive box labeled "FAD-IO, 68–72."

12. Henry J. Steiner, *Diverse Partners: Non-Governmental Organizations in the Human Rights Movement* (Cambridge, Mass.: Harvard Law School Human Rights Program and Human Rights Internet, 1991), 26.

13. Steiner, *Diverse Partners*, 27.

14. Sidney Liskofsky to Bert Gold, memorandum, "Proposal for a Conference of Experts on the 'Right to Leave,'" January 29, 1971, Bert Gold Memos 1970–1971, FADI, BL.

15. Sidney Liskofsky and Karel Vasak, eds., *The Right to Leave and Return: Papers and Recommendations of the International Colloquium Held in Uppsala, Sweden, 19–20 June 1972* (New York: AJC, 1976); Hurst Hannum, *The Right to Leave and Return in International Law and Practice* (Boston: Martinus Nijhoff Publishers, 1987).

16. For a sustained consideration of American Jewish NGOs activities with regard to the Soviet Jewry movement, see chapter 2; Fred Lazin, *The Struggle for Soviet Jewry in American Politics: Israel versus the American Jewish Establishment* (Lanham, Md.: Lexington Books, 2005); also see William Korey, *NGOs and the Universal Declaration of Human Rights: "A Curious Grapevine"* (New York: St. Martin's Press, 1998), 6, 189–202.

17. The group was initially called the Ad Hoc Group on US Policy toward the UN, and issued its first report, "A New United States Policy toward the United Nations," in April 1976. See "Perspectives on the UN, 79," FAD-IO, BL.

18. See Box 20, FAD-IO, *passim*, BL.

19. *American Jewish Year Book* (New York: Jewish Publication Society of America, 1975), 603.

20. A similar shift in priorities took place in the ICJW. See Nelly Las, *Jewish Women in a Changing World: A History of the International Council of Jewish Women (ICJW), 1899–1995*, trans. Stephanie Nakache (Jerusalem: A. Harman Institute of Contemporary Jewry, 1996), 103–108.

21. Sasson Sofer, *Begin: An Anatomy of Leadership* (New York: Basil Blackwell, 1988), chaps. 9–10; Ilan Peleg, *Begin's Foreign Policy, 1977–1983: Israel's Move to the Right* (Westport, Conn.: Greenwood Press, 1987) and "The Legacy of Begin and Beginism for the Israeli Political System," in *Israel after Begin*, ed. Gregory S. Mahler (Albany: State University of New York Press, 1990), 19–49.

22. Peleg, "The Legacy of Begin," 31.

23. *Amnesty International Report and Recommendations of an Amnesty International Mission to the Government of the State of Israel, 3-7 June 1979: Including the Government's Response and Amnesty International's Comments* (London: Amnesty International Publications, 1980); International League for the Rights of Man, Committee on Mid-East Settlements, draft letter, November 2, 1977, Box 20, "United Nations: Human Rights: Violations in Occupied Territories, 77–78," BL.

24. *Amnesty International Report*; "International Commission of Jurists, 1980," FAD-IO, BL; Sidney Liskofsky to Jerome Shestack, letter, October 13, 1977, Box 22, FAD-IO, BL; "ACRI," FAD-IO, JBI/79-80, BL.

25. Sidney Liskofsky, "Backgrounder on South Africa," Box 21, FAD-IO; "UN: Israel and South Africa, 79–80," BL.

26. Liskofsky, "Backgrounder," 4–5

27. Liskofsky, "Backgrounder."

28. Liskofsky, "Backgrounder."

29. Noam Chomsky, "Open Letter to Roger Baldwin," in *Palestinian Human Rights Bulletin*, August 30, 1977.

30. Sidney Liskofsky to Jerome Shestack, letter, January 11, 1979, Box 22, FAD-IO, BL; ACRI, FAD-IO, JBI/79-80, BL.

31. William Korey, "Scapegoat at the UN," *Jewish Chronicle*, October 31, 1980.

32. David Sidorsky, ed., *Essays on Human Rights: Contemporary Issues and Jewish Perspectives* (Philadelphia: Jewish Publication Society of America, 1979).

33. Sidney Liskofsky to Leo Nevas, letter, February 2, 1979, Box 19, Amnesty International, FAD IO 1978–1979, BL.

34. Abraham Karlikow to Liskofsky, letter, October 18, 1977, Box 20, FAD-IO, BL.

35. Max Ellerin and Abraham Karlikow, *Zionism, Israel, and the New Left* (New York: AJC, 1971); Abraham Karlikow, *The Brussels World Conference on Soviet Jewry: An Analysis* (New York: AJC, 1971).

36. Cotler, "Jewish NGOs," 226, 235.

37. M. Bernard Resnikoff, form letter, October 21, 1977, Box 20, FAD-IO, BL.

38. Resnikoff to Liskofsky, letter, October 30, 1977, Box 20, FAD-IO, BL.
39. Resnikoff to Liskofsky, letter, November 1, 1977, Box 20, FAD-IO, BL.
40. Ruth Bader Ginsburg, Alan Dershowitz, Norman Dorsen, Robert M. Cover, Lawrence M. Friedman, and Alan F. Westin, "The Association for Civil Rights in Israel," fund-raising letter, June 13, 1979, ACRI, FAD-IO, JBI/79-80, BL.
41. Bader Ginsburg et al., "Association for Civil Rights."
42. Resnikoff to Liskofsky, letter, November 1, 1977, Box 20, FAD-IO, BL.
43. Israel Shahak, interview, *Intercontinental Press* (Jerusalem, February 1975): 428–431; "What Are My Opinions," *Zu Haderech* (November 27, 1974); *Fifth of June Society Newsletter* (August 13, 1970); *Israeli League for Human and Civil Rights: The Shahak Papers* (Beirut: NEEBII, 1973); *The Shahak Report* (Tel Aviv: I. Shahak, 1973).
44. Resnikoff to Liskofsky, letter, January 13, 1976, BOX 22, ACRI, FAD-IO, JBI/79-80, BL; Alan Reitman to Norman Dorsen, letter, February 2, 1977, "Israel League for Human Rights, 1976–78," Box 20, FAD-IO, BL.
45. Liskofsky to Shestack, letter, January 23, 1979, with attached memorandum, BOX 22, ACRI, FAD-IO, JBI/79-80, BL.
46. Karlikow to Yoram Dinstein, letter, April 6, 1976, Box 22, "Israel League for Human Rights, 1976-78," FAD-IO, BL.
47. Liskofsky to Shestack, letter, January 11, 1979, Box 22, FAD-IO; ACRI, FAD-IO, JBI/79-80, BL.
48. Resnikoff to Liskofsky, letter, November 1, 1977, Box 20, FAD-IO, BL.
49. M. Bernard Resnikoff, Report from the Israel Office, November 16, 1978, Box 22, ACRI, FAD-IO, JBI/79-80, BL.
50. Liskofsky to Shestack, letter, January 23, 1979, with attached memorandum, Box 22, ACRI, FAD-IO, JBI/79-80, BL.
51. Liskofsky to Shestack, letter, January 23, 1979
52. Liskofsky to Bert Gold, letter, March 16, 1979, Box 22, ACRI, FAD-IO, JBI/79-80, BL.
53. Bader Ginsburg et al., "Association for Civil Rights."
54. Morris Fine to Philip Shamis, letter, March 28, 1979, Box 22, ACRI, FAD-IO, JBI/79-80, BL.
55. Resnikoff to Liskofsky, cable, May 14, 1979, Box 22, ACRI, FAD-IO, JBI/79-80, BL.
56. Liskofsky to Karlikow, letter, September 17, 1979, Box 22, ACRI, FAD-IO, JBI/79-80, BL.
57. Resnikoff to Selma Hirsch, letter, November 16, 1978, Box 22, ACRI, FAD-IO, JBI/79-80, BL. Also see "Jacob Blaustein Institute, Administrative Council, 1980" in Box 22, FAD-IO, BL. Initially, the Association for Civil Rights in Israel limited itself to issues occurring within the Green Line, but by the early 1990s its mission stretched into the occupied territories as well. On its early policy of keeping to pluralism issues, see Henry J. Steiner, *Diverse Partners*, 14–15.
58. Lea Spector to Hirsch, letter, November 21, 1979, Box 22, ACRI, FAD-IO, JBI/79-80, BL.
59. Uri Avneri, *Israel and the Palestinians: A Different Israeli View* (New York: Breira, 1975); Matityahu Peled, "Palestinian or Jordanian Entity?" in *Israel and the*

Palestinians, ed. Shlomo Avineri (New York: St. Martin's Press, 1971); Amos Oz, "Al ha-matsav, 1967–1978" ["On the Situation"] in *Be'or ha-tekhelet ha'azah* [*Under This Blazing Light: Essays*] (Merhavyah, Israel: Sifriyat Poalim, 1979); Yeshayahu Leibowitz, *Judaism, Human Values, and the State* (Cambridge, Mass.: Harvard University Press, 1995).

60. Robin Cohen, *Global Diasporas: An Introduction* (Seattle: University of Washington Press, 1997); Michael Galchinsky, "Scattered Seeds: A Dialogue of Diasporas," in *Insider/Outsider: American Jews and Multiculturalism*, ed. David Biale, Michael Galchinsky, and Susannah Heschel (Berkeley: University of California Press), 185–211; Caryn Aviv and David Schneer, *New Jews: The End of the Jewish Diaspora* (New York: New York University Press, 2005).

61. Liskofsky to Shestack, letter, January 11, 1979, Box 22, ACRI, FAD-IO, JBI/79-80, BL.

62. One piece of evidence that suggests others shared their view is the World Union Blue Ribbon Commission Report of WUPJ, "A Declaration of Progressive Judaism on the Jewish People in the State of Israel," 1983, which declared "concern for the human needs and sensitivities of Palestinian Arabs," and was delivered in person to Israel's president, Chaim Herzog, qtd. in Rabbi Benjamin A. Kamin, "Report on the International Conference of the World Union for Progressive Judaism," July 13, 1983, WUPJ Collection, MS16/G7/2, AJA.

63. Rabbi Hillel, Mishnah, "The Order of Damages," Tractate *Avot* 1:14.

CHAPTER 5. ISRAELI, JEWISH, HUMAN

1. Noah Liben, "Update: NIF's Ongoing Support for Radical NGOs," March 10, 2005, at www.ngo-monitor.org/editions/v3n07/NIFOngoingSupportForRadicalNGOS.htm.

2. Amnon Lord, "Defeatism Is Their Trade," *Yediot Aharonot*, March 7, 1999.

3. Interview with Jessica Montell, executive director of B'Tselem, Jerusalem, July 16, 2006.

4. Uri Orbach, "On the Value of Life, Crossing Red Lines, and Judging Those in Grief," *ynetnews.com*, August 11, 2006, at www.ynetnews.com/articles/0,7340,L-3289760,00.html.

5. Interview with Gila Svirsky, executive director of New Israel Fund, 1985–1991, Jerusalem, June 17, 2006.

6. Financial statements in B'Tselem annual reports, through 1999.

7. Stephen Ellman, "Cause Lawyering in the Third World," in *Cause Lawyering: Political Commitments and Professional Responsibilities*, ed. Austin Sarat and Stuart Scheingold (New York: Oxford University Press, 1998), 354–355.

8. Ellman, "Cause Lawyering," 406, note 164; and 412, note 178.

9. Jack Donnelly, *Universal Human Rights in Theory and Practice*, 2nd ed. (Ithaca, N.Y.: Cornell University Press, 2003), 35.

10. Neve Gordon and Nitza Berkovitch, "Human Rights Discourse in Domestic Settings: How Does It Emerge?" *Political Studies* [advance copy] concur that the human rights discourse "is not automatically imported into the local arena" (10).

11. Theodor Herzl, "The Jewish State" (1896), in *The Zionist Idea: A Historical Analysis and Reader*, ed. Arthur Hertzberg (Philadelphia: Jewish Publication Society, 1997), 223.

12. Max Nordau, "Speech to the First Zionist Congress," in Hertzberg, *Zionist Idea*, 236.

13. Leo Pinsker, "Auto-Emancipation: An Appeal to His People by a Russian Jew" (1882), in Hertzberg, *Zionist Idea*, 181.

14. Gideon Shimoni, *The Zionist Ideology* (Waltham, Mass.: Brandeis University Press, 1995), 372–378.

15. Tom Segev, *1949: The First Israelis* (New York: Free Press, 1986); Paul Mendes-Flor, ed., *A Land of Two Peoples: Martin Buber on Jews and Arabs* (New York: Oxford University Press, 1983).

16. Amos Oz, *A Tale of Love and Darkness: A Memoir*, trans. Nicholas de Lange (Orlando, Fla.: Harcourt Brace, 2003), 437.

17. A. B. Yehoshua, "Facing the Forests," in *Modern Hebrew Literature*, ed. Robert Alter (West Orange, N.J.: Behrman House, 1975), 357–392.

18. Ahmad H. Sa'di, "Catastrophe, Memory and Identity: Al-Nakbah as a Component of Palestinian Identity," *Israel Studies* 7, no. 2 (Summer 2002): 175–198.

19. Ben Halpern and Jehuda Reinharz, *Zionism and the Creation of a New Society* (Hanover, N.H.: Brandeis University Press, 2000), 300–302.

20. Some early dissenting voices include short stories by Y. H. Brenner ("The Way Out"), and S. Yizhar ("The Prisoner"), in Alter, *Modern Hebrew Literature*, 145–157, 294–310.

21. Ephraim Ya'ar, "Continuity and Change in Israeli Society: The Test of the Melting Pot," *Israel Studies* 10, no. 2 (Summer 2005): 91–128; Henriette Dahan-Kalev, "You're So Pretty—You Don't Look Moroccan," *Israel Studies* 6, no. 1 (Spring 2001): 6–14; Uzi Rebhun and Chaim I. Waxman, eds., *Jews in Israel: Contemporary Social and Cultural Patterns* (Lebanon, N.H.: Brandeis University Press, 2004), 3–150, 195–330, 345–370; Susan Sered, *What Makes Women Sick? Maternity, Modesty, and Militarism in Israeli Society* (Hanover, N.H.: Brandeis University Press, 2000), 68–70; Halpern and Reinharz, *Zionism*, 316–318.

22. Gad Barzilai, "War, Democracy, and Internal Conflict: Israel in a Comparative Perspective," *Comparative Politics* 31, no. 3 (April 1999): 317–336; Asher Arian, Michal Shamir, and Raphael Ventura, "Public Opinion and Political Change: Israel and the Intifada," *Comparative Politics* 24, no. 3 (April 1992): 317–334; Ghazi Falah, "The Spatial Manifestation of Threat: Israelis and Palestinians Seek a 'Good' Border," *Political Geography* 14, no. 8 (1995): 689–706.

23. Interview with Dr. Neta Ziv, first legal advisor for ACRI and current NIF vice president, Tel Aviv University, July 18, 2006.

24. Ian S. Lustick, "Israel as a Non-Arab State: The Political Implications of Mass Immigration of Non-Jews," *Middle East Journal* 53, no. 3 (Summer 1999): 417–433.

25. Sam N. Lehman-Wilzig, "Loyalty, Voice, and Quasi-Exit: Israel as a Case-Study of Proliferating Alternative Politics," *Comparative Politics* 24, no. 1 (October 1991): 97–108.

26. Eugene L. Rogen and Avi Shlaim, eds., *The War for Palestine: Rewriting the History of 1948* (Cambridge: Cambridge University Press, 2001); Ilan Pappé, *The*

Israel/Palestine Question: Rewriting Histories (London: Routledge, 1999); Tom Segev, *The Seventh Million* (New York: Holt Paperbacks, 2000); Benny Morris, *The Birth of the Palestinian Refugee Problem, 1947–1949* (Cambridge: Cambridge University Press, 1987).

27. Scott Streiner, "Shooting and Crying: The Emergence of Protest in Israeli Popular Music," *The European Legacy* 6, no. 6 (2001): 771–792.

28. Interview with Gila Svirsky, July 17, 2006; Sered, *What Makes Women Sick?* 165.

29. Gordon and Berkovitch, "Human Rights Discourse," 15.

30. Daphna Golan-Agnon, *Next Year in Jerusalem*, trans. Janine Woolfson (New York: New Press, 2005), 37–38.

31. Mission statement, Coalition of Women for Peace, www.coalitionofwomen.org; www.machsomwatch.org.

32. Interview with Dr. Ruchama Marton, founding director, Physicians for Human Rights, Israel, July 16, 2006.

33. Interview with Neta Ziv; interview with Dan Yakir, current ACRI chief legal counsel, July 19, 2006.

34. Michael H. Posner and Candy Whittome, "The Status of Human Rights NGOs," *Columbia Human Rights Law Review* 25 (1994): 269.

35. Interview with Dorit Karlin, director of programs, strategic planning, grants, and partnerships, NIF, July 17, 2006.

36. New Israel Fund, "Illuminating the Vision," *New Israel Fund Annual Report*, 2005, 8–9.

37. New Israel Fund, "Illuminating the Vision," 7.

38. Interview with Neta Ziv.

39. Yuval Yoaz, "The Quiet Revolution: The Israel-U.S. Civil Liberties Law Program, Spearheaded by the New Israel Fund and American University in Washington, D.C., Has Changed the Map of Human Rights in Israel," haaretz.com, May 25, 2004; interview with Neta Ziv; interview with Dan Yakir; interview with Dorit Karlin.

40. B'Tselem, annual reports, 1993-1999; Interview with Jessica Montell.

41. Interview with Rabbi Arik Ascherman, executive director, Rabbis for Human Rights, July 19, 2006.

42. Interview with Neta Ziv.

43. Interview with Jessica Montell.

44. Jack Donnelly, *Universal Human Rights,* 191–192.

45. For original documents and commentary on this question, see Michael Walzer et al., *The Jewish Political Tradition*, vol. 1 (New Haven, Conn.: Yale University Press, 2000), 501–523.

46. Aharon Barak, "The Role of the Supreme Court in a Democracy," *Israel Studies* 3, no. 2 (Fall 1998): 6–29.

47. Ziv Maor, "Arab Family Finally to Get an ILA Offer for a Katzir Plot," *Haaretz*, January 10, 2003; HC 6698/95, *Ka'adan v. Israel's Land Administration,* 54 P.D. 258 (2000); Association for Civil Rights in Israel, "Ka'adan Family Allowed to Build Home in Jewish Residential Community," www.acri.org.il/english-acri/engine/story.asp?id=177.

48. Aharon Barak, "The Constitutional Revolution: Protected Basic Rights," qtd. in Walzer et al., *Jewish Political Tradition,* 502.

49. Yael Tamir, "A Jewish Democratic State," in Walzer et al., *Jewish Political Tradition*, 523.

50. Menachem Fisch, "Living Dangerously," in Walzer et al., *Jewish Political Tradition*, 332.

51. As'ad Ghanem, Nadim Rouhana, and Oren Yiftachel, "Questioning 'Ethnic Democracy': A Response to Sammy Smooha," *Israel Studies* 3, no. 2 (Fall 1998): 253–267.

52. Ghanem, Rouhana, and Yiftachel, "Questioning," 265.

53. Golan-Agnon, *Next Year in Jerusalem*, 205.

54. Dr. Yousef T. Jabareen, "The Legal Status of the Arab-Palestinian Community in Israel," presentation to the Brandeis University Summer Institute for Israel Studies, Barta'a, July 11, 2006. He has compiled a list of other arenas (legal, socioeconomic, and political) in which Arab citizens either suffer formal discrimination or adverse effects.

55. Sammy Smooha, "The Model of Ethnic Democracy: Israel as a Jewish and Democratic State," *Nations and Nationalism* 8, no. 4 (2002): 475–503; Smooha, "Is Israel Western?" in *Comparing Modernities: Pluralism versus Homogeneity: Essays in Homage to Shmuel N. Eisenstadt*, ed. Eliezer Ben Rafael and Yitzhak Sternberg (Boston: Brill Academic Publishers, 2005), 413–442.

56. Yuval Yoaz, "The Quiet Revolution."

57. Justice Itzhak Zamir, presentation to the Brandeis University Summer Institute for Israel Studies, Sheraton Plaza Hotel, Jerusalem, July 10, 2006.

58. According to the Supreme Court registrar, in 2006, 2,306 petitions were filed with *bagatz*. The subject matter was noted in the computer for 1,254, out of which 714 were with regard to the occupied territories. In 2005 there were a total of 2,431 petitions with *bagatz*, the subject matter was noted for 1,490, out of which 817 regarded the occupied territories. Thanks to Dan Yakir for checking with the registrar on this information.

59. For details, see Michael Galchinsky, "The Jewish Settlements in the West Bank: International Law and Israeli Jurisprudence," *Israel Studies* 9, no. 3 (Fall 2004): 115–136.

60. See Antigona Ashkar, *Perpetual Limbo: Israel's Freeze on Unification of Palestinian Families in the Occupied Territories* (Jerusalem: B'Tselem and HaMoked, 2006). In May 2006 the Supreme Court dismissed by a 6-5 majority petitions brought by Adalah and ACRI against the constitutionality of the Citizenship and Entry into Israel law—HC 7052/03 *Adalah v. Minister of the Interior*; HC 8099/03 *Association for Civil Rights in Israel v. Minister of the Interior* (2006).

61. Interview with Dr. Ruchama Marton.

62. Rabbis for Human Rights, "Preventing Home Demolitions Trial," www.rhr.israel.net/projects/trial.shtml.

63. Itzhak Zamir, presentation.

64. Interview with Jessica Montell.

65. Herbert Hirsch, *Anti-Genocide: Building an American Movement to Prevent Genocide* (Westport, Conn.: Praeger, 2002), 58.

66. Interview with Dan Yakir; Golan-Agnon, *Next Year in Jerusalem*, 9; interview with Daphna Golan-Agnon, Jerusalem, July 18, 2006.

67. Ellman, "Cause Lawyering," 353.

68. Interview with Rabbi Arik Ascherman, executive director of Rabbis for Human Rights, July 19, 2006.

69. Lilach Chelnov, *Masekhet Atzma'ut* [Tractate Independence], (Jerusalem: Rabbis for Human Rights, 2006).

70. Interview with Rabbi Arik Ascherman.

71. The WUPJ's activity and perspective on religious pluralism issues was reflected in S. Z. Abramov, *Perpetual Dilemma: Jewish Religion in the Jewish State* (New York: World Union for Progressive Judaism, 1976).

72. Israel Religious Action Center website, irac.org/advocacy/irac/aboutirac/; Israel Religious Action Center, Annual Report, 1989–1990, WUPJ Collection, MS16/I4/37.

73. Donnelly, *Universal Human Rights*, 100.

74. Interview with Ruchama Marton.

75. Interview with Tamar Hermann, Faculty of Sociology and Political Science, Open University of Israel, director, Tami Steinmetz Center for Peace Research at Tel Aviv University, July 20, 2006.

76. See David Kretzmer, *The Occupation of Justice: The Supreme Court of Israel and the Occupied Territories* (Albany: State University of New York Press, 2002).

77. Interview with Rabbi Arik Ascherman.

78. Interview with Tamar Hermann.

79. Interview with Rolly Rosen, SHATIL organizational consultant, coordinator of international relations, and coordinator of assistance to human rights organizations, Jerusalem, July 17, 2006.

80. For a helpful list of ACRI's most important human and civil rights cases through 2005, see "Hitdaynuyot ha-agudah—piskeh din akronim" [Litigation of the Association for Civil Rights in Israel—Principle Decisions], compiled by Dan Yakir, December 26, 2005; for an English list of ACRI's "Legal Landmarks," see www.acri.org.il/english-acri/engine/story.asp?id=369.

81. Interview with Gila Svirsky.

82. Interview with Dr. Ruchama Marton.

83. Interview with Dan Yakir.

84. Interview with Dr. Ruchama Marton.

85. Neve Gordon, "Human Rights as a Contingent Foundation: The Case of Physicians for Human Rights," *Journal of Human Rights* 5, no. 1 (April 2006): 1–22.

86. Interview with Jessica Montell.

87. Interview with Dan Yakir.

88. Interview with Rolly Rosen.

89. Ellman, "Cause Lawyering," 383.

90. Interview with Jessica Montell.

91. Interview with Gila Svirsky; interview with Daphna Golan-Agnon; interview with Arik Ascherman.

92. On handling multiple constituencies, I learned much from my interview with Dan Yakir. Neve Gordon, in "Social Space and Power: Why Do Some Human Rights

NGOs Exert More Influence Than Others?" criticizes ACRI for compromising its principles, rather than acknowledging the significant role ACRI has played in giving a trusted face to human and civil rights work in Israeli society and within the overall dynamic of the network.

93. For another example of the way conflict among NGOs sometimes works to their common advantage, see Stephen Spector, *Operation Solomon: The Daring Rescue of the Ethiopian Jews* (New York: Oxford University Press, 2005), 53–54.

94. Interview with Dan Yakir.

95. Mark Melman, qtd. in interview with Rolly Rosen.

96. B'Tselem Annual Report, 2003, 16.

97. For example, see B'Tselem, *Through No Fault of Their Own: Israel's Punitive House Demolitions in the al-Aqsa Intifada,* information sheet, November 2004.

98. For an example of a PowerPoint presentation, see B'Tselem's report, *Under the Guise of Security: Routing the Separation Barrier to Enable the Expansion of Israeli Settlements in the West Bank,* joint report with Bimkom—Planners for Planning Rights, December 2005. Its website, www.btselem.org, includes links for maps, videos, and a photo archive.

99. B'Tselem Annual Report, 2003.

100. B'Tselem Annual Report, 2005.

101. Interview with Gila Svirsky.

102. Doug McAdam, John D. McCarthy, Mayer N. Zald, eds., *Comparative Perspectives on Social Movements: Political Opportunities, Mobilizing Structures, and Cultural Framings* (Cambridge: Cambridge University Press, 1996).

103. B'Tselem Annual Report, 1995, 1.

104. B'Tselem Annual Report, 2002, 2.

105. B'Tselem Annual Report, 2002, 18.

106. Elie Rekhess, "The Arabs of Israel after Oslo: Localization of the National Struggle," *Israel Studies* 7, no. 3 (Fall 2002): 1–44; Nadim Rouhama, "The Political Transformation of the Palestinians in Israel: From Acquiescence to Challenge," *Journal of Palestine Studies* 18, no. 3 (Spring 1989), 38–59; Robert Berger, "Israeli Inquiry Clears Police Who Killed 13 Israeli Arabs in 2000," *Voice of America News*, September 18, 2005, at www.voanews.com/english/archive/2005-09/2005-09-18-voa37.cfm?CFID=13945231&CFTOKEN=12316649..

107. Interview with Dr. Tamar Hermann.

108. In an interview with Rabbi Arik Ascherman, he described RHR's olive tree campaign as an outgrowth of the second intifada. The olive tree issue was also addressed by the High Court of Justice decision on the separation barrier, HC 2056/04, *Beit Sourik Village Council v. The Government of Israel*, 860; on stopping the IDF's use of Palestinians as hostages and human shields, see HC 3799/02, *Adalah—The Legal Center for Arab Minority Rights in Israel et al. v. GOC Central Command, IDF et al.* (2005), elyon1.court.gov.il/files_eng/02/990/037/a32/02037990.a32.HTM; on improvement of detention conditions, see HC 3278/02, *The Center for the Defence of the Individual, et al. v. Commander of the IDF Forces in the West Bank* (2005), elyon1.court.gov.il/files_eng/02/780/032/a06/02032780.a06.HTM; and HC 5591/02, *Halel Yassin et al. v. Yoni Ben-David—Commander of the Kziot Military Camp—Kziot*

Dention Facility (2005); and HC 3239/02, *Iad Ashak Mahmud Marab et al. v. IDF Commander in the West Bank et al.* (2003), elyon1.court.gov.il/files_eng/02/390/032/a04/02032390.a04.HTM.

109. Interview with Dan Yakir. Also see Galchinsky, "The Jewish Settlements."

110. HC 785/87, *Abd el Afu et al. v. Commander of the IDF Forces in the West Bank et al.* (1988); see also HC 5973/92, *Association for Civil Rights in Israel v. Minister of Defence and others* (1993), elyon1.court.gov.il/files_eng/92/730/059/z01/92059730.z01.HTM.

111. See HC 7052/03, *Adalah v. Minister of the Interior*; HC 8099/03, *Association for Civil Rights in Israel v. Minister of the Interior* (2006). See also Yael Stein, *Forbidden Families: Family Unification and Child Registration in East Jerusalem* (Jerusalem: B'Tselem, 2004); Ashkar, *Perpetual Limbo*.

112. Interview with Daphna Golan-Agnon.

113. The High Court of Justice agreed that nineteen miles of the barrier should be rerouted in HC 2056/04, *Beit Sourik Village Council v. The Government of Israel* (2004), elyon1.court.gov.il/files_eng/04/560/020/a28/04020560.a28.HTM; HCJ 7957/04, *Zaharan Yunis Muhammad Ma'arebe et al. v. Prime Minister of Israel et al.* (2005), elyon1.court.gov.il/files_eng/04/570/079/a14/04079570.a14.HTM.

114. Interview with Daphna Golan-Agnon.

115. B'Tselem Annual Report, 1999; HC 5100/94, *Public Committee against Torture in Israel v. The State of Israel and the General Security Service*; HC 4054/95, *The Association for Civil Rights in Israel v. The Prime Minister of Israel, the Minister of Justice, the Minister of Police, the Minister of the Environment, the Head of the General Security Service* (1999), elyon1.court.gov.il/files_eng/94/000/051/a09/94051000.a09.HTM. In addition, five individual petitioners brought separate claims, two represented by HaMoked—Center for the Defence of the Individual (founded by Dr. Lotte Salzberger), three by the Public Committee against Torture in Isael. The individual petitions asked the court to issue an order nisi directing the GSS to stop the use of shaking, sleep deprivation, the "Shabach position," and other forms of "moderate physical pressure."

116. See PCATI website: www.stoptorture.org.il/eng/activities.asp?menu=4&submenu=2.

117. Neve Gordon, "Outsourcing Violations: The Israeli Case," *Journal of Human Rights* 1, no. 3 (September 2002): 328; *Yidiot Ahronot*, February 4, 2000.

118. HC 5100/94, *The Public Committee against Torture in Israel v. The Government of Israel and the General Security Service.*

119. PCATI press release, November 7, 2001.

120. Yuval Ginbar, *Back to a Routine of Torture: Torture and Ill-treatment of Palestinian Detainees during Arrest, Detention and Interrogation September 2001–April 2003* (Jerusalem: PCATI, 2003).

121. Neve Gordon and Ruchama Marton, eds., *Torture: Human Rights, Medical Ethics and the Case of Israel* (London: Zed Books, 1995).

122. B'Tselem Annual Report, 1999, 16.

123. Interview with Jessica Montell.

124. Ronen Shnayderman, *Through No Fault of Their Own: Israel's Punitive House Demolitions in the al-Aqsa Intifada* (Jerusalem: B'tselem, 2004).

EPILOGUE: THE ROAD FROM DURBAN

1. Barbara Crossette, "U.N. Labels Anti-Semitism as Racism for the First Time," *New York Times*, December 10, 1998.

2. UN Press Release, "Kofi Annan Says 'Healing of Wounds' between Jewish Community and United Nations among His Priorities as Secretary General," SG/SM/7260, December 15, 1999.

3. Anthony Julius, Robert S. Rifkind, Jeffrey Weill, and Felice Gaer, "Antisemitism: An Assault on Human Rights," memorandum submitted to the UN World Conference against Racism, Racial Discrimination, Xenophobia, and Related Intolerance, Durban, South Africa, Jacob Blaustein Institute, August 2001; Felice Gaer, "Antisemitic Incidents Are Not Hooliganism—They Are Human Rights Abuse: The United Nations Should Address Them as Such," remarks to "Confronting anti-Semitism: Education for Tolerance and Understanding," UN Headquarters, New York, June 21, 2004.

4. UN General Assembly Resolution, "Elimination of All Forms of Intolerance and of Discrimination Based on Religion or Belief," A/RES/60/166, December 16, 2005.

5. UN News Centre, "UN Human Rights Council Should Broaden Its Focus beyond the Middle East—Annan," November 21, 2006, at www.un.org/apps/news/story.asp?NewsID=20686&Cr=rights&Cr1=council.

6. UN, "Human Rights Situation in the Occupied Palestinian Territory," Doc. A/HRC/S-1/L.1/Rev.1, July 6, 2006.

Bibliography

ARCHIVES

a. Jacob Rader Marcus Center of the American Jewish Archives, Cincinnati, Ohio (cited as "AJA"):

Coordinating Board of Jewish Organizations Collection
Raphael Lemkin Papers
Louis E. Shecter Papers (1921–1985)
US Holocaust Memorial Museum Collection
World Jewish Congress Collection
World Union for Progressive Judaism Collection

b. American Jewish Committee Archive, Jacob and Hilda Blaustein Research Library, New York (cited as "BL"):

Consultative Council of Jewish Organizations Papers
Memoranda, Statements, Releases, Etc., 1947–1953
Reports, 1947–1953
Foreign Affairs Department—International Organizations
Bert Gold Papers
World Conference against Racism, Racial Discrimination, Xenophobia and Other Intolerance (file)

INTERVIEWS

Rabbi Arik Ascherman, Executive Director, Rabbis for Human Rights, Jerusalem, July 19, 2006.

Liliane Kshensky Baxter, Director, The Lillian & A. J. Weinberg Center for Holocaust Education, William Bremen Jewish Heritage Museum, Atlanta, October 23, 2006.
Felice D. Gaer, Executive Director, Jacob Blaustein Institute for the Advancement of Human Rights, American Jewish Committee, New York, July 9, 2002.
Daphna Golan-Agnon, founding Research Director, B'Tselem, founder, Bat Shalom, Professor, Hebrew University Law School, Jerusalem, July 18, 2006.
Lev Goradetsky, Lecturer in Hebrew, Aramaic, and Mishnah studies, Russian State University for the Humanities, Moscow, September 12, 2005.
Tamar Hermann, Faculty of Sociology and Political Science, Open University of Israel, Director, Tami Steinmetz Center for Peace Research at Tel Aviv University, July 20, 2006.
Dorit Karlin, Director of Programs, Strategic Planning, Grants, and Partnerships, New Israel Fund, Jerusalem, July 17, 2006.
Leonid Lvov, Executive Director, Harold and Selma Light Center for Human Rights Advocacy, St. Petersburg, September 16, 2005.
Dr. Ruchama Marton, founder, Physicians for Human Rights—Israel, Tel Aviv, July 16, 2006.
Ruth Messinger, Executive Director, American Jewish World Service, email, November 8, 2006.
Jessica Montell, Executive Director, B'Tselem, Jerusalem, July 16, 2006.
Rolly Rosen, SHATIL Organizational Consultant, Coordinator of International Relations, and Coordinator of Assistance to Human Rights Organizations, Jerusalem, July 17, 2006.
Dr. Harris Schoenberg, former UN Affairs Director, B'nai B'rith International, United Nations Plaza Hotel, New York, July 10, 2002.
Gila Svirsky, Executive Director of New Israel Fund (1985–1991), Jerusalem, July 17, 2006.
Dan Yakir, Legal Advisor, Association for Civil Rights in Israel, Jerusalem, July 19, 2006.
Neta Ziv, Professor, Tel Aviv University Law School and first Legal Advisor of the Association for Civil Rights in Israel, Tel Aviv, July 18, 2006.

UNITED NATIONS BODIES AND OTHER INTERNATIONAL FORUMS

General Assembly

Convention against Torture and Other Cruel, Inhuman or Degrading Treatment or Punishment, 1984.
Convention on the Rights of the Child, 1989.
Convention on the Elimination of All Forms of Discrimination against Women, 1979.
Convention on the Elimination of All Forms of Racial Discrimination, 1966.
Declaration on the Elimination of All Forms of Intolerance and of Discrimination Based on Religion or Belief, 1981.

"Elimination of All Forms of Intolerance and of Discrimination Based on Religion or Belief," A/RES/60/166, December 16, 2005.
"Human Rights Situation in the Occupied Palestinian Territory," A/HRC/S1/L.1/Rev.1, July 6, 2006.
International Covenant on Civil and Political Rights, 1966.
International Covenant on Economic, Social, and Political Rights, 1966.
Special Committee to Investigate Israeli Practices Affecting the Human Rights of the Palestinian People and Other Arabs of the Occupied Territories, A/RES/2443/23, December 19, 1968.
Universal Declaration of Human Rights, 1948.

Security Council

"Former Yugoslavia," S/RES/771, August 13, 1992.

Economic and Social Council

E/RES/75(V), August 5, 1947 [a.k.a. "the self-denying rule"].
E/RES/1296 (XLIV), May 1968 [the public procedure].
E/RES/1503 (XLVIII), May 27, 1970 [the secret procedure].
"Genocide: Communication from the Government of Pakistan," E/660, February 12, 1948.
"Grave and Massive Violations of the Human Rights of the Palestinian People by Israel," E/CN.4/RES/S-5/1, October 17, 2000.
"Report of the Commission on Human Rights on Its Fifth Special Session," E/2000/112, November 9, 2000.

Commission on Human Rights and Subcommission on the Promotion and Protection of Human Rights

UN Secretary-General, "Declaration of the Right of Asylum: Comments of Non-Governmental Organizations," E/CN.4/794/Add.2, February 26, 1960.
E/CN.4/NGO/136, March 18, 1966.
E/CN.4/NGO/140, May 5, 1966.
"Situation in Occupied Palestine," E/CN.4/RES/2001/2, April 6, 2001.
"Human Rights in the Occupied Syrian Golan," E/CN.4/RES/2001/6, April 18, 2001.
"Question of the Violation of Human Rights in the Occupied Arab Territories, including Palestine," E/CN.4/RES/2001/7, April 18, 2001.
"Israeli Settlements in the Occupied Arab Territories," E/CN.4/RES/2001/8, April 18, 2001.
"Situation of Human Rights in the Occupied Palestinian Territory," E/CN.4/RES/2002/1, April 5, 2002.
"Situation in Occupied Palestine," E/CN.4/RES/2002/3, April 12, 2002.

"Human Rights in the Occupied Syrian Golan," E/CN.4/RES/2002/6, April 12, 2002.
"Israeli Settlements in the Occupied Arab Territories," E/CN.4/RES/2002/7, April 12, 2002.
"Question of the Violation of Human Rights in the Occupied Arab Territories, including Palestine," E/CN.4/RES/2002/8, April 15, 2002.
"Human Rights Situation of Lebanese Detainees in Israel," E/CN.4/RES/2002/10, April 19, 2002.
"The Situation of Human Rights in the Occupied Palestinian Territory," E/CN.4/RES/2002/90, April 26, 2002.
"Situation in Occupied Palestine," E/CN.4/RES/2003/3, April 14, 2003.
"Human Rights in the Occupied Syrian Golan," E/CN.4/RES/2003/5, April 15, 2003.
"Question of the Violation of Human Rights in the Occupied Arab Territories, including Palestine," E/CN.4/RES/2003/6, April 15, 2003.
"Israeli Settlements in the Occupied Arab Territories," E/CN.4/RES/2003/7, April 15, 2003.
"Human Rights Situation of the Lebanese Detainees in Israel," E/CN.4/RES/2003/8, April 16, 2003.
Francesco Capotorti, Special Rapporteur on the Question of Minorities for the UN Subcommission on Prevention of Discrimination and Protection of Minorities, *Study on the Rights of Persons Belonging to Ethnic, Religious, and Linguistic Minorities* (New York: United Nations, 1991).
John Dugard, Special Rapporteur, "The Situation of Human Rights in the Palestinian Territories Occupied since 1967," 1993–present.
Nicodème Ruhashyankiko, Special Rapporteur, "Study of the Question of the Prevention and Punishment of the Crime of Genocide," report to the UN Subcommission on Prevention of Discrimination and Protection of Minorities, 25th Session, E/CN.4/Sub.2/L.565, May 23, 1972.

International Criminal Court

Rome Statute of the International Criminal Court (Rome, 1998), Art. 8(2)(b)(viii), 12, 13, 14, 15.

International Court of Justice

"Legal Consequences of the Construction of a Wall in the Occupied Palestinian Territory," Advisory Opinion, General List No. 131 (The Hague, July 9, 2004).
Democratic Republic of the Congo v. Belgium, (The Hague, February 14, 2002), Separate Opinion of Judge Guillaume, President.

Other Conference Proceedings, Treaties, Decisions, and Working Papers

1949 Geneva Convention IV Relative to the Protection of Civilian Persons in Time of War, Art. 33, 49.

Asian Preparatory Meeting, World Conference against Racism, Racial Discrimination, Xenophobia and Related Intolerance. "Declaration and Plan of Action." Tehran, Islamic Republic of Iran, February 19–21, 2001, at www.unhchr.ch/html/racism/02-recomtehr.html.

United Nations News Centre, "UN Human Rights Council Should Broaden Its Focus beyond the Middle East—Annan," November 21, 2006, at www.un.org/apps/news/story.asp?NewsID=20686&Cr=rights&Cr1=council

United Nations News Centre, "Kofi Annan Says 'Healing of Wounds' between Jewish Community and United Nations among His Priorities as Secretary General," SG/SM/7260, December 15, 1999.

ISRAEL SUPREME COURT DECISIONS

Abd el Afu et al. v. The Commander of the IDF Forces in the West Bank et al., HC 785/87.

Adalah—The Legal Center for Arab Minority Rights in Israel et al. v. GOC Central Command, IDF et al., HC 3799/02.

Association for Civil Rights in Israel v. Minister of Defence and others, HC 5973/92.

Association for Civil Rights in Israel v. The Prime Minister of Israel, The Minister of Justice, The Minister of Police, The Minister of the Environment, The Head of the General Security Service, HC 4054/95.

Beit Sourik Village Council v. The Government of Israel, HC 2056/04.

The Center for the Defence of the Individual, et al. v. Commander of the IDF Forces in the West Bank, HC 3278/02.

Iad Ashak Mahmud Marab et al. v. IDF Commander in the West Bank et al., HC 3239/02.

Ka'adan v. Israel's Land Administration, HC 6698/95.

Zaharan Yunis Muhammad Ma'arebe et al. v. Prime Minister of Israel et al., HC 7957/04.

Public Committee against Torture in Israel v. The State of Israel and the General Security Service, HC 5100/94.

Halel Yassin et al. v. Yoni Ben-David—Commander of the Kziot Military Camp—Kziot Dention Facility, HC 5591/02.

HEBREW BIBLE AND MISHNAH

Gen. 1:27; 6:7–10

Exod. 12:49; 22:21; 23:9

Lev. 19:10; 19:33–34; 24:22; 25

Num. 15:15–16; 21:21–25; 31:7–18; 33–35

Deut. 2:32–25, 10:19, 12:1

Josh. 10:28–40; 11:11–12, 21

2 Sam. 12:1–14

Jer. 7:6
Zech. 7:10
Mal. 3:5
Amos 5:24
Pss. 94:6, 146:9
Mishnah *Avot* 1:14

OTHER SOURCES

Abramov, S. Z. *Perpetual Dilemma: Jewish Religion in the Jewish State*. New York: World Union for Progressive Judaism, 1976.

Alexander, Jeffrey. *The Civil Sphere*. New Haven, Conn.: Yale University Press, 2007.

Alter, Robert, ed. *Modern Hebrew Literature*. West Orange, N.J.: Behrman House, 1975.

Altshuler, Stuart. *From Exodus to Freedom: The History of the Soviet Jewry Movement*. Lanham, Md.: Rowman and Littlefield, 2005.

American Jewish World Service, "Disaster Response," at www.ajws.org/disaster.cfm.

American Jewish Year Book. Philadelphia: Jewish Publication Society, 1908, 1929, 1942–1943, 1962, 1975.

Amnesty International. *Broken Lives—A Year of Intifada: Israel/Occupied Territories/Palestinian Authority*. London: Amnesty International Publications, 2001.

———. *Report and Recommendations of an Amnesty International Mission to the Government of the State of Israel, 3–7 June 1979: Including the Government's Response and Amnesty International's Comments*. London: Amnesty International Publications, 1980.

Anderson, Benedict. *Imagined Communities: Reflections on the Origin and Spread of Nationalism*, revised ed. (New York: Verso, 2006).

Andreopoulos, George J., ed. *Genocide*. Pennsylvania Studies in Human Rights. Philadelphia: University of Pennsylvania Press, 1994.

Arian, Asher, Michal Shamir, and Raphael Ventura. "Public Opinion and Political Change: Israel and the Intifada." *Comparative Politics* 24, no. 3 (April 1992): 317–334.

Ashkar, Antigona. *Perpetual Limbo: Israel's Freeze on Unification of Palestinian Families in the Occupied Territories*. Jerusalem: B'Tselem and HaMoked, 2006.

Association for Civil Rights in Israel. "Ka'adan Family Allowed to Build Home in Jewish Residential Community," at www.acri.org.il/english-acri/engine/story.asp?id=177.

Aviv, Caryn, and David Schneer. *New Jews: The End of the Jewish Diaspora*. New York: New York University Press, 2005.

Avneri, Uri. *Israel and the Palestinians: A Different Israeli View*. New York: Breira, 1975.

Banerjee, Neela. "Muslims' Plight in Sudan Resonates with Jews in U.S." *New York Times*, April 30, 2006, 19.

Barak, Aharon. "The Constitutional Revolution: Protected Basic Rights," in Michael Walzer, Menachem Lorberbaum, and Noam J. Zohar, *The Jewish Political Tradition*, vol. 1. New Haven, Conn.: Yale University Press, 2000.

———. "The Role of the Supreme Court in a Democracy." *Israel Studies* 3, no. 2 (Fall 1998): 6–29.

Barzilai, Gad. "War, Democracy, and Internal Conflict: Israel in a Comparative Perspective." *Comparative Politics* 31, no. 3 (April 1999): 317–336.

Baskin, Judith. "Journal of Professional Proceedings, Jewish Studies Delegation to Russia, Sept. 9–18, 2005" [unpublished].

Becker, Avi. "Superpower Relations and Jewish Identity in the Soviet Union." In *Jewish Culture and Identity in the Soviet Union*, edited by Yaacov Ro'i and Avi Becker, 445–462. New York: New York University Press, 1991.

Berger, Robert. "Israeli Inquiry Clears Police Who Killed 13 Israeli Arabs in 2000." *Voice of America News*, September 18, 2005, at www.voanews.com/english/archive/2005-09/2005-09-18-voa37.cfm?CFID=13945231&CFTOKEN=12316649.

Biale, David, Michael Galchinsky, and Susannah Heschel, eds. *Insider/Outsider: American Jews and Multiculturalism.* Berkeley: University of California Press, 1998.

Blaustein, Jacob. "Human Rights—A Challenge to the United Nations and to Our Generation." Dag Hammarskjold Memorial Lecture, Columbia University, December 4, 1963.

Bookbinder, Hyman. *Off the Wall: Memoirs of a Political Junkie*. Washington, D.C.: Seven Locks Press, 1991.

Brandeis, Louis D. "Zionism is Consistent with American Patriotism" (June 1915). In *The Jew in the Modern World: A Documentary History*, 2nd ed., edited by Paul Mendes-Flohr and Jehuda Reinharz, 496. New York: Oxford University Press, 1995.

Boyarin, Jonathan, and Daniel Boyarin. *Powers of Diaspora: Two Essays on the Relevance of Jewish Culture*. St. Paul: University of Minnesota Press, 2002.

Brachman Shoup, Sarai. "From Leadership to Community: Laying the Foundation for Jewish Community in Russia." In *Jewish Life after the USSR*, edited by Zvi Gitelman, with Musya Glants and Marshall I. Goldman, 127–140. Bloomington: Indiana University Press, 2003.

Brownlie, Ian, ed. *Basic Documents on Human Rights*, 3rd ed. New York: Oxford University Press, 1998.

Broyde, Michael. "The Bounds of Wartime Military Conduct in Jewish Law: An Expansive Conception." Herbert Berman Memorial Lecture, Center for Jewish Studies, Queens College, CUNY, November 3, 2004.

Brym, Robert J. "Russian Anti-Semitism, 1996–2000." In *Jewish Life after the USSR*, edited by Zvi Gitelman, with Musya Glants and Marshall I. Goldman, 99–113. Bloomington: Indiana University Press, 2003.

B'Tselem. "Torture during Interrogations: Testimony of Palestinian Detainees and Israeli Interrogators." Information sheet. November 1994.

———. "Through No Fault of Their Own: Israel's Punitive House Demolitions in the al-Aqsa Intifada." Information sheet. November 2004.

———. *Under the Guise of Security: Routing the Separation Barrier to Enable the Expansion of Israeli Settlements in the West Bank*. Joint report with Bimkom–Planners for Planning Rights. Jerusalem: December 2005.

———. Annual Reports, 1993–2005.

Buergenthal, Thomas. *International Law in a Nutshell*, 2nd ed. St. Paul, Minn.: West Publishing, 1995.

Buwalda, Petrus. *They Did Not Dwell Alone: Jewish Emigration from the Soviet Union, 1967–1990*. Baltimore, Md.: Johns Hopkins University Press, 1997.

Carey, Henry F., and John Carey. "Hostility in United Nations Bodies to Judaism, the Jewish People and Jews as Such." *Israel Yearbook of Human Rights* 17, 29–40. Dordrecht: Martinus Nijhoff, 1987.

Cassin, René. "From the Ten Commandments to the Rights of Man," at www.udhr50.org/history/tencomms.htm.

Chalidze, Valery. *The Soviet Human Rights Movement: A Memoir*. New York: AJC, 1984.

Chanes, Jerome A. "Who Does What? Jewish Advocacy and Jewish Interest." In *Jews in American Politics: Essays*, edited by L. Sandy Maisel and Ira N. Forman. Lanham, Md.: Rowman and Littlefield, 2004.

Charny, Israel W. "Leo Kuper: A Great Pioneer." In *Pioneers of Genocide Studies*, edited by Samuel Totten and Steven L. Jacobs. New York: Transaction Publishers, 2002.

———. "Toward a Generic Definition of Genocide." In *Genocide*, edited by George J. Andreopoulos, 64–94. Philadelphia: University of Pennsylvania Press, 1994.

———, ed. *Toward the Understanding and Prevention of Genocide: Proceedings of the International Conference on the Holocaust and Genocide*. Boulder, Colo.: Westview Press, 1984.

———, ed. *The Widening Circle of Genocide: A Critical Bibliographic Review*. New Brunswick, N.J.: Transaction Publishers, 1994.

Chelnov, Lilach. *Masekhet Atzma'ut* [Tractate Independence]. Jerusalem: Rabbis for Human Rights, 2006.

Chomsky, Noam. "Open Letter to Roger Baldwin." *Palestinian Human Rights Bulletin*, August 30, 1977.

Clapham, Andrew. "Creating the High Commissioner for Human Rights: The Outside Story." *European Journal of International Law* 5 (1994): 556–568.

Clinton, Bill. *My Life*. New York: Alfred A. Knopf, 2004.

Coalition of Women for Peace. Mission statement, at www.coalitionofwomen.org.

Cohen, Allison S. "Crisis in Darfur: Determining Genocide." JBI Human Rights Discussion Paper. November 2004.

———. "We Must Halt the Genocide in Darfur, Sudan, Now." JBI Human Rights Discussion Paper. June 2005.

Cohen, Robin. *Global Diasporas: An Introduction*. Seattle: University of Washington Press, 1997.

Cohn, Haim. *Human Rights in the Bible and Talmud*. Tel Aviv: MOD Books, 1989.

———. *Human Rights in Jewish Law*. London: Institute of Jewish Affairs, 1984.

Coordinating Board of Jewish Organizations. *Memorandum on Discrimination in the Matter of the Right of Everyone to Leave Any Country Including His Own and to*

Return to His Country. New York: Coordinating Board of Jewish Organizations, 1960.

Cotler, Irwin. "Jewish NGOs and Religious Human Rights: A Case Study." In *Human Rights in Judaism: Cultural, Religious, and Political Perspectives*, edited by Michael J. Broyde and John Witte, Jr. Northvale, N.J.: Jason Aronson, 1998.

——, ed. *Nuremberg Forty Years Later: The Struggle against Injustice in Our Time*. International Human Rights Conference, November 1987, Papers and Proceedings, and Retrospective, 1993. Montreal: McGill-Queen's University Press, 1995.

Council of Europe. *Human Rights in International Law: Basic Texts*. Strasbourg, 1991.

Crossette, Barbara. "U.N. Labels Anti-Semitism as Racism for the First Time." *New York Times*, December 10, 1998.

Dahan-Kalev, Henriette. "You're So Pretty—You Don't Look Moroccan." *Israel Studies* 6, no. 1 (Spring 2001): 6–14.

DellaPergola, Sergio, and Amos Gilboa, project heads, and Rami Tal, ed. "The Jewish People 2004: Between Thriving and Decline." Annual Assessment No. 1. Jerusalem: Jewish People Policy Planning Institute (JPPPI), 2004.

DellaPergola, Sergio. "Demography in Israel at the Dawn of the Twenty-first Century." In *Jews in Israel: Contemporary Social and Cultural Patterns*, edited by Uzi Rebhun and Chaim I. Waxman, 24. Hanover, N.H.: University Press of New England, 2004.

Dinstein, Yoram. "Soviet Jewry and International Human Rights." In *Essays on Human Rights: Contemporary Issues and Jewish Perspectives*, edited by David Sidorsky, with Sidney Liskofsky and Jerome Shestack, 126–143. Philadelphia: Jewish Publication Society of America, 1979.

——. "The International Law of Belligerent Occupation and Human Rights." *Israel Yearbook on Human Rights* 8 (1978): 104–43.

Donnelly, Jack. *Universal Human Rights in Theory and Practice*, 2nd ed. Ithaca, N.Y.: Cornell University Press, 2003.

Economist. "The 'Jews of Africa.'" August 19, 2004.

Eisen, Arnold. *Galut: Modern Jewish Reflection on Homelessness and Homecoming*. Bloomington: Indiana University Press, 1986.

Ellerin, Max, and Abraham Karlikow. *Zionism, Israel, and the New Left*. New York: AJC, 1971.

Ellman, Stephen. "Cause Lawyering in the Third World." In *Cause Lawyering: Political Commitments and Professional Responsibilities*, edited by Austin Sarat and Stuart Scheingold, 354–355. New York: Oxford University Press, 1998.

Essas, Eliahu. "The Moscow Symposium: Ten Years Later." In *Jewish Culture and Identity in the Soviet Union*, edited by Yaacov Ro'i and Avi Becker, 262–265. New York: New York University Press, 1991.

Falah, Ghazi. "The Spatial Manifestation of Threat: Israelis and Palestinians Seek a 'Good' Border." *Political Geography* 14, no. 8 (1995): 689–706.

Fein, Helen. *Accounting for Genocide*. New York: Free Press, 1979.

——. "Genocide, Terror, Life Integrity, and War Crimes: The Case for Discrimination." In *Genocide*, edited by George J. Andreopoulos, 95–108. Philadelphia: University of Pennsylvania Press, 1994.

———. "States of Genocide and Other States." In *Will Genocide Ever End?* edited by Carol Rittner, John K. Roth, and James M. Smith, 47. St. Paul, Minn.: Paragon House, 2002.

Ferencz, Benjamin. "Opening Statement of the Prosecution." *Trial of the Major War Criminals*, vol. 1 (Neuremberg, Germany: Secretariat of the Tribunal, 1947), 32.

———. Website, at www.benferencz.org/bio.html.

Fink, Carole. *Defending the Rights of Others: The Great Powers, the Jews, and International Minority Protection, 1878–1938*. New York: Cambridge University Press, 2004.

Fowler, Jerry. "Out of the Darkness: Responding to Genocide in the Twenty-first Century." In *Century of Genocide*, 2nd ed., edited by Samuel Totten, William S. Parsons, and Israel W. Charny, 456. New York: Routledge, 2004.

Frankel, Jonathan. "The Soviet Regime and Anti-Zionism: An Analysis." In *Jewish Culture and Identity in the Soviet Union*, edited by Yaacov Ro'i and Avi Becker, 310-354. New York: New York University Press, 1991.

Fuchs, Lawrence. *The Political Behavior of American Jews*. Glencoe, Ill.: Free Press, 1956.

Gaer, Felice D. "Antisemitic Incidents Are Not Hooliganism—They Are Human Rights Abuse: The United Nations Should Address Them as Such." Remarks to "Confronting Anti-Semitism: Education for Tolerance and Understanding." UN Headquarters, New York, June 21, 2004.

———. "And Never the Twain Shall Meet?" In *The International Rights of Women: Instruments of Change*, ed. Carol Elizabeth Lockwood, Daniel Barstow Magraw, Margaret Faith Spring, and S. I. Strong. Washington, D.C.: ABA, 1998. 1–89.

———. *NGOs and the U.N. High Commissioner for Human Rights*. Atlanta: Carter Center, 1997. 81–96.

———. "Reality Check: Human Rights NGOs Confront Governments at the UN." In *NGOs, the UN, and Global Governance*, edited by Thomas G. Weiss and Leon Gordenker. Boulder, Colo.: Lynne Rienner, 1996.

Galchinsky, Michael. "Gaer, Felice D." *Encyclopedia Judaica*, 2nd ed., v. 7. Detroit, Mich.: Thomson Gale, 2006.

———. "The Jewish Settlements in the West Bank: International Law and Israeli Jurisprudence." *Israel Studies* 9, no. 3 (Fall 2004): 115–136.

———. *The Origin of the Modern Jewish Woman Writer*. Detroit, Mich.: Wayne State University Press, 1996.

———. "Scattered Seeds: A Dialogue of Diasporas." In *Insider/Outsider: American Jews and Multiculturalism*, edited by David Biale, Michael Galchinsky, and Susannah Heschel, 185–211. Berkeley: University of California Press, 1998.

Gardner, Richard N. *In Pursuit of World Order*. New York: Praeger, 1964.

Genocide Watch. Directors and Advisors, at www.genocidewatch.org/DirectorsAdvisors.htm.

Ghanem, As'ad, Nadim Rouhana, and Oren Yiftachel. "Questioning 'Ethnic Democracy': A Response to Sammy Smooha." *Israel Studies* 3, no. 2 (Fall 1998): 253–267.

Ginbar, Yuval. *Back to a Routine of Torture: Torture and Ill-treatment of Palestinian Detainees during Arrest, Detention and Interrogation September 2001–April 2003*. Jerusalem: Public Committee against Torture in Israel, 2003.

Gitelman, Zvi. "The Evolution of Jewish Culture and Identity in the Soviet Union." In *Jewish Culture and Identity in the Soviet Union*, edited by Yaacov Ro'i and Avi Becker, 10–14. New York: New York University Press, 1991.

———. "Thinking about Being Jewish in Russia and Ukraine." In *Jewish Life after the USSR*, edited by Zvi Gitelman, with Musya Glants and Marshall I. Goldman, 59. Bloomington: Indiana University Press, 2003.

Gitelman, Zvi, ed., with Musya Glants and Marshall I. Goldman. *Jewish Life after the USSR*. Bloomington: Indiana University Press, 2003.

Golan-Agnon, Daphna. *Next Year in Jerusalem*. Translated by Janine Woolfson. New York: New Press, 2005.

Gold, Steven J. *The Israeli Diaspora*. Seattle: University of Washington Press, 2002.

Goldberg, David Theo, ed., *Multiculturalsm: A Critical Reader*. Oxford: Basil Blackwell, 1994.

Goldberg, Paul. *The Final Act: The Dramatic, Revealing Story of the Moscow Helsinki Watch Group*. New York: William Morrow and Company, 1988.

Goldstein, Yossi. "The Jewish National Movement in the Soviet Union: A Profile." In *Jewish Culture and Identity in the Soviet Union*, edited by Yaacov Ro'i and Avi Becker, 27–41. New York: New York University Press, 1991.

Goodman, Lenn E. *Judaism, Human Rights, and Human Values*. Oxford: Oxford University Press, 1998.

Gordon, Neve. "Human Rights as a Contingent Foundation: The Case of Physicians for Human Rights." *Journal of Human Rights* 5, no. 1 (April 2006): 1–22.

———. "Outsourcing Violations: The Israeli Case." *Journal of Human Rights* 1, no. 3 (September 2002): 328.

———. "Social Space and Power: Why Do Some Human Rights NGOs Exert More Influence Than Others?" [unpublished].

Gordon, Neve, and Nitza Berkovitch. "Human Rights Discourse in Domestic Settings: How Does It Emerge?" *Political Studies* 55 (2007): 243–266.

Gordon, Neve, and Ruchama Marton, eds. *Torture: Human Rights, Medical Ethics, and the Case of Israel*. London: Zed Books, 1995.

Green, Leslie C. "Jewish Issues on the Human-Rights Agenda in the First Half of the Twentieth Century." In *Essays on Human Rights: Contemporary Issues and Jewish Perspectives*, edited by David Sidorsky, with Sidney Liskofsky and Jerome J. Shestack, 297–308. Philadelphia: JPSA, 1979.

Greenberg, Anna, and Kenneth D. Wald. "Still Liberal after All These Years? The Contemporary Political Behavior of American Jewry." In *Jews in American Politics: Essays*, edited by Sandy Maisel and Ira N. Forman. Lanham, Md.: Rowman and Littlefield, 2004.

Halliday, Fred. "Global Governance: Prospects and Problems." In *The Global Transformations Reader: An Introduction to the Globalization Debate*, edited by David Held and Anthony McGrew, 431–441. Malden, Mass.: Polity Press, 2000.

Halpern, Ben. "Jewish Nationalism: Self-Determination as a Human Right." In *Essays on Human Rights: Contemporary Issues and Jewish Perspectives*, edited by David Sidorsky, with Sidney Liskofsky and Jerome J. Shestack, 317. Philadelphia: JPSA, 1979.

Halpern, Ben, and Jehuda Reinharz. *Zionism and the Creation of a New Society*. Hanover, N.H.: Brandeis University Press, 2000.

Haas, Peter J. *Human Rights and the World's Major Religions, Volume 1: The Jewish Tradition*. Westport, Conn.: Praeger Publishers, 2005.

Hannum, Hurst. *The Right to Leave and Return in International Law and Practice*. Boston: Martinus Nijhoff Publishers, 1987.

Harff, Barbara. "Early Warning and Genocide Prevention." In *Will Genocide Ever End?* edited by Carol Rittner, John K. Roth, and James M. Smith, 127–130. St. Paul, Minn.: Paragon House, 2002.

Harris, David. *In the Trenches: Selected Speeches and Writings of an American Jewish Activist, 1979–1999*. New York: Ktav Publishing House, 2000.

———. "Letter from a Diplomatic Marathoner," October 13, 2003, at www.ajc.org/site/apps/nl/content3.asp?c=ijITI2PHKoG&b=845459&ct=1089261.

Harris, David, and Ruth Messinger. "Bitter Jewish Experience Means Community Can't Be Silent on Darfur." *Jewish Telegraphic Agency*, July 18, 2005.

Held, David. "Regulating Globalization?" In *The Global Transformations Reader: An Introduction to the Globalization Debate*, edited by David Held and Anthony McGrew, 425–429. Malden, Mass.: Polity Press, 2000.

Held, David, and Anthony McGrew, eds. *The Global Transformations Reader: An Introduction to the Globalization Debate*. Malden, Mass.: Polity Press, 2000.

Helsinki Watch Committee. *Glasnost in Jeopardy: Human Rights in the USSR*. New York: Human Rights Watch, 1991.

Henkin, Louis, ed. *The International Bill of Rights: The Covenant on Civil and Political Rights*. New York: Columbia University Press, 1981.

———, ed. *World Politics and the Jewish Condition: Essays Prepared for a Task Force on the World of the 1970s of the American Jewish Committee*. New York: Quadrangle Books, 1972.

Hertzberg, Arthur. *The French Enlightenment and the Jews: The Origins of Modern Anti-Semitism*. New York: Columbia University Press, 1968.

———, ed. *The Zionist Idea: A Historical Analysis and Reader*. Philadelphia: Jewish Publication Society, 1997.

Herzl, Theodor. "The Jewish State" (1896), in *The Zionist Idea: A Historical Analysis and Reader*, ed. Arthur Hertzberg. Philadelphia: Jewish Publication Society, 1997.

Hirsch, Herbert. *Anti-Genocide: Building an American Movement to Prevent Genocide*. Westport, Conn.: Praeger, 2002.

Hirsch, Richard G. "There Shall Be No Poor." In *Judaism and Human Rights*, edited by Milton Konvitz, 234–246. New York: W. W. Norton, with the B'nai B'rith Commission on Adult Jewish Education, 1972.

Hirsch, Samson Raphael. "Do Not Destroy!" in ed. Milton Konvitz, *Judaism and Human rights*. New York: W. W. Norton with the B'nai B'rith Commission on Adult Jewish Education, 1972.

Hoar, Jennifer. "Jews for Justice in Darfur." *CBS News*, May 1, 2006, at www.cbsnews.com/stories/2006/05/01/world/main1567410.shtml.

Hobsbawm, E. J. *Nations and Nationalism since 1980*. New York: Cambridge University Press, 1990.

Hoffman, Stefani. "Jewish Samizdat and the Rise of Jewish National Consciousness." In *Jewish Culture and Identity in the Soviet Union*, edited by Yaacov Ro'i and Avi Becker, 88–111. New York: New York University Press, 1991.

Human Rights Watch/Middle East. *Torture and Ill-Treatment: Israel's Interrogation of Palestinians from the Occupied Territories*. New York: Human Rights Watch, 1994.

Human Rights Watch. *Kosovo: Rape as a "Weapon of Ethnic Cleansing."* New York: Human Rights Watch, 2000.

———. *Yugoslavia: Human Rights Abuses in Kosovo, 1990–1992*. New York: Human Rights Watch, 1992.

Humphrey, John. *Human Rights and the United Nations: A Great Adventure*. Dobbs Ferry, N.Y.: Transnational Publishers, 1984.

Hunt, Lynn. *Inventing Human Rights: A History*. New York: W. W. Norton, 2007.

Huttenbach, Henry R. "Anticipating Genocide." In *Will Genocide Ever End?* edited by Carol Rittner, John K. Roth, and James M. Smith, 123–126. St. Paul, Minn.: Paragon House, 2002.

Ingles, José D. *Study of Discrimination in Respect of the Right of Everyone to Leave Any Country, including His Own, and to Return to His Country.* New York: United Nations, 1963.

International Council of the World Conference on Soviet Jewry in cooperation with the Jewish Communities concerned, *The Position of Soviet Jewry, 1983–1986: Report on the Implementation of the Helsinki Final Act since the Madrid Follow-Up Conference*. London: Institute of Jewish Affairs, 1986.

International Criminal Court. "Rome Statute of the International Criminal Court," at www.un.org/law/icc/general/overview.htm.

Israel Religious Action Center. Website, at irac.org/advocacy/irac/aboutirac/.

Israel Yearbook on Human Rights. Boston: Martirnus Nijhoff Publishers, 1971–present.

Jabareen, Yousef T. "The Legal Status of the Arab-Palestinian Community in Israel." Presentation to the Brandeis University Summer Institute for Israel Studies, Barta'a, July 11, 2006.

Jacob Blaustein Institute for the Advancement of Human Rights. *Twenty-five Years on the Cutting Edge of Human Rights: JBI's 25th Anniversary Review*. New York: AJC, May 1997.

Jacobs, Steven Leonard. "Genesis of the Concept of Genocide According to Its Author from the Original Sources." *Human Rights Review* 3, no. 2 (January–March 2002): 98–103.

The Jewish Monthly. "Is Genocide Here to Stay?" December 1996–January 1997, 27.

The Jewish Week. "Herzog to Diaspora Jews: Keep Israel Criticism to Ourselves." July 15, 1983.

Jewish World Watch. "Jewish World Watch . . . A Call to Conscience," at www.jewishworldwatch.org/about/.

Julius, Anthony, Robert S. Rifkind, Jeffrey Weill, and Felice D. Gaer. "Antisemitism: An Assault on Human Rights." Memorandum submitted to the UN World Conference against Racism, Racial Discrimination, Xenophobia, and Related Intolerance, Durban, South Africa. Jacob Blaustein Institute, August 2001.

Kallen, Horace M. "Democracy versus the Melting-Pot." In *Jewish American Literature: A Norton Anthology*, edited by Jules Chametzky, John Felstiner, Hilene Flanzbaum, and Kathryn Hellerstein, 207–216. New York: W. W. Norton, 2007.

Kant, Immanuel. "Toward Perpetual Peace: A Philosophical Project." In *Practical Philosophy*, Cambridge Edition of the Works of Immanuel Kant, translated and edited by Mary J. Gregor, 326. New York: Cambridge University Press, 1996.

Karlikow, Abraham. *The Brussels World Conference on Soviet Jewry: an Analysis*. New York: AJC, 1971.

Kissinger, Henry A. "The Pitfalls of 'Universal Jurisdiction.'" *Foreign Affairs* (July–August 2001): 86–96.

Knisbacher, Mitchell. "The Jews of Iraq and the International Protection of the Rights of Minorities (1856–1976)." In *Essays on Human Rights: Contemporary Issues and Jewish Perspectives*, edited by David Sidorsky, with Sidney Liskofsky and Jerome J. Shestack, 157–178. Philadelphia: JPSA, 1979.

Konvitz, Milton, ed. *Judaism and Human Rights*. New York: W. W. Norton with the B'nai B'rith Commission on Adult Jewish Education, 1972.

Korey, William. *An Epitaph for Raphael Lemkin*. New York: AJC, June 2001.

———. *NGOs and the Universal Declaration of Human Rights: "A Curious Grapevine."* New York: St. Martin's Press, 1988.

———. "Scapegoat at the UN." *Jewish Chronicle*, October 31, 1980.

Kretzmer, David. *The Occupation of Justice: The Supreme Court of Israel and the Occupied Territories*. Albany: State University of New York Press, 2002.

Kristof, Nicholas D. "If Not Now, When?" *New York Times*, October 29, 2006, 13.

———. "Walking the Talk," *New York Times*, October 9, 2005, 13.

Kuper, Leo. *Genocide: Its Political Use in the Twentieth Century*. New Haven, Conn.: Yale University Press, 1981.

———. "Reflections on the Prevention of Genocide." In *Genocide Watch*, edited by Helen F. Fein, 135–161. New Haven, Conn.: Yale University Press, 1992.

———. "Theoretical Issues Relating to Genocide: Uses and Abuses." In *Genocide*, edited by George J. Andreopoulos, 31–46. Philadelphia: University of Pennsylvania Press, 1994.

Kymlicka, Will. *Multicultural Citizenship: A Liberal Theory of Minority Rights*. New York: Oxford University Press, 1996.

Landau Commission Report. 1987, paragraphs 2.25-2.46.

Las, Nelly. *Jewish Women in a Changing World: A History of the International Council of Jewish Women (ICJW), 1899–1995*. Translated by Stephanie Nakache. Jerusalem: A. Harman Institute of Contemporary Jewry, 1996.

Lasensky, Scott. "A System of Its Own? Mapping Jewish Foreign Policy and World Politics." Paper given at the Association of Israel Studies annual meeting, May 2005.

Lauterpacht, Hersch. *The International Bill of the Rights of Man*. New York: Cambridge University Press, 1944.

——. *International Law*. Cambridge: Cambridge University Press, 1978.

Lawyers Committee for Human Rights. *Human Rights and Legal Reform in the Russian Federation*. New York: Lawyers Committee for Human Rights, 1993.

Lazin, Fred A. *The Struggle for Soviet Jewry in American Politics: Israel versus the American Jewish Establishment*. Lanham, Md.: Lexington Books, 2005.

Leaning, Jennifer. "Identifying Precursors." In *Will Genocide Ever End?* edited by Carol Rittner, John K. Roth, and James M. Smith, 117–122. St. Paul, Minn.: Paragon House, 2002.

Lehman-Wilzig, Sam N. "Loyalty, Voice, and Quasi-Exit: Israel as a Case-Study of Proliferating Alternative Politics." *Comparative Politics* 24, no. 1 (October 1991): 97–108.

Leibowitz, Yeshayahu. *Judaism, Human Values, and the State*. Cambridge, Mass.: Harvard University Press, 1995.

Lemkin, Raphael. *Axis Rule in Occupied Europe*. Washington, D.C.: Carnegie Endowment for International Peace, 1944.

Lerner, Natan. "Religious Human Rights under the United Nations." In *Religious Human Rights in Global Perspective: Legal Perspectives*, edited by Johan D. van der Vyver and John Witte, Jr., 79–134. Cambridge, Mass.: Kluwer Law International, 1996.

——. *The U.N. Convention on the Elimination of All Forms of Racial Discrimination*. Rockville, Md.: Sijthoff and Noordhoff, 1980.

——. "The World Jewish Congress and Human Rights." Pamphlet. Geneva: World Jewish Congress, 1978.

Liben, Noah. "Update: NIF's Ongoing Support for Radical NGOs." March 10, 2005, at www.ngo-monitor.org/editions/v3n07/NIFOngoingSupportForRadicalNGOS.htm.

Lillich, Richard B. *A United States Policy of Humanitarian Intervention and Intercession*, Qtd. in *International Human Rights: Law, Policy, and Process*, 3rd ed., edited by David Weissbrodt, Joan Fitzpatrick, and Frank Newman, 346–348. Cincinnati, Ohio: Anderson Publishing, 2001.

Liskofsky, Sidney. "Human Rights in the Twenty-third United Nations General Assembly." *Bulletin of the International League for the Rights of Man* (Fall 1968): 2.

Liskofsky, Sidney, and Karl Vasak, eds. *The Right to Leave and Return: Papers and Recommendations of the International Colloquium Held in Uppsala, Sweden, 19–20 June 1972*. New York: AJC, 1976.

Longford, Michael. "NGOs and the Rights of the Child." In *The Conscience of the World: The Influence of Non-Governmental Organizations in the UN System*, edited by Peter Willetts, 214–240. Washington, D.C.: Brookings Institution, 1996.

Lord, Amnon. "Defeatism Is Their Trade." *Yediot Aharonot*, March 7, 1999.

Los Angeles Times. "Former President Reagan Dies at 93." June 6, 2004.

Lustick, Ian S. "Israel as a Non-Arab State: The Political Implications of Mass Immigration of Non-Jews." *Middle East Journal* 53, no. 3 (Summer 1999): 417–433.

Maas, Richard. Letter to American Jewish Committee members. December 27, 1979, at www.ajcarchives.org/AJC_DATA/Files/735.PDF.

Mace, James E. "Soviet Man-Made Famine in Ukraine." In *Century of Genocide*, 2nd ed., edited by Samuel Totten, William S. Parsons, and Israel W. Charny, 93–111. New York: Routledge, 2004.

Manor, Y. *To Right a Wrong: The Revocation of the UN General Assembly Resolution 3379 Defaming Zionism*, 2nd ed. New York: Shengold Publishers, 1977.

Maor, Ziv. "Arab Family Finally to Get an ILA Offer for a Katzir Plot." *Ha-aretz*, January 10, 2003.

McAdam, Doug, John D. McCarthy, and Mayer N. Zald, eds. *Comparative Perspectives on Social Movements: Political Opportunities, Mobilizing Structures, and Cultural Framings*. Cambridge Studies in Comparative Politics. Cambridge: Cambridge University Press, 1996.

McGrew, Anthony. "Democracy Beyond Borders?" In *The Global Transformations Reader: An Introduction to the Globalization Debate*, edited by David Held and Anthony McGrew, 405–419. Malden, Mass.: Polity Press, 2000.

Meerson-Aksenov, Michael. "The Influence of the Jewish Exodus on the Democratization of Soviet Society." In *Essays on Human Rights: Contemporary Issues and Jewish Perspectives*, edited by David Sidorsky, with Sidney Liskofsky and Jerome J. Shestack, 144–156. Philadelphia: JPSA, 1979.

Mendes-Flor, Paul, ed. *A Land of Two Peoples: Martin Buber on Jews and Arabs*. New York: Oxford University Press, 1983.

Messinger, Ruth. Letter to the editor. *New York Times*, June 2, 2006.

———. Speech. Ahavath Achim Synagogue, Atlanta, Ga., October 7, 2006.

Morris, Benny. *The Birth of the Palestinian Refugee Problem, 1947–1949*. Cambridge: Cambridge University Press, 1987.

Moskowitz, Moses. *Human Rights and World Order*. Dobbs Ferry, N.Y.: Oceana Publications, 1958.

———. *The Politics and Dynamics of Human Rights*. Dobbs Ferry, N.Y.: Oceana Publications, 1968.

Mosse, George L. *Toward the Final Solution: A History of European Racism*. New York: Harper Colophon Books, 1978.

Mojzes, Paul. "Ethnic Cleansing." In *Will Genocide Ever End?* edited by Carol Rittner, John K. Roth, and James M. Smith, 56. St. Paul, Minn.: Paragon House, 2002.

Neier, Aryeh. *War Crimes: Brutality, Genocide, Terror, and the Struggle for Justice*. New York: Random House, 1998.

New Israel Fund. "Illuminating the Vision." *New Israel Fund Annual Report*. Jerusalem, 2005.

New Israel Fund News. "Shatil Earns Special UN Status." Spring 2006, 6.

Novak, David. *Covenantal Rights*. Princeton, N.J.: Princeton University Press, 2000.

Nyheim, David. "What Can Be Done?" In *Will Genocide Ever End?* edited by Carol Rittner, John K. Roth, and James M. Smith, 113–116. St. Paul, Minn.: Paragon House, 2002.

"On Bosnian War Criminals: An Open Letter." *New York Review of Books* 43, no. 13 (August 8, 1996).

Orbach, Uri. "On the Value of Life, Crossing Red Lines, and Judging Those in Grief." August 11, 2006, at www.ynetnews.com/articles/0,7340,L-3289760,00.html.

Orend, Brian. *Human Rights: Concept and Context*. Calgary: Broadview Press, 2002.

Organization for Security and Cooperation in Europe. *Human Dimension Commitments* v. 2. Warsaw: OSCE Office for Democratic Institutions and Human Rights, 2005.

Otto, Eckart. "Human Rights: The Influence of the Hebrew Bible," *Journal of Northwest Semitic Languages* 25, no. 1 (1999): 1–20.

Oz, Amos. "Al ha-matsav, 1967–1978" [On the Situation, 1967–1978] in *Be'or ha-tekhelet ha'azah* [Under This Blazing Light: Essays]. Merhavyah, Israel: Sifriyat Poalim, 1979.

———. *A Tale of Love and Darkness: A Memoir*. Translated by Nicholas de Lange. Orlando, Fla.: Harcourt Brace, 2003.

Pappé, Ilan. *The Israel/Palestine Question: Rewriting Histories*. London: Routledge, 1999.

Peled, Matityahu. "Palestinian or Jordanian Entity?" In *Israel and the Palestinians*, edited by Shlomo Avineri. New York: St. Martin's Press, 1971.

Peleg, Ilan. *Begin's Foreign Policy, 1977–1983: Israel's Move to the Right*. Westport, Conn.: Greenwood Press, 1987.

———. "The Legacy of Begin and Beginism for the Israeli Political System." In *Israel after Begin*, edited by Gregory S. Mahler, 19-49. Albany: State University of New York Press, 1990.

Permanent Mission of Israel to the United Nations. "Israel and the UN—An Uneasy Relationship," at www.israel-un.org/Israelun/isrun/isrun2.htm.

Petrovsky-Shtern, Yohanan. "The Revival of Academic Studies of Judaica in Independent Ukraine." In *Jewish Life after the USSR*, edited by Zvi Gitelman, with Musya Glants and Marshall I. Goldman, 152–172. Bloomington: Indiana University Press, 2003.

Pinkus, Benjamin. "Soviet Government Policy toward the Extraterritorial National Minorities: Comparison between the Jews and the Germans." In *Jewish Culture and Identity in the Soviet Union*, edited by Yaacov Ro'i and Avi Becker, 290–309. New York: New York University Press, 1991.

Plaut, W. Gunter, ed. *The Torah: A Modern Commentary*. New York: Union of Hebrew Congregations, 1981.

Pomper, Gerald M., and Miles A. Pomper. "Movers, Shakers, and Leaders." In *Jews in American Politics: Essays*, edited by L. Sandy Maisel and Ira N. Forman, 93. Lanham, Md.: Rowman and Littlefield, 2004.

Posner, Michael H., and Candy Whittome. "The Status of Human Rights NGOs." *Columbia Human Rights Law Review* 25 (1994): 269.

Power, Samantha. *"A Problem from Hell": America and the Age of Genocide*. New York: Basic Books, 2002.

Priest, Dana. "Coalition Calls for Action in Bosnia." *Washington Post*, August 1, 1995, A14.

Rabbis for Human Rights. "Preventing Home Demolitions Trial," at www.rhr.israel.net/projects/trial.shtml.

Rackman, Emanuel. "Judaism and Equality." In *Judaism and Human Rights*, edited by Milton Konvitz, 52–54. New York: W. W. Norton, with the B'nai B'rith Commission on Adult Jewish Education, 1972.

Ravitzky, Aviezer. *Messianism, Zionism, and Jewish Religious Radicalism*. Chicago: University of Chicago Press, 1996.

Rebhun, Uzi, and Chaim I. Waxman, eds. *Jews in Israel: Contemporary Social and Cultural Patterns*. Lebanon, N.H.: Brandeis University Press, 2004.

Reeves, Eric. "Cheap Talk: Europe's Indifference to Darfur." *New Republic Online*, October 27, 2006, at www.tnr.com/docprint.mhtml?i=w061023$s=reeves102706.

Rekhess, Elie. "The Arabs of Israel after Oslo: Localization of the National Struggle." *Israel Studies* 7, no. 3 (Fall 2002): 1–44.

Reporters without Borders, ed. *Israel/Palestine: The Black Book*. Sterling, Va.: Pluto Press in association with Reporters without Borders, 2003.

Rieff, David. *Slaughterhouse: Bosnia and the Failure of the West*. New York: Touchstone, 1996.

Rittner, Carol. "Using Rape as a Weapon of Genocide." In *Will Genocide Ever End?* edited by Carol Rittner, John K. Roth, and James M. Smith, 91–97. St. Paul, Minn.: Paragon House, 2002.

Rittner, Carol, John K. Roth, and James M. Smith, eds. *Will Genocide Ever End?* St. Paul, Minn.: Paragon House, 2002.

Roberts, Adam, and Richard Guelff, eds. *Documents on the Laws of War*, 3rd ed. New York: Oxford University Press, 2000.

Robinson, Nehemiah. *The Genocide Convention: A Commentary*. London: World Jewish Congress, 1960.

———. *The Genocide Convention: Its Origins and Interpretation.* New York: Institute of Jewish Affairs, 1949.

———. *The United Nations and the World Jewish Congress*. London: Institute of Jewish Affairs, 1956.

———. *The Universal Declaration of Human Rights*. London: World Jewish Congress, 1958.

Rogen, Eugene L., and Avi Shlaim, eds. *The War for Palestine: Rewriting the History of 1948*. Cambridge: Cambridge University Press, 2001.

Ro'i, Yaacov. "Nehama Lifshitz: Symbol of the Jewish National Awakening." In *Jewish Culture and Identity in the Soviet Union*, edited by Yaacov Ro'i and Avi Becker, 168–190. New York: New York University Press, 1991.

———. "The Role of the Synagogue and Religion in the Jewish National Consciousness." In *Jewish Culture and Identity in the Soviet Union*, edited by Yaacov Ro'i and Avi Becker, 112–135. New York: New York University Press, 1991.

Ro'i, Yaacov, and Avi Becker, eds. *Jewish Culture and Identity in the Soviet Union*. New York: New York University Press, 1991.

Roth, Kenneth. "The Case for Universal Jurisdiction." *Foreign Affairs* (September–October 2001): 150–154.

Roth, Stephen J. "The Right to Jewish Culture in the Soviet Union." In *Jewish Culture and Identity in the Soviet Union*, edited by Yaacov Ro'i and Avi Becker, 355–377. New York: New York University Press, 1991.

Rouhama, Nadim. "The Political Transformation of the Palestinians in Israel: From Acquiescence to Challenge." *Journal of Palestine Studies* 18, no. 3 (Spring 1989): 38–59.

Rubenstein, Joshua. *Soviet Dissidents: Their Struggle for Human Rights*, revised ed. Boston: Beacon Press, 1985.

Rupesinghe, Kumar. "International Alert and the Prevention of Genocide." In *Encyclopedia of Genocide*, edited by Israel W. Charny. Santa Barbara, Calif.: ABC-Clio, 1999.

Rubin, Gary. Memorandum to Irving Levine, "Meeting of the National Coalition for Refugee Resettlement, Washington, D.C., June 18, 1979," at ajcarchives.org/ajcarchive/DigitalArchive.aspx.

Sa'di, Ahmad H. "Catastrophe, Memory and Identity: Al-Nakbah as a Component of Palestinian Identity." *Israel Studies* 7, no. 2 (Summer 2002): 175–198.

Schoenberg, Harris. "Enhancing and Advancing Human Rights: An Essay on Improving UN Human Rights Instruments, Mechanisms, and Procedures Prepared as a Contribution to the UN Decade for Human Rights Education, 1995–2004 in Commemoration of the 50th Anniversary of the Universal Declaration of Human Rights." Center for UN Reform Education, 1999.

———. *A Mandate for Terror: The United Nations and the PLO*. New York: Shapolsky Publishers, 1989.

———. *War No More! A Concrete Action Plan to Revitalize the United Nations Security Council*. New York: Center for Public Policy, 1995.

———. *The World Conference against Racism: The Adoption and Repeal of the Z=R Resolution and the Implications for UN Reform*. Wayne, N.J.: Center for UN Reform Education, 2001.

Segev, Tom. *1949: The First Israelis*. New York: Free Press, 1986.

———. *The Seventh Million*. New York: Holt Paperbacks, 2000.

Sered, Susan. *What Makes Women Sick? Maternity, Modesty, and Militarism in Israeli Society*. Hanover, N.H.: Brandeis University Press, 2000.

Shahak, Israel. Interview. *Intercontinental Press*, Jerusalem, February 1975, 428–431.

———. Interview. *Fifth of June Society Newsletter*, August 13, 1970.

———. *Israeli League for Human and Civil Rights: The Shahak Papers*. Beirut: NEEBII, 1973.

———. *The Shahak Report*. Tel Aviv: I. Shahak, 1973.

———. "What Are My Opinions." *Zu Haderech*, November 27, 1974.

Sharansky, Natan. *Fear No Evil*. Translated by Stefani Hoffman. New York: Random House, 1988.

Shell, Marc. "Marranos (Pigs), or from Coexistence to Toleration." *Critical Inquiry* 17, no. 2 (Winter 1991): 306–335.

Shimoni, Gideon. *The Zionist Ideology*. Waltham, Mass.: Brandeis University Press, 1995.

Shindler, Colin. *Exit Visa: Détente, Human Rights, and the Jewish Emigration Movement in the USSR*. London: Bachman and Turner, 1978.

Shnayderman, Ronen. *Through No Fault of Their Own: Israel's Punitive House Demolitions in the al-Aqsa Intifada*. Jerusalem: B'Tselem, 2004.

Sidorsky, David, ed. with Sidney Liskofsky and Jerome J. Shestack. *Essays on Human Rights: Contemporary Issues and Jewish Perspectives*. Philadelphia: Jewish Publication Society of America, 1979.

Silverman, Rachel. "On Rwanda Visit, Students Learn of the Consequences of Genocide." United Jewish Communities website, April 25, 2006, at www.ujc.org/content_display.html?ArticleID=182205.

Smooha, Sammy. "Is Israel Western?" In *Comparing Modernities: Pluralism versus Homogeneity: Essays in Homage to Shmuel N. Eisenstadt*, edited by Eliezer Ben Rafael and Yitzhak Sternberg, 413–442. Boston: Brill Academic Publishers, 2005.

———. "The Model of Ethnic Democracy: Israel as a Jewish and Democratic State." *Nations and Nationalism* 8, no. 4 (2002): 475–503.

Sofer, Sasson. *Begin: An Anatomy of Leadership*. New York: Basil Blackwell, 1988.

Sorkin, David. *The Transformation of German Jewry, 1780–1840*. Oxford: Oxford University Press, 1987.

Spector, Stephen. *Operation Solomon: The Daring Rescue of the Ethiopian Jews*. New York: Oxford University Press, 2005.

Spinoza, Baruch. *Theological Political Treatise*. Qtd. in *The Jewish Political Tradition* v. 1, edited by Michael Walzer, Menachem Lorberbaum, and Noam J. Zohar, 216. New Haven, Conn.: Yale University Press, 2000.

Stein, Yael. *Forbidden Families: Family Unification and Child Registration in East Jerusalem*. Jerusalem: B'Tselem, 2004.

Steiner, Henry J. *Diverse Partners: Non-Governmental Organizations in the Human Rights Movement*. Cambridge, Mass.: Harvard Law School Human Rights Program and Human Rights Internet, 1991.

Streiner, Scott. "Shooting and Crying: The Emergence of Protest in Israeli Popular Music." *The European Legacy* 6, no. 6 (2001): 771–792.

Tamir, Yael. "A Jewish Democratic States," in Michael Walzer, Menachem Lorberbaum, and Noam J. Zohar, *The Jewish Political Tradition*, vol. 1. New Haven, Conn.: Yale University Press, 2000.

Tanenbaum, Marc H. Partial transcript of testimony before the House of Representatives Subcommittee on Asian and Pacific Affairs of the Foreign Affairs Committee. December 18, 1979, ajcarchives.org/ajcarchive/DigitalArchive.aspx.

Taub, Michael. *Torn at the Roots: The Crisis of Jewish Liberalism in Post-War America*. New York: Columbia University Press, 2002.

Tolts, Mark. "Demography of the Jews in the Former Soviet Union." In *Jewish Life after the USSR*, edited by Zvi Gitelman, with Musya Glants and Marshall I. Goldman, 173–206. Bloomington: Indiana University Press, 2003.

Totten, Samuel. "Non-governmental Organizations Working on the Issue of Genocide." In *The Widening Circle of Genocide: A Critical Bibliographic Review*, edited by Israel W. Charny, 325–357. New Brunswick, N.J.: Transaction Publishers, 1994.

———. "The Role of Nongovernmental Organizations in Addressing the Prevention, Intervention, and Punishment of Genocide in the 1980s, 1990s, and Early 2000s." In *Genocide at the Millenium*, edited by Samuel Totten, 75–101. New Brunswick, N.J.: Transaction Publishers, 2005.

Totten, Samuel, William S. Parsons, and Israel W. Charny, eds. *Century of Genocide*. 2nd ed. New York: Routledge, 2004.

Troen, Ilan. *Imagining Zion: Dreams, Designs, and Realities in a Century of Jewish Settlement*. New Haven, Conn.: Yale University Press, 2003.

Union of Councils for Soviet Jews. *UCSJ Quarterly Report* (Winter 1986).

Union of Councils for Jews in the Former Soviet Union. "Public Campaign to Combat Racisim, Xenophobia, Antisemitism and Ethnic Discrimination in the Multi-National Russian Federation," at www.fsumonitor.com/EC/aboutproject.shtml.

United States Commission on International Religious Freedom. *Annual Report of the United States Commission on International Religious Freedom*. Washington, D.C.: May, 2002.

———. Press release. "Anti-Semitism: USCIRF Vice Chair Gaer on U.S. Delegation to Berlin OSCE Meeting." April 23, 2004.

———. Press release. "Anti-Semitism: Commissioner Gaer Addresses OSCE Rights Meeting." October 15, 2003.

———. Press release, "Commission Asks Clinton to Raise Religious-Freedom Issues in Meeting with Russian President." October 26, 2003.

———. Press release. "Russia: Religious Communities, Extremist Movements, and the State." January 31, 2005.

United States Commission on Security and Cooperation in Europe. *Implementation of the Helsinki Accords*. 101st Cong., 2nd sess. East-West Trade and the Helsinki Process, June 13, 1990, CSCE 101-2-18 (Washington, D.C.: GPO, 1990).

———. Activities Report: 98th Congress (Washington, D.C.: n.d. [circa 1984]).

United States House of Representatives. Subcommittee on International Organizations of the Committee on International Relations. *Anti-Semitism and Reprisals against Jewish Emigration in the Soviet Union*, 94th Cong., 2nd sess. (Washington, D.C.: GPO, 1976).

———. Committee on Foreign Affairs. Hearing before the Subcommittees on Europe and the Middle East and on Human Rights and International Organizations. "Religious Persecution in the Soviet Union, Part I—Soviet Jewry," 99th Cong., 2nd sess., Sept. 11, 1985 (Washington, D.C.: GPO, 1985) and "Religious Persecution in the Soviet Union, Part II, July 30, 1986 (Washington, D.C.: GPO, 1986).

United States Mission to the United Nations. Press release. "Remarks Delivered by U.S. Representative Mrs. Rita E. Hauser during Discussion of Question of Jews in Soviet Union." March 10, 1969.

van der Vyver, Johan, and John Witte, Jr., eds. *Religious Human Rights in Global Perspective: Legal Perspectives*. Cambridge, Mass.: Kluwer Law International, 1996.

Voronel, Alexandr. "Jewish Samizdat." In *Jewish Culture and Identity in the Soviet Union*, edited by Yaacov Ro'i and Avi Becker, 255–261. New York: New York University Press, 1991.

———. "The Subject and Object in a Study of the National Character." In *Jewishness Rediscovered: Jewish Identity in the Soviet Union*, edited by Aleksandr Voronel and Viktor Yakhot, pref. Irving Louis Horowitz, ed. Harris O. Schoenberg, 15–32. US Anti-Defamation League of B'nai B'rith, Washington, D.C.: 1974.

Walker, Robert. "Rwanda Remembers the Holocaust." *BBC News*, January 27, 2005, at news.bbc.co.uk/1/hi/world/africa/4211621.stm.

Walzer, Michael, Menachem Lorberbaum, and Noam J. Zohar. *The Jewish Political Tradition* vol. 1. New Haven, Conn.: Yale University Press, 2000.

Weinbaum, Laurence. "Righting an Historic Wrong: Restitution of Jewish Property in Central and East Europe." Jerusalem: World Jewish Congress, 1995.

Wiesel, Elie. *The Jews of Silence*. Philadelphia: Jewish Publication Society, 1967.

World Jewish Congress. *The Black Book: The Nazi Crime against the Jewish People*. New York: Nexus Press, 1946.

——. *Restitution of Jewish Property in Central and Eastern Europe*. Jerusalem: Institute of World Jewish Congress, 1994.

World Union for Progressive Judaism. "Zionism: One of the Earliest Examples of a National Liberation Movement." UN Doc. E/CN.4/2004/NGO/89 (1989).

Ya'ar, Ephraim. "Continuity and Change in Israeli Society: The Test of the Melting Pot." *Israel Studies* 10, no. 2 (Summer 2005): 91–128.

Yakir, Dan, ed. "Hitdaynuyot ha-agudah—piskeh din akronim" [Litigation of the Association for Civil Rights in Israel—Principle Decisions]. December 26, 2005 [unpublished].

Yedidya, Vera. "The Struggle for the Study of Hebrew." In *Jewish Culture and Identity in the Soviet Union*, edited by Yaacov Ro'i and Avi Becker, 154. New York: New York University Press, 1991.

Yehoshua, A. B. "Facing the Forests," in *Modern Hebrew Literature*, ed. Robert Alter. West Orange, N.J.: Behrman House, 1975.

Yoaz, Yuval. "The Quiet Revolution: The Israel-U.S. Civil Liberties Law Program, Spearheaded by the New Israel Fund and American University in Washington, D.C., Has Changed the Map of Human Rights in Israel." haaretz.com, May 25, 2004.

Zamir, Itzhak. Former Israeli Supreme Court justice, presentation to the Brandeis University Summer Institute for Israel Studies, Sheraton Plaza Hotel, Jerusalem, July 10, 2006.

Index

About the Author

Michael Galchinsky has published books and articles on a wide range of human and civil rights questions. In *The Origin of the Modern Jewish Woman Writer*, he recounted the struggles of novelists, poets, and pamphleteers who argued for Jews' emancipation in the Victorian world and women's emancipation in the Jewish world. With David Biale and Susannah Heschel he coedited *Insider/Outsider: American Jews and Multiculturalism*, in which he reflected on the Diaspora's changing relations with Israel concerning Palestinians' rights. Recent essays include a comparative study of the rights of Jews and other minorities in the British Empire, and an assessment of the international and Israeli law bearing on the West Bank settlements. He is an associate professor of English and director of the Program in Jewish Studies at Georgia State University in Atlanta.